D0919651

WITHDRAWN

PRE-INDUSTRIAL ENGLAND:
Economy and Society, 1500–1750

PRE-INDUSTRIAL ENGLAND
Economy and Society
1500–1750

B. A. Holderness

J. M. DENT & SONS LTD LONDON
ROWMAN & LITTLEFIELD TOTOWA, N.J.

First published in 1976
© B. A. Holderness, 1976
All rights reserved
Made in Great Britain at
the Aldine Press, Letchworth, Herts
for
J. M. DENT & SONS LTD
Aldine House, Albemarle Street, London

This book is set in 11 on 13 point Baskerville 169

Dent edition
Hardback ISBN 0 460 10157 8
Paperback ISBN 0 460 11157 3

Rowman & Littlefield edition
Hardback ISBN 0-87471-910-0
Paperback ISBN 0-87471-911-9

Contents

Preface

Twenty years ago F. J. Fisher felt justified in describing the sixteenth and seventeenth centuries as the 'Dark Ages of English economic history'. That this description no longer applies to the period is due not so much to the improved quality of recent contributions to the subject but to a change in emphasis from the legal and institutional framework of the economy and society of Tudor and Stuart times to the practical problems of the men and women who lived and worked in the pre-industrial world.

The mainsprings of technical change, economic diversification and investment, the management of labour or the recruitment of entrepreneurs, the contemporary realities of accounting, of profit- or loss-making, and the nature of the market and its organization, are all now better understood than they were before the last war. The great themes of a more institutional economic history—the rise of the gentry, the triumph of the yeomanry, the ascendancy of business interests over feudal or communal traditions—are seen now in a different perspective, and historians are less perplexed by the recurrence, or continuity, of these sub-plots in English political history from the thirteenth to the nineteenth centuries.

The economic history of early modern England broke the fetters which had bound it to constitutional history in the 1940s, and for all the deficiencies of statistical information before 1700—a dearth serious enough to move Professor Fisher to make his observations on the Dark Ages in 1956—careful, painstaking, and sometimes quite esoteric, research, in business records, wills, probate inventories, estate muniments and the like, has produced results which have, in every branch of the subject, deepened our knowledge and stimulated our imagination of each century before the present one, but especially of the period from

1450 to 1750. Moreover, the simultaneous development of post-medieval archaeology in England has equally reinforced the empirical, factual preoccupation of modern economic historians of the pre-industrial period.

It is too much to say that we can yet measure or quantify economic change in England before the Industrial Revolution, and for everyone who tries, three or four spring up to scorn his presumption. Certain new lines of inquiry, however, have been opened up. One trend during the last three or four decades has been to attempt the estimation of a linear progression in national income or per capita output backwards from the nineteenth century into the pre-industrial period. Other writers have equally obtained nourishment from the comparison of early modern England with third-world countries of the present, applying models of underdevelopment, or divining, in the setbacks and blockages of development, much the same kind of problem as afflicts modern Mexico or Nigeria. Pre-industrial Europe has always been a battleground of historical controversy, and the consequence of some recent work has been merely to change or enlarge the field of contention. But leaving aside the pretexts upon which controversy flourishes, the empirical basis of most modern research, the studies of particular industries, the fundamental reorientation of agricultural history before 1750, and the exposition of changing patterns in commodity trades, both inland and overseas, have provided the means for a balanced, if still incomplete, restatement of both the potentialities and the pitfalls of development in early modern England. Exploration will continue, perhaps with greater vigour, and new discoveries of great importance will still be made for many years to come, but there is already more than enough material for an interpretation of pre-industrial society and the economy which supported it.

This book, therefore, is a personal interpretation of a long and far from homogeneous period in English economic history. A good deal of modern research has been left out in the process of selection and presentation, but I have tried, as far as I am able, to give a picture of the more outstanding trends and currents of change and diversification, without resort to economists' model building or excessive commitment to a doctrinaire philosophy of history. In the compass of such a book, however, several issues in which I am especially interested have been relegated to minor places in the text or excluded altogether. This is as it should be. In a textbook there is no room for anything save the central issues of change or continuity, fluctuation or stability, growth or regression, as they affected the principal sectors of the economy or its social organization. There is naturally some scope for different opinions in the choice of these principal themes, as in their treatment, but that is the essential justification for a multiplicity of textbooks or guides to the research literature.

The debt which I owe before all others is to the distinguished body of economic and social historians who have already extended and deepened our knowledge and understanding of the era from 1500 to 1750. Those whose work I have made direct use of are acknowledged in the notes or reading lists appended to each chapter, but to the greater number who have informed my mind or stimulated my thoughts I feel the same gratitude. To two men, one of whom I never had the pleasure of meeting, I feel a particular obligation. The first is the late David Chambers whose approach and interests in economic history I have consciously or unconsciously assimilated. The second, not really an economic historian at all, is the late K. B. MacFarlane, whose writings have done much to form my attitudes to certain critical aspects of English social organization and first encouraged me to look beyond 1500 to find the roots of so much which grew and flourished in the seventeenth and eighteenth centuries. Neither appears in the text as much as he should, so both are gratefully acknowledged here.

In the presentation of the text, notes have been employed minimally, and then mainly to identify quotations or allusions taken from modern historians' published work. Where the source is obvious from reference to the bibliography attached to each chapter a note has generally been dispensed with. The reading lists have been compiled mainly to indicate to students where they can find more information on the subject of each chapter. A comprehensive bibliography for much of the period can be found in M. Levine, ed., *Tudor England 1485–1603* and W. L. Sachse, ed., *Restoration England 1660–1689* (C.U.P. for Conference on British Studies, Bibliographical Handbooks) [1] and it is now as unnecessary as it is confusing to equip a brief textbook with a complete bibliographical apparatus.

---

[1] These will soon be supplemented by volumes covering the other periods of history in the same series.

Acknowledgments

Special thanks are due to Miss Patricia Charman whose prompt and efficient typing of the manuscript and my textual amendments was much appreciated.

The author and publishers wish to thank: the Editors and the London School of Economics for permission to reproduce material in Fig. 1 and Table I, from E. H. Phelps Brown and S. V. Hopkins, 'Seven Centuries of the Prices of Consumables, as Compared with Builders' Wage Rates', from *Economica*, NS, XXIII, 1956; the President and Fellows of Harvard University for permission to reproduce material in Table I from E. B. Schumpeter, 'English Prices and Public Finance, 1660–1822', in *Review of Econ. Statistics*, vol. XX, 1938; the Editors and the Economic History Society for permission to reproduce material in Fig. 2 from E. Kerridge, 'The Movement of Rent, 1540–1640', in *Economic History Review*, second series, vol. VI, 1953; the Syndics of the Cambridge University Press for Figs. 3–6 from H. C. Darby, ed., *A New Historical Geography of England*; and Messrs Routledge and Kegan Paul, for material in Table IV, from H. Perkins, *The Origin of Modern English Society 1750–1880*.

I

Seasons, Prices and Population

ECONOMIC FLUCTUATIONS AND THE MUTABILITY OF THE SEASONS

The structure of English life when George III ascended his throne in 1760 bore many points of resemblance to that of Elizabethan England. England was still a country of several distinctive regions. Though the differences narrowed after 1500, each county still revelled in its own particularity and fostered its own partisans in Hanoverian England. The underlying concept of social hierarchy survived throughout the period from 1500 to 1750, and the family as the unit of both social and economic organization continued to shape most human relationships. Above all, the rural framework of both life and thought influenced the age of Johnson as much as the age of More or Shakespeare. One great city and a handful of modest provincial towns formed the urban nation at both ends of this period. Most towns were still supported by gardens or cow-runs, and many were still surrounded by their own open-fields. The bulk of the people still lived in villages or small towns, and most men expected to work within the family grouping or in units of employment seldom exceeding five or six individuals. The largest employers of labour under one roof in 1750 as in 1500 were the great noble households. Work, like social status, was founded upon degree and order. This world has been described as essentially 'hand-made'.

The great watershed which divides us from the Elizabethans or even from Chaucer had not in 1750 been crossed. Fruitful changes which modified everyday life were comprehended within the continuity of experience. Even great upheavals like the Civil War obeyed the precept of *plus ça change, plus c'est la même chose*. The French historian Pierre Goubert has declared that because England never had its Revolution

I

so it has never lost its *ancien régime*. In effect, the structure of this society was also flexible enough to assimilate a modest degree of economic growth and to sustain a larger volume of commercial expansion. Its pulse, however, oscillated between great extremes of plenty and dearth or of prosperity and recession, which overlaid not only the trends of growth or expansion, but also the structure of the economic order in the pre-industrial world. It was no accident that intelligent men should have been obsessed by the mutability of their lives. That there was a divine intercession in the affairs of man few doubted, but the effect, as they realized, was to make everyday life uncertain and haphazard.

In such a world, the natural elements were a matter of grave concern, even in the cities. The state of the harvest was one of the most important independent variables of the pre-industrial economy, but even in years when the food supply was assured, seasonal or short-run conditions still influenced the tempo of social and economic action. England was fortunate in having a damp but equable climate, but few men, then or now, planned for the extremes which surprised them. Wind and water ruled economic life before the age of steam, and an excess or a shortage of either could bring business to a standstill and reduce the employment of labour. Mills were destroyed in storms, livestock killed in floods, blizzards or gales, merchandise lost or damaged under the hammer blows of nature. London was several times half-starved when ships bearing essential commodities of coal or grain failed to arrive because the wind blew persistently from the wrong quarter. Because water was used for so much more than navigation, a drought might stop wheels, damage equipment and interrupt preparatory washing or cleansing processes in several trades. Corn millers and fullers were often at loggerheads in the textile districts when river levels were low. In ironmaking also, dry summers forced entrepreneurs to shut down their furnaces as the quality of metal produced was so poor. We cannot estimate the effect of such elemental disturbances upon business activity except to note the accidents which occurred, but to judge from the consequences of unexpected weather conditions upon the modern economy, economic man before 1800 is likely to have found them deeply perturbing.

The fluctuations of the seasons, if not their extremes, were obviously more predictable and led to a rhythm of activity which greatly influenced the pattern of work (and idleness) in the pre-industrial world. Agriculture was naturally busiest from May to September when the fruits of the farmer's annual investment were gathered. In winter and early spring, tillage, threshing, dung-spreading, hedging and ditching kept many men more or less in employment but work was less regular and always worse paid than in summer. Indoor work like threshing could proceed at any time, but for the rest, heavy rain, snow and frost necessarily enforced idleness upon agriculturists in a northern climate. Similar fluctuations applied to fishing and seafaring, and even to the conduct of war, for armies and navies were stood down in the autumn. Some industrial processes were similarly restricted by the state of the weather to summer operation—bleaching which required strong sunlight, and fabric-printing among others which were interrupted by the onset of frost. Building came to a halt in the autumn and winter, and wage rates were reduced after Michaelmas; quarrying, brickmaking, coalmining and the coal trade from the pithead, road repairs and shipbuilding similarly ran down as the bad weather set in. A large body of labourers and much productive equipment in some districts spent most of the winter in idleness. Moreover, the problems of accommodating the rival claims for labour, horses or waggons at seasonal peaks were chronic in areas of rural industrialization.

Things could have been worse if many trades had not reached the peak of their annual production at times when agriculture was relatively slack. Brewing (following the annual harvest), milling, tanning, soap boiling, rope-making (especially active at night) and many trades which required the use of watermills were concentrated in the months from autumn to spring. Weaving, nail-making and other cottage crafts were less dependent upon the seasons, but tended to be suspended in high summer when the calls of the farm or of neighbouring farmers were pressing. Industrial entrepreneurs grew accustomed to the summer break in production, not least because many of them were also farmers who needed casual labour in the hay or the corn fields. Moreover, the prevalence of dual occupations in the countryside was sustained by the ease of transfer from one kind of employment to another. Even substantial capitalists saw little conflict of interest in their diverse commitments; thus a Wiltshire linen draper in the eighteenth century held up an order for his cloth, because 'a plenty of apples now imploys many workmen making syder'. This ability to comprehend different kinds of employment in the course of the year did not solve the problem of underemployment as such in the pre-industrial economy. For minds attuned to the disciplines of industrial capitalism, to regularity of work and to a

3

high degree of specialization, the rhythm of economic activity before 1750 seems discontinuous and fragmentary. An unusually hard winter might make thousands redundant or half-starve a city, and we can see from the seasonal nature of price changes, particularly of foodstuffs, that physical restraints upon production might well directly influence the level of demand for industrial goods or imports.

Nevertheless the commercial community was acclimatized to the predictable movement of the seasons. Patterns of distribution and the behaviour of the exchanges, the flow of credit and the placement of orders, were all adjusted according to the season, or to allow for the length of supply lines or the speed of delivery. Even overseas merchants were hemmed in by the dictates of seasonality. It was important, for example, in the oceanic trades to have one's ships in the Indian Ocean in time to catch the south-westerly monsoons, and to have them back in the Atlantic before the hurricane season began in August, when insurance rates doubled. Long experience taught merchants how advantageously to exploit the sea routes and also taught those who remained in port how to predict the flow of trade or the degree of risk. Hence the mercantile support services of Amsterdam or London were almost as seasonal as cloth production by the eighteenth century. The European pattern of the seasons was not overcome by commercial intervention until the later nineteenth century when the resources of the whole world were offered up to the merchant for exploitation.

But if the seasons of the year imposed their own discipline upon English men throughout the ages at least until 1850, there were other vicissitudes repetitive in their occurrence which nearly always caught them off-balance. One in particular was inescapable for merchants and manufacturers as much as for statesmen.

'War . . .' wrote Sir George Clark, 'may be said to have been as much a normal state of European life as peace . . .' Between 1494 and 1763 there were fewer than fifty years when the Continent was at peace. On English soil, a handful of armed rebellions of short duration, and the Civil War from 1642 to 1651, were insufficient to interrupt the tenor of normal life. Most men remarked on England's singular good fortune, and not a few historians have since taken war, by mobilizing resources or by conquest of new territories or new markets, to represent a dynamic element of growth in countries not devastated by fighting. Some merchants, who saw military and naval prowess as a means of extending or defending their commercial interests, impressed a similar point of view upon seventeenth- or eighteenth-century governments. War, however, was a complex influence upon economic change. As F. J. Fisher has noted of the early sixteenth-century trade statistics of London, 'With an almost cyclical regularity war, or the danger of war, produced a depression at the beginning of every decade save one.' Eighteenth-century wars, too, 'tended to accentuate the short-term oscillations of activity' (T. S. Ashton), especially those which tended downwards. Ironically, the return of peace itself often brought a recession, simply because it was a change of direction which caused instability. Active merchants, however, feared war rather than peace, for war not only broke chains of communication and brought privateers, as well as hostile navies, into the trade routes, but increased risks and lessened the chances of obtaining insurance, reduced purchasing power for consumption goods and sometimes caused ships and seamen to be impressed into service. For Englishmen, war was a distant prospect affecting trade rather than agriculture, and the consequences of war were often felt in manufacturing output and therefore in employment. In summary, when war threatened, the volume of trade at first increased in order to move stocks before communications were interrupted—clearly apparent in 1701 (War of Spanish Succession, 1702–13), 1741 (War of Austrian Succession, 1740–8), and 1756 (Seven Years War, 1756–63), and probably also in earlier periods. Trade then fell away sharply in the early period of a war until merchants accustomed themselves to changed conditions. Some wars, by reducing competition, actually stimulated production and trade, but in others the level of commercial activity remained low. Strategic industries, munitions, dockyards, and the metal trades of course, were expanded to supply military needs, but the idea that warfare stimulated economic growth generally before 1750 is difficult to justify. War was an element of instability in which capital was destroyed, productive employment reduced and confidence undermined.

The influence of war or the rumour of war upon public confidence is well illustrated in certain of the great financial crises which resounded across the country and across the Continent between 1550 and 1800. The disruption of Antwerp's trade after 1562 and its collapse in the 1570s, when it was the economic hub of Europe, reverberated across the Channel and drew England into the political arena of the long conflict between the Dutch and the Spaniards. Some of the long series of recessions or financial crises which afflicted England after 1690 were directly attributable to war, in 1701, 1715, 1734, 1739 and 1745. To some extent, the connection between war and finance was simply the need of government to pay its way in an emergency. The exigencies to which even well-conducted states like the United Provinces were often reduced when war threatened were like a sword of Damocles for their paymasters. Business confidence, therefore, was never inured to war, but, as always, merchants' sensibilities were touched no less by other events, the Fire of London in 1666 or the great Lisbon earthquake of 1755, for instance, both of which caused panics in the business community. The incompetence of government finance, especially in the seventeenth century, produced a number of similar tremors particularly in London. The 'Stop of the Exchequer' in 1672, when Charles II imposed a moratorium on the repayment of loans to his money-lenders, staved off a real disaster but also upset long-term confidence in public lending. The complex international crisis of 1710 was a compound of harvest failure, credit expansion and political intrigue, and the worse one in 1720 was retribution for the mania which took 'boldness to the point of sharp practice and downright fraud', known as the South Sea Bubble. Adam Smith rightly attributed a good deal of the instability of the eighteenth century to speculative manias. Crises which were the result of multiple causes were especially serious. The 'depression' of the 1550s and the slump of 1622–3 were compounded of harvest failure, epidemics, currency manipulation and structural deficiencies in the clothing trades of the time.

It is probably mistaken to describe the events which culminated in crises as random, but however frequently the peaks of prosperity and the troughs of depression recurred across the centuries, it is straining logic to see in these fluctuations a circular flow in which the rhythms are as clearly marked as in the trade cycles of the nineteenth century. Scholars have rather ignored the patterns which a careful analysis of such pre-industrial fluctuations can plausibly reveal; perhaps wisely, because the application of modern tools of economic analysis to the movement of diverse economic variables before 1800 has often produced results in Continental scholarship which are confusing or indistinct. Thus even the forty-month cycle which is particularly characteristic of industrial capitalism has been discerned in the pattern of Spanish-American commerce before 1650. Too many hypothetical cycles exist for the sake of coherence, and, with two exceptions, it is perhaps best to assume that pre-industrial fluctuations were essentially adventitious.

Their repetitiveness owes more to the persistence of meteorological or political influences than to any innate tendency for phenomena to recur. The two exceptions, however, stand out like sentinels in no-man's-land. First, the rhythm of the harvest produced consequences for the economy which were perhaps literally a matter of life or death. Secondly, the economy of the whole of Europe between 1500 and 1750 was bounded by certain very long-range fluctuations, notably of population and of price-trends, just as the tide of the sea contained in its dominant motion the movement of the waves—the backwash or the surges which befall mankind in any age.

THE INFLUENCE OF THE HARVEST

W. G. Hoskins has called the annual harvest the 'heart-beat of the whole economy'. Since bread and beer were of vital importance to at least three-quarters of the English people, a serious harvest failure spelt hunger and misery for thousands in the sixteenth or seventeenth centuries. The frequency of food riots, the almost universal unpopularity of grain dealers [1] and the policies which central and local government adopted to prevent unfair trading, to fix maximum prices or to assuage social unrest indicate the surpassing importance of the food supply to an economy dependent upon its own agriculture. Imports successfully relieved the larger towns from time to time, but the attempts repeatedly made by the Privy Council before 1640 to discover aggregate corn stocks, and the obsession of justices of the peace with the prevention of hoarding, were typical of a country living on a narrow margin above its subsistence needs. In general local people lived upon what corn the soil yielded, and the long-range corn trade was organized to supply the few large towns or 'industrial' regions like Lancashire and the West Riding (from the seventeenth century) which were normally deficient in grain.

Between 1480 and 1759 Hoskins has calculated that one harvest in four was at least deficient and 46 out of 280 were really bad. By contrast 111 were good or abundant, so that two in every five years produced crops well above average. Distribution of bad or good harvests through time was fairly equal, thus in each 70-year period after 1480 the number of failures was: 1480–1549, 18; 1550–1619, 17; 1620–89, 18; 1690–1759, 19. On the other hand, bad and good harvests were often clustered

---

[1] Grain dealers were unpopular, both among the people and with governments, because they were suspected of hoarding grain to force up prices, especially in times of crisis.

together, and certain decades, the 1520s, 1590s, 1630s, 1690s, stand out as hard times. There was indeed a 'marked tendency for good or bad harvests to run in series', 1519–21, 1549–51, 1594–7, 1657–61, 1708–11 (all bad) and 1537–42, 1601–6, 1618–20, 1704–7 and 1741–4 (good). Because yields were still very low, the surplus over and above the seed-corn in normal years was painfully small, and in bad years reached danger levels. Thus a bad crop 'almost automatically ensured another bad harvest from sheer deficiency of seed'. This vicious circle was then broken only when the weather intervened to produce an abundant crop. The 'mechanism' of nature adjusted itself remarkably well— three or four bad harvests were often followed immediately by three or four abundant ones, as in 1519–26 or 1646–55.

The pattern of English harvest fluctuations lends little direct support to those historians who have seen important trends in climate affecting the length of the growing season in the north temperate zone, like the so-called 'little ice age' of 1550–1650, for the range in quality of the harvests throughout the period changed very little. But weather obviously played a major role in the yield of particular years, and we know from contemporary accounts of great harvest failures like 1596, 1622, 1709 or 1740 that cold late springs or incessant summer rains destroyed or blighted the crops in the field.

The short, not the long, term is the critical dimension in which to discuss such movements, for the effects of two or three bad years in a row were calamitous not only for the farmers but also for townsmen and industrial workers who depended upon the market. The concurrence of trade depressions and poor harvests was particularly serious in years such as 1622 when the price of corn in Wiltshire and the north of England did not fully reflect its scarcity 'because of want of monies and want of employment and labour for the poor', or 1693–8 when dislocation as a result of the War of League of Augsburg, 1689–97, high taxation and the re-coinage added to the miseries of repeated dearths. A causal relationship between food shortage and commercial recession is difficult to establish, however often the two coincided after the trauma of 1549–57, when hunger, sickness and a major slump in the clothing trade provoked widespread disorder.

As for the effects of improved productivity in cereal farming the evidence of yield ratios between 1500 and 1750 is ambiguous. On the face of it output per acre was notably greater at the end than at the beginning of the period, but when the improvement took place is still in dispute. But if, as seems likely, yields doubled between the fifteenth and late seventeenth centuries, this was barely sufficient to keep pace with even the most conservative estimate of population growth. Yet in the middle decades of the eighteenth century Britain was an important exporter of grain, reaching a peak of almost 1,000,000 quarters in 1750. This suggests that however often poor harvests recurred, England had freed itself from the incubus of what the French call *crises de subsistance*, crop failures so severe that men starved or suffered from fevers caused by malnutrition. Indeed for some historians the ghost of Malthus, who first proposed that population has an inherent tendency to outrun the resources to sustain it, has been completely exorcized from recent British history. This may be a mistake, for in years such as 1727–9 there is some evidence to indicate that severe malnutrition provoked the fevers which carried off large numbers of the population, at least in some parts of England. But there are few examples of starvation *recorded* in England after the Restoration, comparable to the horrors of 1556–7, 1596–7 or 1622–3. We can say that in the seventeenth century the margin between deficiency and disaster widened, although men had not solved the problem of the harvest as the most vital influence upon their daily existence. The recurrence of food riots in the eighteenth century, even though some of them were designed chiefly to prevent exports, underlines the precariousness of the achievement even in the midst of plenty.

We shall return to the question of malnutrition and epidemic diseases later, but one other connection must be brought in at this point. Years of scarcity in grain were often also years when meat and dairy produce were in short supply. A deficient harvest in 1719 in the north and west, caused by a long drought, was matched by a wholesale slaughter of livestock weakened by the dry weather, which drove up the prices of butter, cheese and eventually of meat. In wet years, for example, in 1556, 1595–6, 1695–6, 1710–14, 1736, 1740, sheep-rot, 'murrain' and other distempers of livestock were visited upon a prostrate people. The great cattle plague of 1746–58 was 'autonomous'—like bubonic plague it fell upon a population of cattle without immunity and spread like wildfire. We shall probably find from further research that endemic animal diseases raged at either extreme of English weather, in droughts or in cold, wet seasons, so that to the menace of a deficient supply of corn was often added a disaster to the nation's livestock.

POPULATION

Between 1500 and 1750 the population of England grew substantially, probably from something over 2,000,000 to about 5,700,000. There are no proper statistics before the census of 1801 and several plausible estimates have been made for various periods, based on data drawn from contemporary enumerations for different purposes, or upon the analysis of the parish registers of baptisms, burials and marriages. After 1660, however, a number of 'political arithmeticians'—Sir William Petty, Gregory King, Charles Davenant—provided a more accurate base for calculations. King is especially renowned for his work as a demographer, but even his data are no more than well-informed guesses. Even so, the above rate of growth between 1500 and 1750 seems about right and may have been appropriate for the level of economic activity.

It is generally assumed that population increase before the late nineteenth century occurred in spite of very high death rates, because the rate of reproduction remained equally high and in most years ran slightly ahead of mortality. Thus a population almost but not quite static reputedly typified Europe in the centuries before the Industrial Revolution. A major calamity was repaired by increased fertility within one or two generations and any spurt in numbers out of key with necessary replacement rates was cut off by the operation of natural checks like disease or famine. Vital rates were held roughly in equilibrium and growth proceeded slowly but surely. 'The gross birth rate was usually about 30–35 per thousand [and] with death rates at around 25–35 per thousand, this gave a population growth rate of 0·5–1·5 per cent per annum' (Cipolla).[1] Birth and death rates tend to vary directly, as one adjusts to changes in the other. Through a millennium of time such a view may be justified, but it can apply neither to the repeated oscillations of growth and recession which characterized particular decades or generations nor to the even longer fluctuations which shaped the demographic increase, stagnation or decline of a century or more. Although population grew satisfactorily between 1500 and 1750, closer examination reveals that, within the period, two protracted phases, one of rapid expansion until the early decades of the seventeenth century, and another, of much slower growth or even of stagnation between 1640 and 1740, succeeded each other. Such great swings are more characteristic of population change in the pre-industrial, or settled agrarian world

[1] C. Cipolla, in W. W. Rostow, ed. *The Economics of Take-off into Sustained Growth* (Macmillan 1963), p. 401.

10

of Europe and Asia, than either equilibrium or steady increase. Indeed, although English population did not fall after 1630–50, it is possible to discern, in the ups and downs of long-run change, alternating phases of expansion and recession which affected the conduct and constitution of the whole economy.

The first problem is to estimate the contribution of the two phases to English population growth. For 1600 most acceptable estimates vary around the figures of 4,000,000 to 4,500,000. Thirty or forty years later the population of England was certainly greater, and might well have reached 5,000,000. An increase from about 2,000,000 to about 5,000,000, between 1500 and 1640, is not inordinate in an expansionary age, for even then the annual rate of increase did not exceed one per cent. Most authorities would take the view that the figure of 5,000,000 is too great for the eve of the Civil War, but it is quite plausible, if we assume that the *rate* of growth in the next hundred years was notably slower than in the 'long sixteenth century'. But even in the age of expansion, the impulse of growth varied considerably. When the upswing began, after the doldrums of the late fourteenth and fifteenth centuries, is still not clear—some suggest that the turning point was in 1470–80; others postpone it until the mid-sixteenth century—but by 1525, most agree, population growth was in full flood. In the 1550s and 1560s this surge was suppressed, and numbers may have declined by as many as 20 per cent especially among the 'lower orders', who were always very susceptible to epidemics due to the squalor in which they lived or to hunger crises. By the 1570s, however, expansion again resumed, and some villages like Wigston Magna, Leicestershire, apparently increased in numbers by 50 per cent in the forty years before 1603. When the next ebb occurred is in doubt and it probably set in differently in various places. After 1640, moreover, all was not uniformly bleak. The period from 1685 to 1720 was probably favourable to population growth, but fluctuations in the two quarter-centuries surrounding it were sufficient to hold down any major upswing in the century before 1750. Even so, 500,000 people were perhaps added to the population of England between King's estimate in 1688 and 1750, especially in favoured areas where urban or industrial expansion was in full swing.

For the question how the population could have increased so substantially before 1750 and why there should have been the two distinct phases of demographic change, there are unfortunately no simple or unambiguous answers. External influences, the incidence of epidemics, war or hunger, obviously contributed much to changes in the population at various times, but the absence of significant warfare on English soil, except during the 1640s, and the recurrent fluctuations of the harvest throughout the early modern period, do not suggest that military destructions or famine seriously affected the long-term trend of population change in England. The worst which widespread hunger achieved was to inhibit a rising trend for a short period, after which growth was often resumed at an even faster rate. The influence of particular famines upon the size of population cannot be dismissed out of hand, but the general proposition that population before the nineteenth century was held in check by the recurrence of dearths at more or less regular intervals is very doubtful, if only because it cannot account for differing secular rates of demographic expansion in the midst of recurrent variations from plenty to want in the food supply. It is possible to argue that hunger did play an intermittent part in aggravating or even provoking the epidemic diseases by which thousands fell before the scythe of the grim reaper. Some diseases, especially ergotism,[1] uncommon but not unknown in England after 1500, were directly linked to poor harvests. Most of the great epidemics, however, plague, typhus, influenza, smallpox, were merely made worse by falling upon an undernourished people. Some historians, notably J. D. Chambers, have argued against any connection between great mortality and hunger crises, and sought to pin almost all the evidence of abnormally high death rates upon the 'autonomous' effects of epidemics. But the coincidence of many great epidemics with phenomenally bad harvests suggests that one cannot be dogmatic even for well-favoured England.

Epidemics, of course, often irrupted with great suddenness in many populations and possessed characteristics unconnected with malnutrition. What mattered was whether the population possessed sufficient biological immunity to the disease. Many of the great epidemics, bubonic plague, influenza, the so-called 'sweating sickness' of the fifteenth and early sixteenth centuries, struck as 'pandemics' across wide territories and whole peoples, but their impact, however virulent, was not continual, and without new strains of their bacteria they tended to decline as time passed. Thus the long run of plague in England from 1348 to 1666 was sustained by at least one mutation in 1563 which reinvigorated the virus, and diseases like influenza are prone to quite

---

[1] Ergotism is a disease cased by eating rye-bread contaminated by a fungus which produces convulsions and, in acute cases, mutilation of the limbs and death.

frequent mutations, so although some strains became endemic, virulent outbreaks apparently continued to carry off large numbers in certain years throughout the period. The impact of plague had not been solely responsible for the sequence of lethal epidemics in England after 1348, so in the century after 1666, a combination of old complaints and 'new delights' ensured that new outbreaks of fevers in years like 1677–82, 1727–9 and 1740–1 were little less serious than in the plague era. Epidemics usually came in a bewildering variety and often with several diseases in combination. They spread like a conflagration because of poor hygiene, squalor and overcrowding, and although country people were certainly afflicted, it was in the towns, large villages or crammed, often sordid, public institutions like prisons, barracks and even hospitals, that epidemics caused most harm. Typhus was often called 'gaol fever', and long before bubonic plague had been traced to the rat flea (*xenopsylla cheopis*), observant physicians attributed its spread to the filth and overcrowding which defiled the air men breathed.

Terrible as were these visitations of God, the direct influence of epidemics upon long-term population change is less than straightforward. No one would deny that, whatever the causes underlying the late medieval decline of population, plague in 1348 did most of the damage. Equally the demographic setback of the 1550s has been attributed to a major outbreak of influenza which upset the tenor of economic life significantly and brought about, at least temporarily, that shortage of labour which provoked the so-called Statute of Artificers in 1563. Something similar has been proposed for the years 1725–45, as a restraint upon growth before the later eighteenth-century surge. Epidemics and food crises together, as in 1622–3, most affected those not directly producing food, whose employment was then further threatened as consumers cut back on industrial products in order to buy foodstuffs. Then, by tramping around in search of work, labourers often carried the infection with them. The social implications of epidemics are equally interlocking. Great mortalities cut down the weakest and most vulnerable, so that the survivors enjoyed some Darwinian advantages of biological fitness. Moreover, when epidemics decimated mature occupants of established businesses, the way was opened for earlier marriages among the waiting generation, and therefore for a higher level of fertility. On the other hand, when epidemics receded, the decline in the death rate was confined to the peaks and did not necessarily affect the underlying trend of either mortality or fertility.

13

Not all historians agree that the precipitant of change was rising or falling mortality. There are equally cogent arguments for the view that the critical factor was fertility. To some extent the discussion turns upon the severity of known epidemics, especially after 1650, but the essence of the argument is the ability of populations to moderate their own growth rate. Since little could be done by human agency before 1750 to reduce excessive mortality, the variable must needs have been the birth rate. Pre-industrial societies knew something of primitive techniques of birth control, *coitus interruptus*, prolonged lactation, above all simple continence, and they operated, as a rule, a principle of late marriage. Since the birth rate varies inversely with the age of fertile women, postponement of marriage beyond twenty-five reduced potential childbirth very effectively. This only applied if pre-nuptial chastity was generally enforced, but most of the available evidence suggests that illegitimacy was low, by nineteenth-century standards, between 1540 and 1750. Domestic service, apprenticeship, farm service, extended education and the need to wait upon inheritance before setting up as family men restrained young people from early or improvident marriages. It is significant that in industrial districts and the larger towns, where accommodation and day labour were plentiful, marriages tended to be earlier for both partners. Moreover, it is possible that the age at marriage was lowered in periods of rapid population growth, such as between 1570 and 1610, and after 1750, but the proof for the earlier period is elusive.

Recent research has added to these institutional checks upon fertility the idea of 'homoeostatic techniques of adjustment', a complex of psychological and physiological influences intended to prevent the worst combination of overpopulation and scarce resources from causing disaster. The evidence for this is the fact that for quite lengthy periods family size was being limited by other than purely biological means, while in other periods no such restraints were imposed by local populations. Thus the century from 1540 to 1640 is generally characterized by the prevalence of large families, and the next century by rather smaller families, owing not to differences of child mortality but to some kind of choice by the parents. In fact there are numerous variations of detail but the pattern in the Devon village of Colyton is impressive enough to suggest a clear trend. Why such a choice should have been exercised is uncertain. But it is not unlikely, as Professor Chambers expressed it, that there existed 'a population able to recognize economic opportunities when it saw them, and ready to adjust marriage and child-bearing propensities more quickly, and to a greater extent, than is commonly allowed by those who assume that . . . birth rates were more or less constant at the limits of biological potential'.[1] In other words, smaller families were likely to be the result of rising material expectations before 1750, as they were after 1880, in which children could be viewed as a liability rather than as the asset they were in other peasant societies. That does not explain why the mentality of pre-industrial populations changed, unless we assume that when conditions were so favourable, for the comparatively poor, the restraints upon family size could be released. Such a view is impossible to prove, and we must conclude merely that if men chose the size of family they required in any sense at all, the elements were compounded both of fear of what fate might bring and of hope for better things. We can at least accept the evidence of modern demographers that the birth rate in the pre-industrial world was variable enough to set off different secular trends at different periods, so that even if a long-run decline of the average death rate did occur, it was not alone in creating the greater natural increase of population upon which the sixteenth- and eighteenth-century expansions depended.

Another element of importance in the constitution of regional or local populations was migration. This barely affected the national total before 1750, for neither emigration nor immigration was statistically significant, but internally it was often of great moment. London, which increased more than tenfold before 1700, when it contained at least half a million inhabitants, grew largely by immigration. Indeed, because the metropolitan death rate was already higher than its average birth rate by 1600, immigrants were required to replace as well as to enlarge the population. The unhealthiness of London and other great towns continued even after the plague had disappeared. By 1700–50 the death rate of the Great Wen may have exceeded 50 per thousand, twice as high as in 1801–30, and the number of immigrants into Middlesex, 1700–50, has been estimated at more than 460,000. The newcomers came from all over the British Isles, but perhaps chiefly from the agricultural counties of the south and midlands of England. In general the share of the urban population increased steadily, from 12 per cent in 1500 to about 20 per cent in 1600 and 25 per cent in 1700, presumably

[1] J. D. Chambers, *Population, Economy and Society in Pre-Industrial England* (O.U.P. 1972), p. 65.

almost all by means of immigration. Towns like Bristol, Norwich, Newcastle, Hull, Manchester or Liverpool formed hinterlands like miniature Londons from which to draw upon their human resources for immigration. Much immigration, however, was casual or adventitious in the manner of Dick Whittington. Towns drew men either because wages were higher or because economic (and social) opportunities seemed inherently greater. Alternatively, men emigrated from the home district because they were driven out by hunger, unemployment or disease. They became wanderers out of pessimism, and they flocked into the towns, where the municipal authorities or rich merchants often relieved acute distress in times of famine. The line between 'betterment migration' and 'subsistence migration' is difficult to draw, but the two concepts are none the less useful in interpreting pre-industrial mobility.

In the countryside, an equally high degree of personal mobility is evident throughout the early modern period. Movement from village to village, or from village to market town, was already ancient by the sixteenth century, to judge from the work of medieval historians like J. A. Raftis or H. E. Hallam.[1] By the reign of Elizabeth even freeholders were often highly mobile. In Nottinghamshire, in 1612, at least half the freeholders appear to have held their land for less than two generations, and evidence for Nottinghamshire, Lincolnshire, Bedfordshire, Kent and Sussex reveals that movement was continuous. Many immigrants to particular places were from quite distant parishes, but the great majority, especially of the poor, were from within 10 or 15 miles of the place of settlement. Dorset experienced a remarkable immigration of small farmers from Devon around 1600, and in some villages of the fens, hard hit by epidemics, an almost wholesale turnover of population took place at certain times in the seventeenth century. Landlords could expect applications for vacant farms often from considerable distances. Local or rural migration after the Civil Wars was therefore very marked, and in this respect the Settlement Law of 1662 was as irrelevant as Elizabethan statutes restraining movement and vagrancy, for people continued to move about in defiance of the law as it stood. The issuing of certificates authorizing such movement from the 1690s, for instance, never encompassed the whole extent of rural mobility at that time. Large numbers of adolescents left the villages and small towns of their birth to enter

[1] J. A. Raftis, *Tenure and Mobility* (Pontifical Institute of Medieval Studies, Toronto, 1964); H. E. Hallam, *Settlement and Society* (C.U.P. 1965).

service and a great many never returned. Service indeed seems to have contributed to another phenomenon of English social history before 1750, the relatively wide range of choice for marriage partners. Inter-village marriages were very common in this period, and this obviously assisted in elaborating the pattern of mobility. On the other hand, the expansion of industries in the countryside did not necessarily require a significant increase of immigration, partly because their development usually occurred within an established agrarian framework and partly because many such areas apparently grew more rapidly than the national average, between 1600 and 1800, because of their superior fertility.

The effect of these complex patterns of growth and mobility resulted in some geographical redistribution of English population. Lancashire, the West Riding and Durham, among the poorest and least peopled counties in 1500, had become, two and a half centuries later, as densely populated as counties in the once-dominant south-east region. The north and west, as far south as Gloucestershire, grew much faster in general than all save the 'metropolitan' counties of the south between 1600 and 1801. The share of the national population in the north and west Midlands (excluding Lincolnshire) and northern England and probably increased from 33 per cent in 1600–30 (average of two esti-mates) to 42 per cent in 1801. The direction of change, however, almost certainly originated in the century before 1600, and was not worked out completely until 1850.

THE MOVEMENT OF PRICES

The food supply and changes in the size or growth rate of population are obviously major variables in economic life, for even in societies not yet fully monetized, the existence of gluts or dearths closely affects the price mechanism, if only in the short term. Whether or not prices had a direct significance for many households in the sixteenth and seventeenth centuries, they provide a historical frame of reference for general trends of economic activity. Prices, however, are not necessarily a reflection of the supply and demand of consumable or marketable commodities. What happened between 1500 and 1750 were two very long-term price trends, one persistently upward before the mid-seventeenth century and the other a period of stable or even falling prices for the century after 1660. By and large, there are two schools of opinion on the causes of these long periods of concurrence. The first is essentially monetarist;

17

that is to say, the root cause is attributed to changes in the supply of money or bullion. The second is concerned to find 'physical' explanations for the phenomenon, which is to say that it emphasizes the supply of material commodities and changes in the schedule of secular demand for them.

The monetarists have drawn strength from the apparent coincidence of a vast influx of silver (and gold) from the New World from the 1520s and European movements of general prices. The argument is that significant changes in the money supply, without a comparable increase or decline in the supply of commodities which entered the market, must inevitably alter the price level because too much (or too little) money begins to chase too few (or too many) goods. A vast increase in the media of exchange, when physical output was limited by restraints upon productivity, was bound to cause inflation. Moreover, the exchange value of the currency was affected by the actual quantity of precious metals in the coinage. Debasement, that is to say dilution, of the silver content in coins by the addition of more base metals, or clipping (depreciation of minted coins by cutting at their edges to reduce the weight of silver), both raised prices for commodities, because silver was regarded as fixing the standard of exchange. Debasement meant that more coins could be struck out of the same stock of silver. Furthermore, since the use of money is essentially fiduciary, tampering with the exchanges might in itself reduce the credit of money in common trade. The upshot of any decline of the standards of the coinage in circulation was that bad (debased or clipped) money irresistibly drove out good money, which disappeared into hoards, and thus depreciated still further the aggregate value of the currency in use. The sixteenth century saw not only the vast influx of American bullion into Europe but also several attempts by government to alter the ratio of silver to base metals in the coinage. How far does this support the monetarist explanation of secular inflation in the period?

The most difficult problem is to assign dates for the opening of particular trends, for even in a 'century' of inflation, short-period fluctuations against, or notably greater than, the secular trend are to be expected. Thus, as the graph (Fig. 1) shows, the pattern before 1650–60 is one of several sharp inclines, followed by plateaux and occasionally by short downslopes, though in general each plateau is on a higher plane than the previous one. Many recent writers have assumed that this upward trend began as far back as 1475–80 and was running strongly

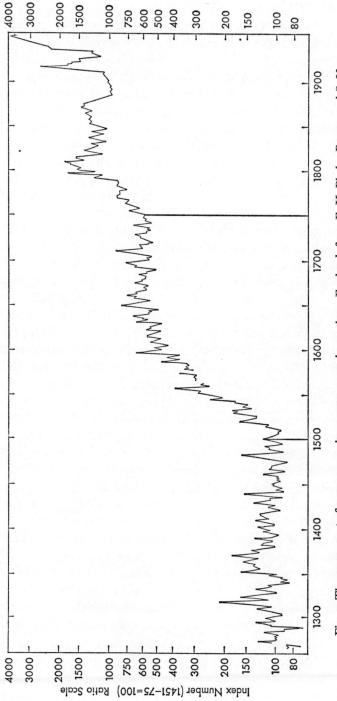

Fig. 1. The movement of consumer prices, 1250–1950, in southern England, from E. H. Phelps Brown and S. V. Hopkins, 'Seven Centuries of the Prices of Consumables, as Compared with Builders' Wages,' *Economica*, XXIII, 1956, Fig. 1.

Index Number (1451–75=100) Ratio Scale

in 1509–22, although it was only from the 1520s, 'when prices failed to descend to the sort of levels which had earlier prevailed, that signs of anything exceptional occurring are evident' (Outhwaite).[1] Thereafter movement was increasingly rapid. The period from 1540 to 1557 marks the next sharp incline, and there were others for agricultural products, from 1593 to 1600 and from 1631 to 1652. Industrial commodity prices moved upward more slowly but more steadily from 1510 to 1650, as did wage-rates (Table I). By 1560, agricultural prices were 198 per cent and industrial prices 106 per cent higher than in 1500; by 1600 the increase was 413 per cent and 152 per cent respectively, and by 1650 agricultural prices stood 585 per cent and industrial prices 224 per cent above the level around 1500.

The earliest monetary explanations of inflation before 1650 merely stressed that the increase in prices was the direct outcome of increases in the quantity of money, as a result of debasement or of the inflow of bullion. Y. S. Brenner, however, has proposed a more sophisticated analysis: 'The rise in prices in England during the first half of the sixteenth century was due to the concatenation of an increasing velocity and volume of currency circulation with a relatively decreased supply of and intensified tightness of demand for agricultural products.'[2] In this increase of the velocity of circulation, credit expansion, through relaxation of the usury laws, and the increased use of bills of sale and exchange and of promissory notes, played a significant part. Debasement appears as the prime mover of monetary expansion before 1550, followed by the increased output of the Mint after the Elizabethan restoration of the coinage in 1560–1. The factor of credit was obviously significant in enlarging the media of exchange, but must have been ancillary to other influences because credit expansion showed no sign of slackening after 1650, when the inflationary bubble had been pricked. The difficulties multiply when we try to quantify the components in the equation. Thus even if we can estimate the increase of prices, we cannot know the amount of money actually in circulation, for merchants were accustomed to use a variety of foreign coins as well as the products of the English mint; and for the velocity of circulation or the number of transactions undertaken, there is nothing of any utility with which to fit historical experience into the frame of economic theory. Problematical as the strict hypothesis may

[1] R. B. Outhwaite, *Inflation in Tudor and Early Stuart England* (Macmillan 1969), p. 13.
[2] Y. S. Brenner, 'Prices and Wages in England, 1450–1550', *Bulletin of the Institute of Historical Research*, XXXIV, 1961, p. 103.

Table I. *Price Trends and Real Wage Movements 1451–1750: Decennial Averages*

	I Cost of Living	II Industrial Prices a	II Industrial Prices b	III Real Wages
1451–60	99	99		102
1461–70	105	103		97
1471–80	94	100		107
1481–90	116	103		89
1491–1500	100	97		100
1501–10	105	98		96
1511–20	115	102		88
1521–30	151	110		67
1531–40	154	110		..
1541–50	203	127		..
1551–60	290	186		..
1561–70	(283)	218		(59)
1571–80	(319)	223		..
1581–90	362	230		56
1591–1600	478	238		44
1601–10	479	256		42
1611–20	527	274		38
1621–30	527	264		(39)
1631–40	611	281		..
1641–50	647	306		..
1651–60	621	327		(49)
1661–70	636	343	109	48
1671–80	614	351	98	49
1681–90	571	310	85	(51)
1691–1700	663	331	103	..
1701–10	603	..	101	..
1711–20	647	..	93	58
1721–30	604	..	92	61
1731–40	558	..	86	..
1741–50	593	..	91	68

Figures in parentheses ( ) are averages of incomplete decennial data. The mark .. signifies that the data are too deficient for use. The indexes in I, IIa and III are based in 1451–75 (=100). The index in IIb is based in 1701 (=100).

SOURCES:

Cols. I & III: E. H. Phelps Brown and S. V. Hopkins, 'Seven Centuries of the Prices of Consumables, Compared with Builders' Wage Rates', *Economica*, XXIII, 1956, App. B. Col. I is made up of a 'basket' of consumer goods available in southern England and weighted as follows: cereals 20%; meat, fish 25%; butter, cheese 12½%; drink 22½%; fuel and light 7½%; textiles 12½%. Col. III is an index of building craft wages (Oxford and London) related to the price of consumables in Col. I, thus suggesting the purchasing power of money wages at different times. Col. II (a), from E. H. Phelps Brown and S. V. Hopkins, 'Wages Rates and Prices: Evidence for Population Pressure in the Sixteenth Century', *Economica*, XXIV, 1957, p. 306, consists of an unweighted selection of industrial products, some canvas, charcoal, candles, oil, shirting, woollen cloth, laths, plain tiles, bricks, lead and solder (see *ibid.*, p. 301 for explanation). Col. II (b) is a crude fusion (by this author) of two indexes of producer prices (products similar to Col. II (a)), 1661–1698 (based in 1697 and 1696–1801 based in 1701) in E. B. Schumpeter, 'English Prices and Public Finance 1660–1822', *Review of Economic Statistics*, 1938, which will serve to show the trend of industrial prices beyond 1700.

be for the period, common sense suggests that changes in the money supply must have influenced the movement of prices directly.

Debasement, which became an instrument of short-term public policy in 1542, undoubtedly reduced the silver content of the coinage dangerously, and may have precipitated the great rise of the 1540s, but the fact that price rises affected different segments of the commodity market very unevenly suggests that this is unlikely, except in a tributary sense. Moreover, the upward trend of prices had set in long before even the minor devaluation of 1526, and indeed continued beyond the restoration of the coinage in 1561, although Cecil's work may have contributed to the temporary downturn of prices in the 1560s. American silver has proved even more contentious. For England, no one presumes that it was of any moment until after 1550. Privateering in Spanish America was spectacular but apparently unimportant as a source of bullion into England. The two sources usually cited are, first, a favourable trade balance with Spain, as a result of which specie was used to pay for the surplus of exports from England to Spain, and secondly an influx of silver brought about by divergence in bimetallic ratios between gold and silver, although since these ratios tended to be self-adjusting, an inflow of one metal was likely to be balanced by an outflow of the other, so that the end result was equilibrium. For the balance of trade, there is not yet sufficient evidence to state categorically that the Spanish trade was either in surplus or in deficit in the century between 1550 and 1650, so that we do not know whether there was a net influx of silver, especially since we have no information about shipping or other commission earnings. In a general way throughout Europe, the correlation of price movements and flows of treasure is doubtful. While it is true that agricultural prices rose much higher than can be explained simply in monetary terms, the increase in industrial commodity prices across Europe was not only more modest, but virtually disappears when converted to silver prices. The vast analysis of Braudel and Spooner is essentially inconclusive in what is, to date, the most complete and wide-ranging survey of price and wage data for Europe after 1450.[1] But all modern historians are now required to consider the schedules of supply and demand for material commodities as factors of at least equal importance to the supply of money.

Physical explanations of the historic experience of inflation have

[1] F. Braudel and F. Spooner, 'Prices in Europe 1450–1750', *Cambridge Economic History of Europe*, vol. IV (1967), pp. 430–42.

become increasingly fashionable since the 1930s. Indeed, a few writers have argued that monetary expansion was the effect, not the cause, of much inflationary pressure, as the consequence of increasing *demands* for money and credit in the sixteenth century. The effects of harvest fluctuations, since good and bad harvests tended to run in sequences, have always been considered important, but only in the short term, because long climatic trends do not seem to have changed the periodic level of prices. Coupled with the incontrovertible evidence of long-term phases of population change, in which a major increase or decrease of numbers immediately influenced the consumption of necessary commodities, such as food, firewood, clothing and accommodation, glut or dearth could indeed change the level of prices beyond the term of their exigency. But population was certainly not the only influence at work, even if its growth before 1630–50 underlay most of the others. The increase of rents, for instance, was itself an independent inflationary force to be reckoned with, but at bottom rents could be raised only because landlords were able to find prospective tenants willing, or at least not reluctant, to pay the increase demanded. At the same time the potential and the pitfalls of foreign trade, especially the sequence of commercial depression and expansion, generated their own pressures upon the price level, if only by being superimposed upon tendencies already evident in the domestic economy. Commercial vicissitudes owed much both to changes in the demand schedules for the goods handled and to independent political events, which, like the state of the harvest, affected the price mechanism at least briefly.

The simple view that population pressure *caused* the inflation before 1630 gained support from the apparently solid evidence of a major decline in real wages, on the assumption that this reflected a widespread reduction of living standards. Thus the purchasing power of building craft wages fell from 1510–20 to 1595–1605 by 46 per cent.[1] But this decline reflects the very great inflation in the prices of food or other basic consumables. Wages fared much better if compared with industrial commodity prices. The opinion that the growth of capitalism after 1540 was stimulated by an inflation of profits, as businessmen gained from the price rise at the expense of their labourers' incomes, has by now been demolished. Industrial wages in some trades apparently grew even faster than product prices. For agriculture there may be much to be

[1] From E. H. Phelps Brown and S. V. Hopkins, 'Seven Centuries of the Price of Consumables compared with Builders Wages', *Economica* XXIII, 1956.

said for the view that a polarization of wealth between rich and poor villagers occurred before 1630, as farmers with considerable surpluses for sale profited from the century of inflation. The most cogent of the 'real' explanations of inflation is demographic pressure upon food resources. No long-run Malthusian crisis of acute overpopulation had afflicted English society by 1600–50, thanks to some improvement in agricultural productivity, but the fact that prices for foodstuffs settled on a higher plane after each period of shortage implies that many of the preconditions of acute hunger existed from 1590 to 1650.

Physical explanations certainly seem to account better for the long period of more or less stable prices after 1660 than monetarist theories. It is true that the influx of Spanish silver declined significantly in the middle third of the seventeenth century, and there is something in the argument that for two centuries after 1640 supplies of bullion comparable to those put into circulation by the Spaniards in the previous century were much diminished. The fluctuations follow quite closely such real events as the state of the harvest or the incidence of war. Even in the 1690s, when the state of the currency was so bad that a recoinage was required, the temporary price rise is more likely to have been the result of commodity shortages in years of war and bad harvests. More-over, the price level fell back after the emergency was over. The large but immeasurable expansion of credit after 1650 may be seen in part as a mere adjustment to an inadequate coinage, but most of the pressure for credit expansion came from the increasing turnover of business activity which occurred in the context of a stable price level. Many important commodities—wool, coal, meat, glass, tobacco, sugar—showed some tendency to fall in price in the period before 1750. The percentage change of consumer prices, 1660–1750, as compared with 1570–1660, was under fifteen. Real wages perhaps increased by 20 per cent between the same two periods. But the century 1660–1750 stands between two long periods both of substantial population increase and of price inflation.

When all is said, however, the question remains whether the un-doubted rise of prices before 1650 actually amounted to a 'revolution'. From our standpoint, at the end of sixty years in which the consumer price-index has risen twelvefold, the inflation between 1500 and 1650 was not excessive. But in a society in which supply and demand were both relatively quite inelastic, and in which the potential for saving and the opportunity for personal credit were much less prevalent, the effects of inflation, and especially the great spurts of price increases, in the 1540s and 1550s, the 1590s and 1640s, were not only materially damaging for the poor or for those who lived on fixed incomes, but psychologically disturbing for everyone from prince to pauper. It is one thing to note the very long-run tendency for money to depreciate in value; or to observe that many of the forces which upheld inflation, from variations in the supply and flow of specie, population pressure, harvest failures, to the gradual, if not persistent, expansion in the market for goods and in the volume of transactions, affected medieval life in the same way as in the sixteenth century. The point, however, is that the upsurge of prices after 1520 came after a long period of near stability, just as from the 1760s onwards, the upward trend set in after Good King George's 'pudding time',[1] and was therefore doubly disturbing. It broke up the pattern of developing expectations. Moreover, the behaviour of food prices is the most sensitive of all indicators of the common man's attitude to economic performance and food prices seemed to have risen before 1650 beyond reasonable expectations.

[1] Cf. 'The Vicar of Bray', fifth stanza:
> 'When George in pudding-time came o'er,
> and moderate men looked big, sir,
> I turned a cat-in-the-pan once more
> and so became a Whig, sir.'

FURTHER READING

T. S. Ashton   *Economic Fluctuations in England 1700–1800* (O.U.P., 1958).

J. D. Chambers   *Population, Economy and Society in Pre Industrial England* (O.U.P., 1972).

E. L. Jones   *Seasons and Prices* (Allen and Unwin, 1965).

R. B. Outhwaite   *Inflation in Tudor and Stuart England* (Macmillan, 1971).

R. Ramsey, ed.   *The Price Revolution in Sixteenth Century England* (Methuen, 1969).

E. A. Wrigley   *Population and History* (Weidenfeld, 1969).

F. Braudel and F. Spooner   'Prices in Europe, 1450–1750', *Cambridge Economic History of Europe*, vol. iv, 1967.

E. J. Buckatzsch   'The Constancy of Local Populations and Migration in England before 1800', *Population Studies*, V, 1951–2.

J. Cornwall   'Evidence of Population Mobility in the Seventeenth Century', *Bulletin Institute of Historical Research*, XI, 1967.

F. J. Fisher   'Commercial Trends and Policy in Sixteenth Century England', *Economic History Review*, X, 1940.

K. F. Helleiner   'The Vital Revolution Reconsidered', in D. V. Glass and D. E. C. Eversley, eds., *Population in History* (Arnold, 1965).

W. H. Hoskins   'Harvest Fluctuations in English Economic History 1480–1619', *Agricultural History Review*, XII, 1964.

W. H. Hoskins   'Harvest Fluctuations in English Economic History, 1620–1759', *Agricultural History Review*, XVI, 1968.

E. A. Wrigley   'Family Limitation in Preindustrial England', *Economic History Review*, XIX, 1966.

2

The Shape of Society: Hierarchy and Social Mobility

The view that English society before the nineteenth century was essentially aristocratic, setting great store by the deference owed to rank, adhering to a chain of authority distinctly outmoded, but hallowed by time and pertinacious in the face of necessary changes, is exaggerated. It takes little account of the social dynamism inherent in post-feudal society in Europe; it neglects the receptiveness of that society to the fertilizing influences of social mobility; it overlooks the extent of intermarriage and the value attached to money and wealth; above all, it suggests an ordered consistency which is belied by differences of opinion and material circumstances, and by the jealousy and factiousness that disturbed every status-group in society between 1400 and 1800.

On the other hand, the foundation of political authority, before as well as after the overthrow of royal 'despotism' in the course of the seventeenth century, was landed property. The men who controlled Parliament, the magistracy, and provincial and central administration, as well as their rivals for office, were rich in land. The expectation that tangible wealth should reflect the rank of its possessors—that earls should be richer than barons and barons richer than knights or esquires, and so on—persisted surprisingly late in public, or at least official, sentiment, long after any such gradation could be maintained in practice. It was part of a body of hierarchical ideas inherited from the past which were repeated time and again by conservatives, 'divine right' apologists and opponents of rational models of society which stressed the connection between power and actual wealth or the relativity of political organization. Hierarchy, that is to say, became an article of faith with adversaries of such writers as Hobbes, Harrington, Locke or Mandeville. In truth, most articulate men expressed a belief of sorts in structured societies, even when they despised the present establishment, from direct memory of internecine tumult or because they accepted the classical, and medieval, fear of upheaval. 'Civility', polite society, 'rational' behaviour clung to the cliff-face with greater tenacity because a fall might let in the 'fourth estate' of men with neither power nor responsibility, who easily outnumbered the rest of society.

The constitution of pre-industrial England grew upon roots firmly bedded in a deep loam of patriarchal and patrilineal authority. Kinship and the associated pattern of clientage were as central to political and social relationships as the hereditary authority of rank. The family and the state were part of the same order, and a link between the two was forged from the rich ore of local or provincial patriotism. One source of strength in English society, and a weakness in the ambition of centralized authority, was the vigour of social and political, as well as economic, life in the counties and leading provincial towns. The network of deference and, conversely, of social opportunity, retained its strength until well beyond 1750, because at every turn men were brought up in the shadow of social discipline and under duty of obedience from their earliest years. Hierarchy, it seemed, was inherent in the society of men. Writers often employed the image of the Great Tree, which not only permitted them to describe the gradations of rank but supplied an object-lesson in stately organic growth to point the moral.

Sir Thomas Smith's celebrated description of the English constitution in the 1560s—in *De Republica Anglorum*—placed the orders of men into four groups—gentlemen, citizens and burgesses, yeomen and artificers, and labourers. The gentry included everyone from the sovereign down to the mass of men with a right to bear arms ('esquires' and 'mere gentlemen'). The middle groups, and especially the yeomanry, Smith admired. The yeomen were equated with the forty-shilling freeholders who had the vote in county elections and served on juries. The fourth sort were 'men which do not rule'—husbandmen and labourers, craftsmen and artificers, even merchants and copyholders without free land. Smith's plan of society is both very artificial and deeply conservative, even by early Elizabethan standards. Members of the fourth class included merchants or farmers of greater wealth than the yeomanry or citizenry. Complete freehold was comparatively rare, and Smith's legalistic description is much too narrowly based. A middle order existed in the sixteenth century but it was not founded upon archaic tenures. Moreover, the gentry, in Smith's definition, was too broad a category and owed a good deal to French ideas of nobility, in which 'those whom their blood and race doth make noble and known' had already many of the characteristics of a caste system.

Birth was a norm of social classification inextricably interwoven in the thought, and occasionally in acts of government, of the pre-industrial world. An attempt was made before 1650 to determine occupation, and throughout to assign legal domicile, by birth, and the ancient nostrum that birth (and breeding) 'will out'—will reveal itself in human character and behaviour—has been an unconscionably long time in dying. Inappropriate as descent or genealogy may have been in fixing a man's place in the firmament of authority and acceptance in early modern England, the restraints upon personal freedom of action imposed by family ties or status were consistently applied. The poor in this respect were relatively free; the rich and exalted, even the modestly well-to-do, were inhibited by the demands of property and loyalty to kin. Richard Pococke, touring Britain in the 1750s, noted that Preston, Lancashire, 'subsists . . . by many families of middling fortune . . . and it is remarkable for old maids, because their families will not ally with tradesmen, and have not sufficient fortunes for gentlemen'. The pseudo-gentry formed a category enormously on the increase after 1600, but the vainglory of descent was not confined to them. Celibacy indeed was enforced widely by social custom among property-owning families whose younger children posed problems of support, when both primogeniture and the rationale of accumulation counteracted the sharing of family possessions. Younger children must make their way in the world to secure independence. Younger brothers of gentry were said to number 16,000 in the early years of Charles II. As one of them, Thomas Wilson, had said in 1600, 'their state is of all stations for gentlemen most miserable; . . . [younger brothers must have] that which the cat left on the maltheap.' The younger children of gentry, however, provided the impetus for much economic enterprise, for success attended upon the industrious. Nevertheless, attendant bachelors and old maids were very much part of many substantial households. In practice the full force of primogeniture was usually tempered by affectionate parents. Among farmers or tradesmen, for example, younger sons were generally set up in business by their fathers or were provided with annuities or portions of movable property. Smaller freeholders, indeed, were by no means so bent upon holding together their landed possessions as gentlemen, and not a few willed their real estate in portions to all their male children. However powerful as solvents of heredity were intermarriage and the sale of property, the theme of 'natural hierarchy' in writers from Sir Thomas Smith to Edmund Burke and beyond, resounded also in popular feelings as a mirror of their belief in respectability. The common idea was that of the social pyramid, with its narrow apex of great magnate families and its enormous base of near propertyless labouring poor. It fitted the concept of the hierarchy of descent and also the more real stratification based upon wealth and political authority.

One theory of social order in pre-industrial England which has gained ground recently is to describe the community as a one-class system. What is meant in effect is that there are two groups, one forming the 'political nation', the propertied and 'responsible', the other excluded from all office and a good deal of the nation's property. The number of Englishmen in the early eighteenth century who were politically significant—who possessed the vote—probably did not exceed 200,000 or one-fifth of the adult male population. The oligarchy which carried the responsibility, and enjoyed the fruits, of government was obviously very much smaller. Political categories of this kind are essential material in the social structure. The lesser freeholders with the vote were not richer as a group than the merchants, tenant farmers, master artisans, etc., who were still excluded, but the prestige of the county franchise was such that many of the latter spent much effort and diverted a fair proportion of their capital into acquiring freehold land. Whatever is said about the decline of the yeomanry in England after 1660, it remains true that in many counties a furious demand for land among the middling new rich continued from the sixteenth to the nineteenth century. The new 'yeomanry' was often somewhat different from the old after the Restoration—it was often non-resident—but the lowest rungs of political society continued to be fully occupied until such time as parliamentary reform changed the basis of qualification. Of course, the men who voted in county or borough elections often had no real independence, and except intermittently no political responsibility, although the constitution of village and small-town élites which comprised those men below the rank of magistrate, who served minor public offices and kept their fingers upon the pulse of local affairs, is an important and still neglected theme of English social organization before the nineteenth century. The pyramid of society had many faces, one of birth and heredity, another of material possessions, a third of political power and authority.

The ruling élite, the gentlemen of England, were an élite only in the sense that they arrogated to themselves most of the substantive political and judicial functions of the state. On occasion too they bestirred themselves as an order to protect this entrenched position, by discountenancing the pretensions of non-armigerous families or by appropriating the principal offices of the county, and once even the House of Commons in 1712, as their private preserve. The gentry were split by faction, by wide discrepancies of wealth, by family, county or metropolitan jealousies, and by religious, political and social ideals. The scramble for office, influence and emoluments was a comedy played over and over again in early modern England, set in a scene of constant social mobility, and articulated by a whole series of dramatists from Ben Jonson onwards. The partisanship of eighteenth-century political life was not a new development of the years after 1688, for precisely the same kind of factions rent the politics of Tudor and Stuart England.

To be a gentleman was to have a path to follow, open to all kinds of services and benefits denied to other mortals, but to become a gentleman was not generally difficult. Powerful and indispensable as the English gentry and nobility were in the period, they did not form an 'estate' in the sense understood by European societies. First, nobility was reserved to a small number of heads of great households, increasing from 50 to 300 between 1540 and 1760 but still infinitesimal by European standards. The peers possessed few privileges denied to other gentlemen or freeholders, except a seat by right in the House of Lords, and although some sense of their exclusiveness was fostered in periods of few ennoblements, under Henry VII, Elizabeth or Sir Robert Walpole, less stringent standards in succeeding ages brought the very rich commoners, from knights to merchants and lawyers, into the fold of English nobility. What was lacking in England was an effective sense of caste, supported by legal barriers or the rules of *dérogeance* (loss of status caused by the adoption of a demeaning occupation), and morganatic alliances (the denial of rank to wives of inferior descent and to their children), which in rigid societies glued together the fixed orders or estates. The English, for all their nice sense of rank and dignity, had no framework of estates, for the collective personality of the nobility and clergy was

31

severely limited. This did not mean that an English earl could not be as arrogant as a French *duc* or a Spanish grandee. It did, however, mean that after the Wars of the Roses, noble English families could no longer expect to obtain military commands or political offices merely because of their birth, although the propensity to defer to rank nevertheless kept the magnates in high office.

We must take up a suggestion of Professors Stone, Mingay and Thompson [1] that the ruling élite of England was in fact divided into magnates, not necessarily peers of the realm, and a larger and less influential group, which we may call the squirearchy, most but not all of whom bore coats-of-arms, but were typically untitled, possessed substantial but not great estates of land, say 500–5,000 acres, and were especially involved in the affairs of their counties, in Quarter Sessions, the shrievalty, petty sessions, county representation at Westminster and county needs. Their politics obviously affected the action of central government, as when, for example, Elizabeth encountered difficulty in enforcing the Anglican church settlement in Lancashire, where a papist gentry retained much power, or in counties at the opposite extremity of belief where Puritans dominated Quarter Sessions.

Between 1560 and 1760 the function, and the fortune, of this squirearchy had been closely related to the swings of power at the centre. Quantitatively the group waxed and waned in wealth and in numbers, but it survived remarkably well until 1914, because it was politically indispensable. As unpaid local administrators, bound by the rule of law and widely accepted by the governed, they obviated the need for a massive bureaucracy sitting heavily upon the fabric of English society. Above all, however, the squirearchy was able to weather both political and economic adversity and to exploit any opportunities which were offered. The gentry established that power upon landownership. The share of English property seems to have remained broadly similar throughout the period. In 1790 the gentry, distinct from the great magnates, probably owned over 40 per cent of the land, and this is unlikely to have changed for at least a century. The best guess for the mid-sixteenth century is that the middling and lower gentry possessed one-third of the cultivated land. Before the Dissolution of the Monas-

[1] See L. Stone, *The Crisis of the Aristocracy, 1558–1641* (O.U.P. 1965), and G. E. Mingay, *English Landed Society in the Eighteenth Century* (Routledge 1963) and F. M. L. Thompson, 'The Social Distribution of Landed Property in England since the Sixteenth Century'. *Economic History Review*, XIX, 1966.

teries, in 1436 and 1523, middling lay estates assessed to the subsidy [1] comprised about 25 per cent of the land areas. As to numbers we can estimate the number of families in the sixteenth century as 8,000 to 10,000 and in the eighteenth as 15,000 to 18,000.

Above the squirearchy was a very small group of very rich, potentially very powerful and influential households. It always included the peerage, for very few peers were created before 1750 who possessed landed estates inadequate for their dignity. Before 1539 bishops and mitred abbots also belonged to the magnate class, and nothing is more striking after the Reformation than the decline of the 'lords spiritual' as a political and economic force. In addition to the titular nobility there were always some families of knights, baronets or plain esquires of great wealth and massive influence. This charmed circle numbered variously 200–500 individuals before the Restoration. The number was greater between 1690 and 1750, but the oligarchy which steered the ship of state into the calm latitudes of the Augustan age was composed of about 800 families including rivals for office. Their power base was proportionally immense. Estates over 5,000 acres, which was the least that a magnate could possess, probably occupied between one-fifth and one-quarter of the kingdom between 1550 and 1750, and, including the great ecclesiastical estates, perhaps even more between 1450 and 1550.

The disadvantage of taking a property qualification to determine social structure is that it does not obviously include social groups of substantial wealth like the merchants and London lawyers whose connection with the land may have been casual. Great merchants of the City, and even of Norwich, Bristol or Newcastle, were at least as rich as many knights or esquires. According to Gervase Holles, indeed, the mayor of London in the sixteenth and seventeenth centuries was regarded as equal to a baron *outside* 'the city and his proper jurisdiction', where he was more like a prince. Thomas Wilson thought that mercantile fortunes in excess of £50,000 in London and of £10,000 to £20,000 in the provinces were not uncommon in 1600, and Gregory King's supposed income for the greater merchants and traders by sea in 1688 nearly equalled that of his esquires (£400 as against £450 p.a.). Recent researches, however, have established that although there were some merchant fortunes of immense size in seventeenth-century Eng-

[1] The subsidy was a direct tax regularly levied by Parliament upon land, goods or incomes between the fourteenth and sixteenth centuries.

land, the majority of even London's merchants were on a par, at best, with the lesser gentry or yeomanry.[1] Since the number of great merchants, lawyers and other important functionaries probably exceeded 5,000 at any particular time in the seventeenth century their aggregate income and wealth were sufficient ostensibly to undermine the absolute primacy of landed property among the élite of wealth by the time of the Glorious Revolution. This, of course, is a false impression because most of the representatives of these groups drew a good part of their revenues from property, buildings or land. The openness of landed society allowed the new rich to accommodate themselves to its expectations by acquiring estates and the trappings of political patronage. In the sixteenth century some great capitalists, like Thomas Sutton, who amassed a fortune in the Northumbrian coal trade, or 'Customer' Smythe, apparently experienced difficulty of admission into the upper ranks of Elizabethan society, although great lawyers were more readily accepted. The merchant-princes of the next century, from Sir Baptist Hickes to Vyner, Chaplin, Child and Heathcote, suffered no such rebuffs. True, society as well as the law took vengeance upon the overweening merchants who floated the fraudulent South Sea Company, but they were exceptional. Although few businessmen made the peerage in the eighteenth century, the opulent and successful ones easily stepped into the charmed circle. An example of the type is Sir Gilbert Heathcote, who was a man of political weight before he became a great landowner in Rutland and Lincolnshire in the 1720s and 1730s. His estates secured the succession of his line socially, politically and economically—an obvious precaution for an ambitious man who could not know his posterity.

The combined total of politically significant families did not much exceed 25,000 magnates, esquires, greater merchants, office-holders and leading lawyers. But the professional *cadres* of English society notably expanded, in London and great provincial centres such as York, Bristol or Chester in the sixteenth century, and elsewhere in provincial England after 1600. Professor Everitt, comparing the size and diversity of the Victorian leisured class with the few 'private residents' in England before 1620, has argued that the rise of this 'pseudo-gentry' between the reigns of Charles I and Victoria 'formed as important a development in English history as the . . . rise of the landed gentry'.

[1] R. Grassby, 'Personal Wealth of the Business Community in Seventeenth Century England', *Econ. Hist. Rev.* XXIII, 1970.

Men were heard to complain that lawyers were already too numerous in Elizabeth's day, and the proliferation of clergymen, notaries, attorneys, physicians, schoolmasters after 1540 merged with and created an increasingly unified middle order out of the yeomanry and well-to-do farmers and merchants, middlemen and artisans in trade. The absence of a rigid formation of 'estates', *bourgeoisie* or peasantry, in England is nowhere more marked than in this amorphous, complex and increasingly interlocking group which spanned both town and country. Changing attitudes and opportunities in certain spheres of business as well as a growing demand for educational, medical and legal services, influenced the expansion of this new middle order. Since many if not all of the personnel in this class, as if to prove the absurdity of Sir Thomas Smith's conservative plan of English society, were not enfranchised, they were properly excluded from the political nation as formally constituted. But in reality the essential dividing line socially and politically lay between the rate-payers and the mass of the poor. Hence Gregory King's influential distinction between solvent and insolvent persons. By his reckoning at least 400,000 families were sufficiently well off to pay rates regularly, to give employment and to form a reservoir for village or town offices, constable, churchwarden, overseer of the poor, etc. It was the 800,000 or more families of cottagers and labouring poor who were fully excluded from political and economic responsibility.

King's data are probably not very accurate but they do serve to show that the 'feet of the body politic' were too large for the head and trunk by 1700. The poor had become an immense problem long before the Industrial Revolution. In the early sixteenth century the labouring poor of many towns already comprised half to two-thirds of their total population, often crowded in 'working-class parishes' or slum districts as horrifying in their squalor as in a Victorian city. In the countryside, too, the poor excluded from all taxes or paying their dues upon wages were already numerous enough to cause danger of social unrest in times of hardship. The poor, however, were not formed into a homogeneous working class. Wage-earners included among their number journeymen and skilled craftsmen as respectable as any self-employed master—often waiting for capital or for a vacancy to acquire an independent business. There were also domestic servants, apprentices, farm servants and other retainers, seamen, common soldiers, as well as a half-proletarianized body of labourers employed in the trades such as textiles, metal-working and mining which had moved out into the countryside. The 'stop of work' in the commercial and subsistence crisis of 1622–3, for example, threw thousands of textile workers out of employment, and the effects on Wiltshire or the West Riding were not unlike those which reverberated through nineteenth-century industrial regions in similar recessions. But the poor were no less characterized by tiny smallholders, common-right holders, squatters, who occupied unauthorized cottages on the manorial 'waste', catch-workers and the like, who were not independent of employment by others but who could or would take paid work only at seasonal peaks of demand or when trade was prosperous. These poor, perhaps a quarter of the population in the seventeenth century, caused most of the problems, partly because the livelihood of many of them was being diminished by reclamation or more intensive farming, or because of the threat to order of their precarious standard of living, and of their alleged turbulence and idleness. Hence the long succession of attempts to control the poor by statute or through Quarter Sessions and the Poor Law, and the widespread belief in pre-industrial society that the only way to keep the labouring poor humble and diligent was to pay barely subsistent wages in order to compel them into work.

Countless proposals were produced concerning the best way to make the poor industrious and quiet. There were even writers before 1700 who drew a bow at the labour theory of value, exalting the labourers' contribution to the value acquired by a product in the process of its manufacture and proclaiming the duty of both employers and the state to generate employment for the idle. Indeed, a profound change in the attitude of articulate people to labour and labourers took place in the century after 1680, which was eventually to turn the working man from a 'hewer of wood and drawer of water' to a consumer of goods and services, to be encouraged by high, rather than to be scourged by low, wages. These were attempts to release the pressure building up in society by its increasing body of propertyless poor and to discover a more rational role for the great majority of English subjects in an economic system, to which they were indispensable but in which they had little interest. The fruits of these ideas were not borne until after 1800, and throughout the pre-industrial period the poor remained like a nation within a nation, from which few could escape upwards into a more rarefied atmosphere. They continued to be blown by the mischances of underemployment, dearth, disease and overcrowding, by the vicissitude of poor-relief policies or by the vagaries of attitude among those set above them.

It is scarcely surprising that in the mobile confusion of English society before 1800 social theory should lag behind reality. Adherence to the principle of hierarchy decayed slowly as other elements, always present, became increasingly more obvious and influential. Rank and lineage remained powerful watchwords of social order, but as early as Sir Thomas Smith the fact that gentlemen 'be made good cheap in England', indicates what little chance there was of turning the order into a caste. As Smith went on to say, the man 'who can live idly and without manual labour, and will bear the port, charge and countenance of a gentleman . . . he shall be taken for a gentleman . . .; [and if need be] a king of heralds shall give him for money, arms newly made and invented . . .' All European societies provided for such eventualities, but in none save England was the fabrication of new gentry so widespread, commonplace or so much of a business enterprise. Smith perhaps did not emphasize sufficiently that idleness was not necessarily a badge of gentility even in his day, for many of the successful members of the order, new-made or established, remained active in professional or public duties, while others, merchants or moneylenders, landowners or younger sons in business, cheerfully soiled their hands in trade. The mutability of landed families becomes an oppressive theme for antiquarians in the two centuries after 1550. Thomas Fuller, in the midseventeenth century, repeatedly observed the changes evident in the past three hundred years—'Hungry time has made a glutton's meal on this catalogue of gentry [of 1433 in Bedfordshire] . . . The lands in Berkshire are very skittish, and often cast their owners.'

From this dynamic aspect of social change, a great flood of historical writing has flowed. The importance of social mobility in determining the course of English history between the Reformation and the Restoration is unlikely now to be overlooked, but it is so much involved in considerations of economic change that the main lines of development have still to be examined. The conceptual framework in which social mobility has been made to work in transforming society rests upon two different foundations. First are those theoretical explanations in which class conflict is explicit, in which two 'classes', possessing different economic interests and different social values, fought each other for hegemony until one emerged as dominant. Secondly, there is a similar cluster of hypotheses stressing the jealousies, internal dissensions and the diversity of ostensibly homogeneous social orders or status-groups. Men, it is argued, did not behave as if they were in the midst of a class war, and it has even been suggested that for the kind of people who formed public opinion in pre-industrial England the social order was essentially classless. There are, in addition, many variations upon these themes, but the battle lines have been drawn upon the issue of 'class'.

The most famous expression of the first line of argument is R. H. Tawney's hypothesis of the rise of the gentry between 1540 and 1640. Tawney's gentry expanded at the expense of Crown, Church and aristocracy by a judicious exploitation of the land market, by a much more efficient management of their estates, by raising rents, changing tenures, farming for profit. They prospered in the inflation of the sixteenth and early seventeenth centuries, when the aristocracy—their competitors for hegemony—bound by customary obligations and other limitations upon their freedom of action, was forced to reduce its landed wealth and consequently its political authority. The gentry as a class rose with the massive transfers of land before 1640 and with the increasing authority of the Commons. By 1650 the shift of power had therefore become complete. The weakness of Tawney's statistical methods has itself caused a good deal of controversy among historians, but two substantive objections to his hypothesis undermine many of his premises. First, the extent to which the greatest landowners suffered is less evident than Tawney supposed. Aristocracy did not fall before the rampant agrarian capitalism of the new men, because the aristocrats who survived the buffeting of civil war and royal purges were not as a class any more inhibited from rational economic behaviour than the *parvenu* gentry. Noble behaviour obviously depended upon external conditions, so that in the wild and dangerous north retaining and the trappings of bastard feudalism lingered longer than in the secure south of England, but few noble families were so hidebound as to retain hopelessly uneconomic obligations long after they were redundant. The new Tudor nobility was distinguished by a hard-headedness which would have done the generation of Rockefeller and Carnegie proud. The evidence for growing aristocratic impoverishment is much in dispute. The revenues of many great estates like those of Lord Pembroke at Wilton certainly did not lag behind the general rise in prices before 1600, but others were crippled by extravagance, mismanagement or fecklessness so that some aristocratic households fell, for economic as well as political reasons; but that in itself is a qualification of Tawney's point of view since it implies significant differences *within* the class. The same objection applies to his 'gentry' who were not, as economic and political historians now generally accept, a homogeneous group, but a complex of warring, or interlocking, social and political factions.

Tawney's interpretation was not Marxist, chiefly because he rejected the Marxian emphasis upon purely materialist or economic values to the exclusion of religious conviction or idealism, but the basis of both class-directed theses of social change is remarkably similar. Marxists hold to the same view of an aggressive and individualistic new order which overthrew the old régime of feudal landlords and authoritarian church. Since revolution is indispensable to Marxist concepts of social change, the decisive turning-point—the revolution—in the conflict between feudalism and bourgeois capitalism occurred in the century between the Reformation and the Civil War, which becomes *tout court* the English Revolution. The Reformation demonstrated the emergence of new values and new social forces at work in society. The Civil War was the culmination of the running fight between old and modern economic forces. The parliamentary forces were bound to prevail, by the logic of history, for Parliament drew its strength from the commercial and industrial regions and from the prosperous countryside, and had a preponderance of resources; the Crown was forced to rely upon the backward and impoverished feudality of the north and west. At the time, James Harrington had expressed a similar point of view, that victory in the Civil War was merely a reflection of the obvious correlation between wealth and power which had been working itself out in new social combinations in the past century or so. (Excellent accounts of a Marxist and of a modified Marxist interpretation of the period are to be found in Maurice Dobb's *Studies in the Development of Capitalism* and in Christopher Hill's *The Century of Revolution, 1603–1714.*)

The elements which forged the strength of the bourgeoisie before 1660 were surprisingly consistent. The moral advantage of economic success was reinforced by the Protestant ethic and the growth of scientific rationalism, which as much as the shift of power transformed the beliefs and ideals of society. Protestantism inculcated the virtues of education (primarily of course in order to read the Bible), individualism and self-help, and indirectly those of saving, accumulation and the intelligent management of business. Above all, the Calvinist attitude to the taking of interest—usury in medieval doctrine—had become a keynote of the change in social values. Scientific rationalism, in the broadest sense, not only overturned many ancient superstitions and beliefs, and thereby eventually weakened the grip of tradition upon public sentiment, but by providing a methodology of empiricism for a wide range of inquiries also affected the common way of thinking among progressive intelligent men.

The objections to the revolutionary or cataclysmal view of social change have always been that the thesis is too elegant, too well carpentered to explain the hurly-burly of human behaviour in the crucial period. Just as class is not an appropriate concept for European society before the nineteenth century, so neither Protestantism nor modern science really liberated the chained mind from the inconveniencies of superstition or the just price. Capitalism did not advance on a unified front to the conquest of the material world, armed with the weapons of irresistible ideas and equipped with modern tools of exploitation. Research has established the immense but diffuse diversity of experience. Local issues, religious differences, personal bonds of loyalty, even constitutional ideals, were as important as material advantage. The gentry were divided along lines which defy generalization, and merchants, far from being in unison, were no less faction-ridden than their betters. There was a royalist party among the citizenry of most commercial centres and the Crown controlled such progressive towns as Newcastle and Exeter (with Topsham). Moreover, war was not a foregone conclusion in a dialectic sense. The parliamentary troops were not superior till Fairfax and Cromwell made them so; and the train bands of London were not revolutionary cadres who steeled less committed allies to greater fervour at encounters such as Turnham Green or Newbury. The war was lost by Charles's misjudgment and hesitancy in the first two years, 1642–4, not by parliamentary resolution or enjoyment of superior resources. When the war was over, the opportunity of burying the old régime once for all was never contemplated. Delinquents suffered directly from heavy fines and the sequestration of estates, but it is now known that the majority of former royalists had resumed most of their estates well before 1660, and unless they were overt Catholics were not molested by government.[1] Moreover the royal authority which was re-established in 1660 experienced great difficulties, but retained a great deal of the power enjoyed by the early Stuarts. The Crown, from

[1] J. Thirsk, 'Sales of Royalist Land during the Interregnum', *Econ. History Review*, V, 1952; idem, 'The Restoration Land Settlement', *Journal of Modern History*, XXVI, 1954.

1660 to 1688, was not a constitutional monarchy directed by the gentry in Parliament, and it is only in the eighteenth century that we can talk of a permanent shift in the power of central government from Court to Cabinet and Parliament.

The Civil War was more than an incident in the history of the seventeenth century, but it was not a stage in the revolutionary process of social development. H. R. Trevor-Roper has suggested rather that it was the revolt of a faction excluded from the sweets of office, a mid-seventeenth-century variant of the later conflicts of Court *v.* Country, fomented by the resentment of 'mere gentry' against office-holders, courtiers, monopolists and other favourites of the government. Conflict has thus become a struggle within the 'political nation' over the spoils of office, generalized into an assault upon (and defence of) absolutism and the 'bureaucratization' of public service. The weakness of the argument is that the 'mere gentleman' who suffered so much from pecuniary anaemia has proved very elusive. It is improbable that many such existed in an era when Tawney showed how wide were the opportunities for improved estate management and other occasions of private profit-making. The truth is that a highly selective presentation of the evidence can be made to prove almost anything in a period of so much contrariety and articulate dissension. The Civil War had the effect, whatever its causes, of preserving Parliament and the dialogue between Crown (or central government) and representative institutions, and this, by comparison with the *ancien régime* on the Continent, was itself a notable outcome of the conflict.

The last century of the period was in no sense an anticlimax. The repercussions of the Civil War continued to be felt in political life until 1688 at least, but the shape of political society, and the order upon which it rested, was recognizably similar in both 1600 and 1750, however much the character of central government had changed during the interval. One feature which bound together the mobile confusion of Tawney's century (1540–1640) and the dynamism of the hundred years after 1660 was the heterogeneous nature of the English ruling élite. There were 'ins' and 'outs' in respect of the Crown or the government in being at all times, and the way in which magnates, gentry and commercial classes divided in the peaceful but factious political arena of the Augustan age, from 1720 to 1760, just as much as in the Civil War, is a matter of great importance for historians searching for trees in the woods of hypothesis. What looks like a coherent oligarchy of landed wealth in the eighteenth century turns out to be a complex of conflicting interest groups. Moreover, most of the greater functionaries of state and even of party in the early eighteenth century were 'new men' in much the same sense as the protégés of the Tudor state—the Cecils, Herberts, Pophams, Dudleys, Egertons, Paulets, Russells or Cavendishes, who, incidentally, formed the backbone of the aristocracy after the Restoration—had risen from obscure gentry to magnate rank. Political 'dynasties' were founded by successful families in every age, and we are apt to forget the short lease that the established aristocracy had usually held upon public office and social leadership. The feudal baronage had been as uncertain in its attempt to perpetuate its dynastic ambitions as any latter-day nobility in post-medieval England. Families rose and fell in a steady procession; old families were allowed, by public disgrace or economic attrition, to fall away; new families were absorbed into the charmed circle. This was no less true of the century from 1660 to 1760 than of any other period. If the ferment was less under Sir Robert Walpole this at most was only a brief respite.

The argument for a continuous pattern of social change from the fifteenth until the nineteenth century rests upon the conviction that landownership throughout retained its power to determine the bounds and lineaments of English political society. The whole basis of Tawney's 'rise of the gentry', or of James Harrington's materialist interpretation of his age, clearly expressed in his book *Oceana*, depends upon the effectiveness of large-scale movement in the ownership of real property. It is widely assumed, however, that the immense transfers of wealth which occurred from 1540 to 1660 resulted in a notable and significant slowing down of activity in the land market in the next century. The work of Professor Habakkuk has been especially influential in setting the scene of this new epoch. His evidence appears to reveal first, that the land market fell more and more under the hegemony of the greater magnate families, who bought out their smaller neighbours, gentry or yeomen, and by exploiting marriage alliances acquired other estates and additional bases of power; second, that economic logic in the deflationary era after 1670 favoured the large estate and the large farm (which often went together); and third, that the great estates, by making use of legal provisions such as the entail were able to adhere together better than unsettled estates subject to the vagaries of inheritance. As a result of this increasing oligarchic control over the land market, the prices for the land which did come up for sale increased disproportionately during the eighteenth century, and thereby deterred many individuals from choosing land as an investment. Recent research, however, is beginning to suggest that this hypothesis is too elegant and too precise to fit all the facts, and that, in some regions at least, the land market continued to reflect the same kind of social, political and economic aspirations, right down the social scale from great plutocrats to tradesmen and farmers, as it did in 1600. For the new rich in 1750 land still meant security, political authority and the trappings of status. In other words, the evidence for a change of trend in the direction of social mobility after the Restoration remains to be proved, and in the context of a very long-run pattern of social behaviour, from 1250 to 1850, distinctly unlikely.

The shape of English society in the pre-industrial era was, by contrast with other traditional societies in literate civilizations, remarkably flexible. It had need to comprehend the Renaissance reinterpretation of ancient preoccupations about order and dignity within an open framework receptive to the creation and assimilation of new wealth. Shakespeare's famous speech in *Troilus and Cressida* sums up the question admirably: 'O! when degree is shak'd, Which is the ladder to all high designs, The enterprise is sick. . . . Take but degree away, untune that string, And hark what discord follows.' In an age troubled by vagrancy and turbulence, such sentiments were both convincing and convenient. How many eighteenth- or even nineteenth-century men of property would have disagreed with them? But the essential point is the second line of the quotation; 'the ladder to all high designs', implies, not a fixed order of ancestral rank, but a channel, along which respectable aspirations could legitimately flow. The problem was to reconcile the potentially competitive forces of order and flux. Tensions within society were always under the surface, and the long series of uproars, from Tudor rebellions to Hanoverian food riots, indicates how often they broke out in open conflict. Moreover, there are even distinct signs of what can only be called class hatreds arising out of a lack, or breakdown, of the necessary tolerances between different social orders. The classic example is that of the Game Laws, which not only denied some of the earth's fruits to the men who most needed them, but by reserving the capture of game to the land-owning gentry created a war between magistrates and poachers which embittered social relations in the late

43

seventeenth and eighteenth centuries as much as in the nineteenth. Fortunately, perhaps, such examples of overt class selfishness within the law were few before 1750, and English society managed to avoid ossifying into a rigid and repugnant pattern of legal privileges and obligations of the kind which bedevilled the *ancien régime* in Europe.

FURTHER READING

P. Laslett   *The World We Have Lost* (Methuen, 1965).

C. B. Macpherson   *The Political Theory of Possessive Individualism* (O.U.P., 1962).

G. E. Mingay   *English Landed Society in the Eighteenth Century* (Routledge, 1963).

J. Plumb   *Growth of Political Stability in England 1675–1725* (Macmillan, 1967).

I. Roots   *The Great Rebellion, 1642–60* (Batsford, 1966).

L. Stone   *The Causes of the English Revolution 1529–1642* (Routledge, 1972).

D. C. Coleman   'Labour in the English Economy of the Seventeenth Century', *Economic History Review*, VIII, 1956.

J. P. Cooper   'Social Distribution of Land and Men in England 1436–1700', *Economic History Review*, XX, 1967.

A. Everitt   'Social Mobility in Early Modern England', *Past and Present*, 33, 1966.

H. J. Habakkuk   'English Landownership 1680–1740', *Economic History Review*, X, 1940.

J. H. Hexter   'Storm over the Gentry', in Hexter, *Reappraisals in History* (Longman, 1961).

B. A. Holderness   'The English Land Market in the Eighteenth Century: the Case of Lincolnshire', *Economic History Review*, XXVII, 1974.

L. Stone   'Social Mobility in England, 1500–1700', *Past and Present*, 33, 1966.

R. H. Tawney   'The Rise of the Gentry 1540–1640', *Economic History Review*, XI, 1941.

H. R. Trevor Roper   'The Gentry', *Economic History Review*, supplement 1953.

P. Zagorin   'Social Interpretations of the English Revolution', *Journal of Economic History*, XIX, 1959.

3

Agriculture

In 1600 at least three-quarters of the population of England lived in villages, hamlets or isolated houses in the countryside. There was no uniform agrarian landscape and the regions were still in some ways independent of each other. Rich grazing marshes, meadows and immemorial fields, new closes and ill-kempt commons, sandy heaths and bleak moorlands, fells and plains, slopes and vales—these were, and are, the features and idiosyncrasies of the English landscape.

Although variety everywhere is a keynote, it is customary to distinguish two broad zones of land use in England. First, a Highland zone was formed of the Pennine massif and its outliers together with the moorlands of the west down into Dartmoor and the Cornish peninsula. Altitude and slope as well as climate affected the agriculture which could be practised there. Centuries of rain had leached many valuable trace elements out of the ground, and in the uplands had left a poor, acidic soil little suitable for ploughing. Nevertheless, tillage had long been practised almost everywhere for subsistence production of oats or barley, but except in some of the river vales or broader plains of the zone, ploughing was always subordinate to grazing or meadowland management. On the high moors immense tracts of rough common pasture for sheep (occasionally for cattle) were shared out among the dispersed farmsteads or the village communities settled in the warmer and more fertile valleys beneath. Over much of the Highland zone nucleated settlements were less common than dispersed settlements, clustered in small hamlets or scattered to the wide like broadcast seed. The pastoral products of the Highland zone were usually of less worth than those of the Lowlands, although by 1600 the wool and hides and tallow gave a living not only to upland graziers but also to the manufacturers of cloth and leather goods increasingly to be found at the fringe of the zone. Until the seventeenth century, however, stock-raising for fattening in the Lowlands played a minor part in the economy owing to the small market for meat. The quantity of land under the plough had contracted after 1300 and this decline was only reversed briefly in the Highland zone (in 1795–1815). Thus, the open-field farming which had developed in many Highland fringe areas was abandoned by the seventeenth century.

The Lowland zone was more varied but in general both drier and more fertile. Much of it was well suited to arable farming. Its most characteristic feature was the sequence of scarps and vales which marched across country from south Devon to Yorkshire. Many parishes therefore contained a variety of land from thin high downland to clay in the vale beneath. The scarplands were characteristically pastoral, like the Cotswolds on which grazed enormous flocks of sheep bearing high-grade wool. Tillage, at least until the late sixteenth century, was concentrated upon the more moisture-retentive and deeper soils of the 'vale' or narrow upland river valleys, where the open-fields and the meadows could be laid out satisfactorily. Some upland villages in high 'wold' or downland districts depended upon a pastoral economy almost entirely, but many, even in unpromising areas, ensured some arable production by practising infield-outfield cultivation, which is more characteristic of the Highlands. In this, a small piece of land was kept in continuous cultivation by heavy manuring (the infield) while outlying parts were ploughed and fallowed irregularly as the state of the soil dictated (the outfield). Scarp-and-vale farming systems could be found in most Lowland counties; but since much of the zone consisted of great clay plains without access to scarpland grazing—the Vales of Severn, Trent, York, Ancholme, London or Aylesbury, or the large Midland Plain west of the oolite limestone ridge from the Severn to the Humber, the Cheshire Plain and the west Lancashire Plain—other systems had had to be devised. The plains, in fact, were very diverse, but they were characteristically the home of the open-field farming which most closely resembled the textbook model. The Midland plain, for example, was an area of nucleated villages and coherent, collaborative agriculture, subject to changes of far-reaching importance by 1600, but still in 1750 keeping its medieval inheritance substantially intact.

Another important contrast in the Lowlands existed between 'Felden' and Woodland England. The Felden (plain or 'champion' landscape) was the classic area of the medieval open-fields. The Wood-land included those districts where early deforestation had been slower and more piecemeal, where dispersed settlement remained common in the sixteenth and seventeenth centuries, and where the open-field system had come later, and was less complete and less well organized. Few Woodland counties contained large amounts of standing timber by 1600, though, in many, remnants of old forests remained—Arden in Warwickshire, Dean in West Gloucestershire, Waltham in Essex and Hertfordshire, etc. Mixed farming, but with a special and increasing concentration upon cattle farming (less upon sheep), predominated, but non-agricultural activities were also of increasing importance—iron, charcoal and textiles in the Weald, iron and charcoal in Dean and the West Midland Woodlands, textiles in Suffolk and north-west Essex, leather-working, tallow-boiling, woodworking, in several different forest districts. In particular counties like Warwickshire a sharp local contrast existed between the area south of the Avon (Felden) and Arden (Woodland) to the north. In Suffolk the Woodland district was surrounded by the heaths and scarplands of High Suffolk in the west and the Sandlings, a light-soil area in the east towards the sea.

But Suffolk also contained fen land, which was part of another great tract of distinctive country stretching from Mildenhall to Lincoln, and appearing again in the upper basin of the Humber. Fenland was partly of black soil (peat), partly of alluvial silt deposited by the great rivers like the Great Ouse and the Yorkshire Ouse, the Witham, Welland and Nene, and partly of heavy clay, which underlay all, but reached the surface in the little 'hills' which dotted the Fenland landscape. In addition, the coastlands, especially from the Tees to the Thames, but in parts along the south and west coasts as well, were formed of silt washed down by erosion from 'losing' coasts, like Holderness or east Norfolk and Suffolk, onto 'gaining' coasts like Lincolnshire, north Norfolk or Essex. The coastal marshes were reclaimed by drainage and the constant grazing of newly sprouted herbage. Around 1600 great tracts of perma-nent pasture were 'inned' (reclaimed) from the sea in different parts of England. The silt marsh lay on top of boulder clay on which ancient villages with open-fields and immense common pastures continued to flourish, because of their reputation for stock-raising, throughout the early modern period.

During the centuries after 1400 the inherent diversity of these agrarian 'countries' was accentuated by the increasing commitment of

47

commercial farmers to specialization for the market, especially for the London market. This specialization influenced not only crop-selection and stock-breeding, but also the pattern of land use and the organization of agrarian systems and social relationships on the land.

The social basis of agriculture changed as much as its management. Perhaps the most important element was the proportional decline of the numbers of people employed in the sector. On the basis of a famous calculation made in 1688 by Gregory King and of a similar estimate by Joseph Massie in 1760, it appears, first, that agriculture was already employing a smaller proportion of households than we might expect of an underdeveloped economy; secondly that the percentage was declining in the last two generations of the period; and thirdly that the relative decline was not matched by an absolute fall in the number of farmers and presumably of labourers in husbandry. According to the data of King and Massie the number of families identifiably engaged in agriculture fell from three-fifths to a little over one-half of the total number of all families, which for a period as short as seventy years, 1690–1760, seems rather precipitate. We must presume that no significant shift in the proportion of rural families engaged in part-time farming but described as weavers, nailmakers, innkeepers, furnacemen, colliers, etc., occurred after 1690, which, since the greatest spurt of rural industrialization in England was probably contained in the period from 1400 to 1650, is in fact quite plausible. Earlier information is not available except for Gloucestershire in 1608, when the proportion of able-bodied men in farming in the whole county was already under 50 per cent. In 'mixed counties' like Gloucestershire, full-time employment in agriculture had apparently lost its position of all-embracing dominance before 1600, although in largely agricultural counties such as Lincolnshire or Leicestershire (at least before the Restoration), the numbers primarily dependent upon husbandry for their living probably still exceeded 80 per cent at the same period. It is evident, however, that agriculture was no longer synonymous with rural life in the England of Elizabeth or James I.

The villages in which the rural population lived were as diverse as the landscape. The distinction between nucleated villages and dispersed settlements was as significant as the division between Highland and Lowland zones in Britain. In districts of dispersed settlement like Cornwall the farmsteads were often isolated and relatively remote. Where the villages were typically large and concentrated, as in the Midland plain, the farmhouses, barns and foldyards (in which cattle were kept in winter) lay along the village street or around a green, at least before inclosure, and were usually physically separate from the land worked by the farmers. The relocation of these farmsteads at the heart of their cultivated lands, 'within the ring fence', was a characteristic feature of the era of parliamentary inclosure, although it was certainly not an innovation of the eighteenth century. So far as we can generalize about farms at all before 1750, it is their lack of a logical arrangement, the inconvenience of many of the buildings and yards and the piecemeal dispersion of the fields and grassland which stand out from estate surveys and plans all over the country.

The environment of the village, however, was equally shaped by the social organization of its community. We can distinguish between 'peasant' and 'squirearchal' villages, the one dominated by the wealthier farmers and tradesmen, landowners or tenants, whose position was reinforced by the absence of proprietorial despotism. Peasant villages retained a considerable degree of communal government and self-regulation of agricultural customs, and, even outside the industrial regions, they possessed a social structure which comprehended a wide variety of service trades for the agricultural sector of the neighbour-hood. By contrast, the village under the aegis of the great landed pro-prietor, resident squire or absentee magnate, gave little scope for any kind of peasant independence or communal responsibility. The farmers and labourers lived willy-nilly in an ambience of economic and social authority, which probably did not affect their material well-being, for the relationship between proprietor and tenant was often very fruitful, but which stood in strong contrast to less deferential village communi-ties. At a later date the essential differences were summarized in the terms 'open' and 'close' parishes, which emphasized the degree of proprietorial control exercised over the legal settlement of the labouring poor. Every county, virtually every farming region, contained villages of both types, as well as many less sharply defined, though the 'peasant' villages were most numerous on rich, deep soils, especially in the fens and marshes where great commons still survived in the eighteenth century. The breakdown of the agrarian community and the disappear-ance of the peasant from English life were both less complete and less widespread before 1800 than we should expect from reading nineteenth-century jeremiads about the social dissolution of the countryside.

The social organization of agriculture was equally complex. The tripartite division, between landlords, who owned but in general did not work the land or its fixed capital, the farmer who employed the fixed capital and supplied the stock and implements, managed the business of agriculture and earned sufficient returns to pay both landlord and labourers, and the labourer, who worked on the land for a wage, however paid, and owned almost nothing of the means of production— a division which was so characteristic of nineteenth-century Britain— can be seen in an early form at least as far back as the seventeenth century. Leaving aside for the time being the role of the landlord, the place of labourers and farmers was already well established in the hierarchy of agricultural work by 1688. The men who worked on the land for wages could not be classified under the simple heading of 'The Agricultural Labourer' in the seventeenth century. The labour force, which was not supplied by townsmen or industrial workers persuaded to take a break in the harvest field, was divided into several classes, cottage smallholders, piece-workers, day labourers, very like the type found in England in 1850, and farm servants. But it is evident that well over half the male workers in agriculture by 1700 enjoyed little capital and less land. Before Elizabeth I died there was a numerous group of so-called rural 'labourers' whose holdings were less than one acre in extent and who, to judge from their probate inventories, were without livestock or tillage. Not a few 'yeomen' farmers were indicted before the courts of Quarter Sessions before 1640 for building accommodation for their labourers (virtually farm-tied cottages) without the statutory minimum of four acres of ground prescribed in an Act of 1589. Wholly dependent day-labourers were quite commonplace on the larger farms of southern England by the time of the Civil War, although their employment, being supplementary to that of the yearly-hired farm servants, was generally very uncertain and often irregular. The farm servants, men and women, lived in the farmhouse, had their food and working clothes provided and received a small money payment at the end of their term of service. Hired usually at special fairs, they performed most of the specialist services of the farm as dairymen or maids, cheesewrights, horsekeepers, shepherds, waggoners, ploughmen and so forth. But farm service also provided a kind of apprenticeship in agriculture for the young of the district, and many farm servants were children or adolescents. The piece-workers, casual day labourers, 'running men' or 'darrickers', as they were called, were frequently drawn from the class of half-independent cottagers, who were numerous in the sixteenth century but much less so two centuries later. The cottage smallholding, excluding any common rights which might appertain to it, was usually from 3 to 15 acres in size and for the most part was not self-sufficient without resort to wage-labour to eke out the cottagers' income, at least outside the industrial areas. Some were freeholds, others copy-holds, but the greatest number were probably let at will by landlords and therefore easily subjected to pressure from their rationalizing impulses or from ambitious farmers. The labour requirements of a substantial mixed farm around 1700 probably extended from half a dozen farm ser-vants and two or three dependent day labourers to a shifting number of casual labourers at seasonal peaks or for special tasks like hedge-laying or ditching who were drawn from other local resources of employment.

As for the farms themselves so much changed in the period from 1500 to 1750 that any underlying continuity of structure is overlaid by innova-tions and rearrangements, but one fact can be discerned which seems important. In spite of the persistent tendency for the land to be amalga-mated into larger farms right up until the late nineteenth century, some kind of median farm of 30–60 acres emerges, from a long series of estate surveys and inventories, as characteristic of agriculture in pre-industrial England. Even in the sixteenth century there were larger farms every-where, but as a rule the biggest farms were found on light upland soils, as they were in the nineteenth century, partly because they contained so much hill grazing land, but also because the cultivated land was thin and relatively infertile. At Great Chesterford, on the chalk uplands of north-west Essex, for example, the farms were traditionally large (over 150 acres) and in 1748 the landlord not only found difficulty in letting them, but apparently believed it was impossible to divide them into smaller units to attract poorer tenants. The adage 'the richer the land, the less the [average] holding' was not a bad summary of Western Europe farm size-distribution before 1800, even though in England geological determinism no longer prevailed over other considerations of land management at least by the seventeenth century. Even so, a median farm of around 50 acres was remarkably tenacious in the face of so many changes in the organization of English agriculture between the fifteenth and nineteenth centuries.

INCLOSURE AND THE CONSOLIDATION OF FARMS
The most obvious sign of rural change in the English countryside between 1400 and 1800 was inclosure. As a notion inclosure incorporates

several different practices. Its oldest manifestation was encroachment upon the waste, the usually piecemeal reclamation and fencing of ground not directly part of the village system of tillage or permanent pasture. Intakes of cultivable land from forests, fens, heath or moorland were features of periods when rural population pressure was strongly in evidence. But 'assarting', as medievalists call this process, was superimposed upon other kinds of inclosure by 1350–1500. Large-scale reclamation, undertaken by the landlord or the community, especially in the fens or marshes, was not unknown in medieval England, but it reached a peak between 1570 and 1640. Inclosure of the common fields, wholly or in large part, was also in full flood before 1500, and the tide flowed strongly over much of England until 1830. In addition consolidation of holdings and changes in land use in the fields allowed some landlords and peasants to inclose their estates into compact, fenced farms in the midst of the more traditional landscape of strips and furlongs.

The variety of styles makes it difficult for us to assess the total impact of inclosure before the era of parliamentary inclosure in the eighteenth and nineteenth centuries. A figure for some Midland counties suggests that 8–9 per cent of their total area was inclosed between 1455 and 1607, but this refers not to the aggregate of land converted to inclosed farming after 1300, but to a special category of large-scale inclosure which resulted in a public outcry and sometimes to the extinction of the common fields. Moreover, at least as much land was inclosed in the same way in the Midland counties between 1600 and 1750. From the standpoint of 1750 it is obvious that a good deal of England was already inclosed. In a few areas there is no evidence of an open-field system ever having been established; in others, virtually the whole region had been converted to inclosed farms in the centuries before 1750. Moreover, even in the parliamentary inclosures of the eighteenth and nineteenth centuries hardly a village in the country was free of some piecemeal inclosure of the type mentioned above. In all it is possible that half of the cultivable land in England had been deliberately inclosed at some time before 1750.

The distribution of parliamentary inclosure suggests that the classic ground of open-field farming was the English Midlands. In Kent, Cumberland, Cornwall, Cheshire, Herefordshire or Suffolk not many traces of such farming existed by 1700–1800. Yet this impression of a clear Midlands bias in 'champion' husbandry is a *trompe l'œil*. There is now sufficient evidence of some form of common field agriculture over most of England by 1300. At some time before 1700 whole sections of this medieval inheritance had disappeared. When this occurred is a matter of doubt, but in the counties mentioned (among others) the change was probably progressive, reaching a peak of activity in 1540–1640. There was much less furore than in the central and eastern Midlands, but the motives were probably similar. First was the greater relative value of grassland rather than arable after 1350. In areas where climate or geology were favourable to pasture farming, the recession of population provided an opportunity for conversion. In the peripheral regions it is likely that the medieval field-systems had been neither so tightly organized nor so pervasive of village agriculture as in the Midland plain. Routines were therefore broken with less disruption. Secondly, the disintegration and regrouping of tenements in the fluid land market which was developing from the thirteenth century onwards permitted the consolidation of strips and eventually the creation of private inclosures. This was especially characteristic of the Woodland districts, and they, together with the Highland and Marsh or Fenland zones, were largely inclosed, without evidence of depopulation, before 1750. Arable remained, but was overborne by the commitment of such regions to dairying and other kinds of stock-farming. Tillage was intertwined with pasture in a convertible system, and although there is evidence of particular farms being decayed and their lands thrown together with others all over these regions, there were few deserted villages in the north-west, the Welsh Borders, the south-west Peninsula and in the south-east from Suffolk to Sussex.

The abandonment of village sites is a complex issue, but it does seem that poor soil or declining fertility after 1300 were not of first importance. Many places in the light-soil uplands of eastern and southern England disappeared before 1750, but so also did many others in the rich soils of Oxford, Warwick or Northampton. The correlation between bitterly opposed inclosure and depopulated villages is clear and unequivocal. Several things made this depopulating inclosure in the Midlands especially obnoxious. One was the interruption of communal régimes of cultivation and land management. But much more important was the spectacle of the 'greedy cormorant', who, in order to increase his income by exploiting the wool boom of the fifteenth and early sixteenth centuries, turned out men in favour of sheep. His deeds often bore the colour of illegality, but when poor men had little redress save

the Lord Chancellor's equity, the determinedly appetitive landowner
or leaseholder could usually win his way. After 1520 the incloser's path
was less smooth, for government was more resolute in indicting social
malefactors, but it seems that the great surge of depopulating inclosure,
which reduced hundreds of more or less viable English villages to
desolation, was slackening as the difference between wool and grain
prices narrowed in the 1520s. But not all large-scale inclosure by
pastoralizing landlords was for wool-growing in the sixteenth century.
In Midland counties such as Leicestershire or Warwickshire, where all
inclosure was suspect, dairying and cattle-breeding predominated in
some districts. Livestock farming remained profitable throughout the
period before 1750. Bacon's belief that 'high corn prices invited and
enticed men to break up more corn ground and convert it to tillage,
than all the penal laws could ever by compulsion', could not be trusted
to work, and a great deal of legislative and executive activity was undertaken from the time of Henry VII to that of Charles I's personal rule to
moderate the 'decay of tillage'. Unfortunately the great outbursts of
public outrage against inclosure in the century before the Civil War
probably do not tell us much about the progress of conversion, for most
coincided with runs of bad harvest in which unease about the food
supply was multiplied by fear of uproar.

Even the early Tudors could distinguish between useful and 'anti-
social' inclosure. Thus the anti-inclosure Act of 1536 accepted that
some inclosure was necessary owing to the state of the soil or to local
agricultural practice. In the *Discourse of the Common Weal* (1549), the
Knight observed that, 'Experience should seme plainlie to prove that
Inclosures should be profitable and not hurtfull to the common weale;
for we se that countries, wheare most Inclosures be, are most wealthie,
as essex, Kent, devenshire, and such.' However, much more heat than
light was generated by the energy of the debate until the Civil War.
The same charges were levelled at the avarice of individuals which
harmed the community through the centuries which separated John
Rous (1460s) from Nathaniel Kent (*c.* 1770), and though the truth is not
improved by repetition, sufficient instances could always be found of
illegal proceedings, intimidation, 'decay of ploughs' or destruction of
houses to make good cases. But if the enemies of inclosure remained
intransigent, Professor Beresford has traced a significant change in
public opinion in the century after Elizabeth's accession from near
universal revulsion to an appreciation that inclosure might be important

as a means of improving land use and physical output.[1] Tudor saws such as 'sheep eat men', or 'horne and Thorne shall make England forlorne' were not forgotten but became muted in the seventeenth century.

Even so, opinion, and judicial intercession, lagged behind practice, and the early Stuart period saw more indictments and inquiries concerning inclosure than at any time since Protector Somerset's brief ascendancy. After the Commonwealth in the 1650s the law and the government suffered in silence the continuing current of conversions, and long before the age of parliamentary inclosure, official, but not necessarily peasant, opinion approved or acquiesced in the process of agrarian change. Before 1600 the wind had already backed to a new quarter. Bacon and Raleigh, among others, supported market forces in rural change. The debates preceding the Tillage Act of 1597 clearly reveal the growing influence of those who saw agricultural specialization, and the convertible husbandry, as more beneficial than the preservation of an ancient *status quo*. By 1618, indeed, after the food crisis had temporarily passed, it was admitted that England was more in 'want of pasture and cattle, for much woodland and barren grounds are become fruitful cornelands in steed of pasture'. Moreover, those who were accused before the Privy Council or Star Chamber were likely to defend themselves vigorously, as when Richard Rossiter from upland Lincolnshire in 1608 excused himself on the grounds that his arable was too poor to sustain continuous cultivation and must in part be allowed to fall into grass. Sir Thomas Burton of Frisby, Leicestershire, objected in 1631 to an order to reconvert his land to tillage, because, 'the soil is a cold claie and not so fitt for Corne as grasse'. Whole villages are found approving of inclosure, like Eagle in Lincolnshire, where 'Most of the land now tilled is more proper for grass and ... more ground now eaten as common is fitter for corn as is proved by experience among our next neighbours.' In 1597 the Members of Parliament for Shropshire contrasted their own county in the process of conversion, as most apt to be the nation's 'Dairyhouse', with Herefordshire as a 'Barne'.

The progress of specialist stock farming and, in the plain, and in the scarp-and-vale regions of the Lowland zone, the success of convertible husbandry ensured that inclosure would continue long after the crude despoliation of the sheepmaster had been superseded. Penal laws and

[1] M. Beresford, 'Habitation versus Improvement', in F. J. Fisher, ed. *Essays in the Economic and Social History of Tudor and Stuart England* (C.U.P. 1961).

commissions to prevent depopulation could not stop inclosure, not least because the premises upon which they were effected were often anachronistic or unpractical. The paternalism of government was sometimes admirable but it did not succeed in protecting the poor, who were widely admitted to hate and fear inclosure, because the poor lost ground by due process of law, and influential opinion objected as much to the authorities' disregard of the common law as to their meddling. As such, resistance to executive interference not only brought down Laud, and Charles I, whose attitudes to inclosure were not forgotten in their indictment, but contributed to the fall of both Wolsey and Somerset. But the need for government to moderate the decay of habitation in the countryside remained, even after the desertion of villages had stopped. Large numbers of villages from Northumberland to Devon were reduced in size after 1550, as a result partly of conversion to pasture or convertible farming and partly of a deliberate policy of amalgamating farms. Thus, at Tuggal in Northumberland in 1567, eleven husbandmen, eight cottagers, four cottiers and one smith had been reduced to eight farmers. At Brixton Deverill in Wiltshire three farmers with 26 horses had replaced six with 43 by the mid-seventeenth century. Leicester was reported to be full of displaced agriculturists begging for a farm or a piece of land to employ their teams. The cottage smallholders were especially vulnerable, and had been largely extinguished as landholders in many English villages like Bishop Wilton in Yorkshire, or South Ormsby in Lincolnshire, by 1750. The 'family farm' had been reduced to a residue of insignificant proportions in downland or scarp villages from Hampshire to Northumberland in the seventeenth century. The influence of inclosure was important but not exclusive. Thus land hunger among richer peasants ever since the thirteenth century had polarized rural society between wealthy and poor by 1450 and the pressure upon landlords to amalgamate vacant holdings from appetitive 'yeomen' was often irresistible. Moreover, owners and land stewards were increasingly persuaded to consolidate their farms in the interests of efficiency, especially after 1650 when the *rentier* system was becoming widespread. Much 'ingrossment' occurred before, and as a precipitant of inclosure from the fifteenth century onwards.

Parallel with this kind of depopulation was 'impopulation' of certain agricultural regions, in the fens and marshes, the Highland moors and in the steadily diminishing forests of England. In Lancashire and the West

Riding, new townships were created after 1550 out of a spate of cottage-building in the waste beyond existing settlements. Impopulation was often associated with industrial development, but it was also a feature of agricultural reclamation in the Lowlands. The extension of fenland drainage and disafforestation, saltmarsh intakes and 'mere-drainage' reached its apogee when the general movement of lowland inclosure was also very active, between 1570 and 1640. Depopulation and impopulation, therefore, were coeval if not complementary developments.

The reclamation of vast tracts of fenland around the Wash and in the middle reaches of the Trent and Yorkshire Ouse (Hatfield Chase and the Isle of Axholme) was by far the most important and extensive of these colonizing projects in the seventeenth century. James I, chronically short of money, had made plans, after a detailed survey of Crown lands in 1607, to improve his income by fenland drainage, but the scheme was held up until after his death, not least by the hostility of the 'rude, uncivill and envious' inhabitants of the Fens themselves. By the mid-1620s the chief promoter of drainage was not the Crown but Francis, Earl of Bedford, a great landowner in the southern Fenland of Cambridge and Huntingdon. James I had chosen, and Bedford and Charles I were soon to adopt, Cornelius Vermuyden as engineer of the project. Bedford, Vermuyden and others formed a company of Adventurers in 1630 (chartered in 1634) to reclaim as much as 400,000 acres. Vermuyden's basic method was to improve the general drainage by driving straight channels such as the Old Bedford River (1631–7) which short-cut the Ouse between Earith and Denver. In 1638, Charles I intervened partly to obtain a share of the lands for the Crown and partly to settle some of the bitter disputes which had developed. A new plan, to make 400,000 acres dry enough for winter use, was drawn up, but deferred as a result of the Civil War. Existing installations deteriorated, and when drainage was resumed in 1649–51 much repair as well as new work had to be undertaken. The chief work of the 1650s was the New Bedford River, supplemented by link-drains from the Ouse to the Old Nene south-east of Peterborough. By the time of the 1663 General Drainage Act most of Vermuyden's basic plan had been carried out more or less successfully. The Bedford Level which formed a tract of country from Peterborough to Wisbech, Ely and St Ives, mostly of excellent peat soils, was drained, allocated and put into cultivation. As early as 1655, Thomas Fuller was carried away with enthusiasm:

'The chiefest complaint I hear of is this, that the country thereabout is now subject to a new drowning, even to a deluge and innundation of plenty, all commodities being grown so cheap therein.' On the other hand, drainage was not effected without continual opposition, from the fen men who remained resolute in their suspicion of the Adventurers, from others like Sir John Maynard, who exposed the chicanery and cheating of a good many of the 'projectors', and from critics of the engineer's methods.

The chief difficulty, which nobody foresaw in the seventeenth century, was subsidence of the desiccated peat land. Nevertheless, the Bedford Level remained an outstandingly successful enterprise, especially when the use of wind-pumps reduced the back-flow of waters from the outfalls. It was extended, on a modest scale, in the 1720s by the River Nene Cut, which replaced the late medieval Morton's Leam between Peterborough and Guyhirne, and something similar was attempted, several times, in the seventeenth and eighteenth centuries, in the wilderness of Deeping Fen in South Lincolnshire, where opposition was bitter and often violent.

The drainage of the Lincolnshire fens, except for Axholme, was much less successful. Deeping Fen, the Ancholme Level, various districts around Boston and on the silt soils in South Holland, were organized by groups of Adventurers at different times from the 1630s onwards, or were undertaken by rich local proprietors like Sir John Monson or the Earl of Lindsey, but the really significant improvements had generally to wait for the era of parliamentary inclosure, especially for the series of drainage Acts passed from 1761 to 1801. Indeed, the evidence for the period from about 1670–80 to the 1760s is that it was a Sisyphean struggle to preserve that which was already dry land. The Isle of Axholme, and the neighbouring Hatfield Chase, indeed, had been drained quite effectively, and with similar consequences, by Vermuyden and a group of shareholders in the same period as the Bedford Level, and despite ferocious rioting had returned quite handsome profits to the participants. The rest of the Humber fens were not adequately reclaimed until after 1750.

The consequences of fen drainage were not as beneficial as many projectors believed. The quantity of 'drowned' land was exaggerated in the interests of the reclaimers, and the fen lands had been rich and economically diverse before 1630. A good deal, of course, was done to improve grazing and meadow land, in some areas peat land was made

Agriculture

fit to bear good crops of wheat or oats, beans, hemp and flax, together with new crops such as onions or coleseed. On the other hand, a fair amount of swamp land remained untouched, and there were still nearly all the great meres or deeps intact in 1700 which had given medieval fen men a living from fishing. Moreover, even though many entrepreneurs made fortunes in excess of anything to be obtained from contemporary industry or foreign trade, at least as many lost their investments, and more 'projects' were abortive or failed to mature into profits than there were which made an acceptable return upon the risk-capital invested.

On the other hand, a good many new farms and a few new townships were laid out in the former waste, and parishes such as Hatfield, Deeping, Outwell, Upwell, Thorney, Mildenhall and Manea or Mepal did add substantially both to their populations, after 1630–50, and also to the amount of their land which could be ploughed, cropped and subjected to the discipline of convertible tillage. Moreover, beside the great public undertakings, private and piecemeal drainage schemes, inclosures and conversions were continually being attempted, often successfully, by individual farmers or local landowners. Despite the defects of reclamation, the Fenland had an agrarian economy by 1750 already notably different from that of 1500, and the 'social' or public benefit from the capital invested was sufficient to impress Daniel Defoe and a whole string of his contemporaries. Not the least important aspect of the public debate between 1620 and 1760 was the expectation, which gained ground, that unimproved wastes, however useful in a wild state they were to their denizens, could serve a wider interest by the effort to render them more productive. By 1680 oats, wheat, coleseed, onions, pulses and some root vegetables, as well as much superior grass, had been grown extensively on land a century before not even suitable for winter grazing.

These converging patterns of agrarian change were adapted to fit the framework of legal jurisdiction. The law had always provided some protection against the arbitrary appropriation of communal rights. The aggrieved could always seek redress in Chancery. As a result, Chancery eventually became a means merely of registering inclosures. Large-scale inclosure could always be put to arbitration, and in Chancery the appointment of commissioners and even of surveyors became commonplace. Between 1630 and 1650 a substantial number of large inclosures were enrolled in Chancery. In theory, a decree could be issued only to settle a formal dispute, so that many legally authorized inclosures in the seventeenth century were the result of fictitious contests. Chancery decrees are evidence more or less of inclosure by agreement, which was proceeding also without recourse to the law throughout the period from 1550 to 1750. At the same time statute law was fashioned to serve other requisites of agrarian change. Thus the law was once modified to permit the erection of cottages on the waste without three acres of land, to meet the needs in the industrial districts for accommodation. Subsequently an Act of 1589 reversed this principle. The Tillage Acts of 1597 were repealed in 1624 when grain supply was felt to be adequate. The changeableness of public policy was obviously subject to particular pressure groups, but we must not assume that communal interests were necessarily sacrificed, by legal provision or the lack of it, to the selfishness of that Mammon of Unrighteousness, the agrarian capitalist. Change reflected less prevarication than the response to physical variables in the agrarian landscape.

To sum up: inclosure was the most palpable means of modifying both the landscape between 1300 and 1850 and the organization of agricultural production. It was intertwined with a tendency to enlarge the size and reduce the number of farms. Inclosure before 1750 was most complete and least contentious in regions apt for pasture farming but not fully integrated into the Midland system of two- or three-course communal farming. In the Midlands it proceeded amidst much protest, but after 1520 less and less to satisfy the simple greed of rich wool growers. It was closely associated with the spread of convertible husbandry, and seems in general to have followed the logic of soil geography, being most active both on the light, thin soils of the scarplands and on the cold, heavy clays of the deep plain country between Humber and Thames. Its economic effects are questionable, inasmuch as inclosure may not have promoted major agricultural improvements. On the other hand, there is little evidence that inclosure seriously harmed tillage as far as the supply of cereal products is concerned. The social consequences of inclosure were also ambiguous, but the widespread evidence of opposition among the rural poor in the agricultural counties throughout the period suggests that popular suspicions were not groundless. All in all, inclosure was not an 'autonomous' movement promoted against the grain by anti-social profiteers or accredited improvers, but part of a wide-ranging current of agrarian development drawing together the 'countries' of England into an aggregate market.

THE COURSE OF AGRICULTURAL CHANGE

The Problem and its Setting. The chief deficiency of the traditional, largely subsistent agriculture of early medieval Europe was its low level of productivity. This meant that even the peasantry was vulnerable to recurrent harvest failures. Yields were low, so that even in a moderately good year the quality and quantity of seedcorn carried over to the next were inadequate. Cereal production in almost all regions had priority because the medieval peasant (and townsman) depended for his existence upon his breadcorn and his drink-corn (barley for brewing). The acreage under corn was necessarily large in relation to population not only because transport was insufficient but also because output per acre was often near the minimum which nature would yield. Over a century ago, a long experiment was begun at Rothamsted Agricultural Station to test the effects of continuous cropping without fertilizers upon temperate cereals. The results indicated that although the virgin fertility of the soil was rapidly lost, crop yields settled down to an average of 12 bushels an acre after a few years and remained at that level for decades.

Medieval farmers, who may have had inferior seedcorn, nevertheless applied both a rotation of sowing and a certain amount of fertilizer, so that they should have been able to rely upon a constant minimum above ten bushels year and year about. Early medieval England possessed one great natural advantage, namely ample waste ground of fair quality fit for colonization, which not only brought new land into cultivation but also allowed a rise of population to take place without undue stress upon the technical resources of agriculture. When this avenue was closed, and even inferior land in the Pennines or Breckland was put into tillage, medieval society was faced with a potential imbalance between arable and pastoral management. It was necessary, in order to produce sufficient corn before 1300, to encroach upon grassland on which the cattle and sheep necessary to produce the dung to manure the land were fed. Too little livestock meant insufficient dung, and too little fertilizer meant that yields could not be increased to feed a growing population. This vicious circle is the model of traditional agriculture. To enlarge the circle was the object of much agricultural change in the period after 1500. It could be broken only when extraneous inorganic elements could be introduced in the nineteenth and twentieth centuries, but at least by 1750 English agriculture had entered a more 'virtuous circle' of notably higher productivity. It is a mistake to draw a sharp

61

contrast between the custom-bound, unreflective peasant of the thirteenth century and the enterprising, individualistic farmer of the seventeenth and eighteenth, for medieval agriculture was neither unresponsive to managerial change nor as technically backward as the textbooks still portray. Even so, it was the shock waves that flowed from the Black Death which brought about the changes upon which agriculture after 1450 was reconstructed.

The Progress of Innovation. Nowhere was the problem of striking the right balance between corn and livestock more significant than in the regions in which open-field cultivation still predominated in the sixteenth and seventeenth centuries. This partly explains the great variety of 'champion' régimes in Lowland England by 1600, for much of their operative diversity apparently arose from successive attempts by peasant farmers, at least from the thirteenth century, to adapt their tillage to new needs. Medieval open-field farming was not only more flexible than most textbook models imply, but also foreshadowed, from 1300 to 1600, many of the more far-reaching changes which took place in the century after 1650.

It is possible that some open-field communities had already abandoned collaborative rotations altogether by 1600. At the other extreme, several villages still retained intact a rigid and almost unchanged system of regulated common-field agriculture until the date of their parliamentary inclosure. However, the basis upon which most open-field farming was conducted around 1600 was a rotation established upon a three- or a two-course system of cropping. In the first, winter corn (wheat or rye) was followed by spring-sown corn (barley, oats or pulses), after which the land lay fallow for a year. In any year, therefore, one-third of the tillage was in fallow and two-thirds under crops. Two-field systems operated with half the arable land under fallow at any time, while the cropped field might be in either winter or spring corn. Many such field systems were arranged not by 'fields' but by furlongs or strips within the fields. W. G. Hoskins had rightly observed that 'within certain broad limits, the open-field farmer could do what he liked with his own strips'.[1] Extraordinary differences in the size or arrangement of fields were thus reconciled to the needs of rotation in English villages where the terrain was broken or piecemeal inclosure

[1] W. G. Hoskins, 'The Leicestershire Farmer in the Seventeenth Century', *Agricultural History*, 25, 1951, p. 10.

had decimated the ancient field structure. Peas and beans, which as legumes helped to fix nitrogen in the soil, had been grown for centuries, but in the three centuries after 1300 the acreage under pulse crops, especially in the Midland clays, had greatly increased. Before 1550 pulses were scarcely even sown in the fallow break to increase total output. They competed with barley for a place in the spring shift, but gained ground because they provided valuable fodder where meadow was comparatively scarce. By 1600–50 the indications are that innovation in crop selection was very active. Thus Robert Loder of Harwell in Berkshire was growing vetches in the fallow field for grazing in 1610–20. Such 'hitch' crops, as they were called, were widespread in the Lowlands by mid-century. Because of the importance of fallow for summer pasture, such innovations had necessarily to fit in with local stock-feeding needs, but there are many examples of communal or private agreements to improve the forage supplied by the fallows.

Arable farming was limited before 1600 by the small range of crops, other than 'white corn', which were available for sowing. New crops were becoming widespread after 1640, but they were of little significance in the first half of the period. Tillage, moreover, posed fewer problems for the innovative farmer than the supply of forage for his annuals, and most of the changes before 1600 affected grassland management. The conversion to pasture of immense tracts of the country after 1300 went far beyond the formal process of inclosure. In the Midland counties, where depopulation was most obnoxious, some kind of general 'fodder crisis' may have revealed itself by the mid-sixteenth century. In the aftermath of the Black Death, a good deal of both piecemeal inclosure and temporary field-grass management occurred in communities strong enough to withstand the depopulator. 'Leys', as the plots of field grass were called, were especially important. For various reasons, individuals or groups of villagers opted to take whole furlongs or particular strips out of tillage and to protect them temporarily with fences. The idea was to put this land back under the plough after a period of rest, but leys were often merely excuses to convert field land into permanent inclosures. Ley farming eased the traditional problems of finding adequate forage for livestock in open-field régimes. Together with the culture of pulses, the management of leys ensured that the numbers of livestock kept by peasant farmers were maintained and generally increased even in the period of renewed population pressure upon food resources, 1550–1650. It contributed something to break the vicious circle mentioned above. Furthermore, ley farming opened up a path to a new kind of mixed agriculture in Lowland England. Temporary field-grass plots, subsequently reconverted to plough land, resembled the treatment of the outfield in areas of otherwise marginal fertility, especially in the Highland. What developed out of this practice was a more widespread and systematic convertible husbandry, which came to characterize the farming of many plain and scarp-and-vale districts by the late seventeenth and eighteenth centuries.

Convertible husbandry was adaptable for both inclosed and open-field farming systems. It involved a less regular alternation of grazing and tillage than in the formal two-shift or three-shift system, although in many parishes of the Midland plain the two systems could be worked side by side. It was particularly appropriate in villages where different crops were sown in the same fields by individual farmers. Because fallowing remained necessary on many soils from heavy, wet clays to light, thin gravels or chalks, temporary leys after several years in tillage were particularly attractive. In some of the scarp-and-vale parishes, as in the Lincolnshire Wolds, conversion of ancient open fields to permanent grass was usually followed by ploughing in the sheep-walks or rabbit warrens on the hill slope. This walkland arable was leyed after three or four years in cultivation and another stretch of the slope broken up. The essence of the convertible system was the same all over Lowland England, but in detail, a considerable number of local variations could be incorporated into the system as soil or land management required.

Ley-farming was transformed by the introduction of new crops. In the first phase, field grass was merely a matter of chance, because there were neither the means nor the knowledge to select seeds for the purpose. The sweepings of the hay loft were as much as most farmers could provide, until sainfoin, trefoil or clover were made available in the seventeenth century. The introduction of 'artificial grasses' marked the most profound change in grassland management in pre-industrial England. The poor quality of 'natural' pasture or meadow is a matter of record, so that the introduction of selected grasses or legumes notably improved the feeding of stock. Artificial grasses had been known in the Low Countries for a long time by 1600, and English writers, plagiarizing Continental authorities, were advocating clover, etc., before there is evidence of its growth in England. The most important was Sir Richard Weston (*c.* 1645), who travelled in the Low Countries and reported at first hand upon the culture of root crops and artificial grasses. Over the thirty years, 1640–70, most of the field crops pioneered by the Flemings made headway in English agriculture. Eventually sainfoin and trefoil were found most suitable to semi-permanent leys on light, dry upland soils and were increasingly used to follow tillage in the scarplands. Clover was more adaptable and became a mainstay of ley-farming in the Midlands, in Wales, the south-west and northwards beyond Yorkshire into Northumberland. It was much better adapted to short leys—one to three years in duration—and eventually found a special place as a fallow break crop within an alternating rotation of corn and fodder crops. The new grass crops spread widely, from Kent and East Anglia where they made land fall, although their diffusion was often erratic and depended a good deal upon local example by innovating farmers or progressive landlords. By 1720, clover, sainfoin, trefoil, nonsuch and rye-grass were known by some farmers in every part of England, and in certain districts their culture was already predominant.

The other celebrated introduction, the turnip as a field crop, dates from the same period in East Anglia. Experiments with root crops in agriculture go back to some time before 1618 when John Norden noted that carrots were grown in the Suffolk Sandlings. Soon afterward turnips, which because of their bulk were more suitable for fodder, are recorded on a number of farms in the same county. Turnips are mentioned in places as far apart as the Chilterns and Nottinghamshire before 1680, and were perhaps not uncommon as field crops in East Anglia, Hertfordshire and Kent by 1700. Carrots (and parsnips) continued to be grown in the lightest of soils in Suffolk and Somerset at the same period. One other crop is of great local significance, oil-seed rape or coleseed, grown in some places like Gloucestershire to provide oil for industrial uses, but increasingly in the Fenlands from about 1640 to clean the land and to provide nutritious fodder (oil-cake) for livestock. Rape spread erratically into regions where roots were not found satisfactory, but because it was regarded as an exhaustive crop its diffusion was always somewhat restricted.

It would be true to say of all these new crops that, though widely known, their use was not so widely accepted by English farmers before 1760. This was partly because the use of turnips in farming was apparently not associated with the famous four-course rotation, often known as the Norfolk system on the majority of farms on which they were grown. Farmers seem to have grown them in small quantities before

1750 chiefly to feed their draught oxen or milch cows in the winter. The simultaneous introduction of clover and turnips was largely coincidental. The régime of 'high feeding', the growth of fodder crops to feed large flocks of sheep or for the stall-feeding of beasts intended for meat, had only just begun in East Anglia in 1750. Turnips, however, were grown to cleanse the land, and it is not unlikely that some farmers were growing roots for sale especially on the fringe of the woodland pasture areas. In general, however, the influence of the turnip as an index of agricultural progress has been overrated. It was symptomatic of innovation rather than a prime mover in the transformation of arable management. Much more important are clover and sainfoin and even the very restricted but valuable cash crops produced for industrial use. The new field crops so far mentioned were introduced to increase the supply of fodder available for stock-rearing. Many of the other introductions were the result of attempts to save imports of raw materials, rapeseed, woad, teasels, weld, woodwax, saffron, hemp and flax. The last two had long been grown in England, but the acreage—usually in small plots or closes—probably increased between 1550 and 1700. Most such crops were very localized—saffron at Saffron Walden, or Burwell in Cambridgeshire; woad near Tewkesbury; teasels in Essex or Yorkshire—but weld at least could be sown with corn and so was appropriate to ordinary open-field farming. In addition, cash crops of various kinds were often sown by enterprising farmers near industrial or commercial markets or centres of consumption: vegetables in Kent, the Vale of London, near Bristol and Norwich; tobacco (until 1660–80) in the Vale of Severn around Winchcombe; potatoes (introduced from Ireland about 1650–60) in the Lancashire plain near Wigan.

Market gardening in general was scarcely known in England before 1560 when Flemish immigrants brought the arts they had learned in half-urban Flanders to their land of adoption. Fruit and vegetables of considerable variety were produced around the big cities by 1600, at first often by gardeners organized in gilds. Hops, increasingly used to flavour beer after 1500, were grown in many districts, Kent, Hertfordshire, Hampshire, Devon, the West Midlands, Suffolk, Nottinghamshire and Yorkshire by 1650–1700, frequently by men whose other interests were in mixed husbandry. The specialist gardeners were increasingly challenged by farmers in the supply of the more easily grown vegetables and fruits. Cash cropping encouraged the adoption in agriculture of the intensive techniques of gardening, especially in counties such as Kent or

Hertfordshire which also produced great quantities of grain for the metropolitan market. One result of this was the search for new fertilizers to improve the land under tillage, especially the use of urban waste, night soil, rags, soot, potashes in districts near London, Bristol or Norwich.

The problem of soil fertility remained persistent, and in some sense mysterious until the age of Liebig and agricultural chemistry, from the middle of the nineteenth century onwards. Even when the new balance was struck between grass and tillage in Lowland England, the so-called vicious circle was enlarged rather than broken. But at least one of the specialist agricultural régimes was organized to maximize the provision of dung in the arable fields. The sheep-course or fold-course system typified scarpland and heathland farming in many parts of Lowland England, from East Anglia to Wiltshire. The sheep, which on many farms or in many villages numbered more than 10,000, were grazed out in the downland, but brought in, usually at night, to be folded in the fields or on that part of the heath or hillside due to be ploughed for corn. The sheep, packed closely in their folds, were walking dung heaps intended chiefly to maintain arable fertility. The system was certainly successful, but a good deal of the grazing on leys or in the fallows without benefit of clover or sainfoin probably took as much from the land as was put in by the livestock. A more skilful use of fallows or leys certainly did not inhibit agricultural development, but since dung had never been the only fertilizer available, so the application of more, and more various, fertilizers or top dressings helped to enlarge the productivity of the soil before the use of artificial grasses had become widespread. Inorganic fertilizers had always played some part in the maintenance of soil structure. They were employed to lighten heavy clay soils or to add body to particularly light soils. These included white marl in Norfolk, red marl in the West Midlands and Lancashire, clay or peat or sandy soils, lime and chalk in several scattered places, though knowledge of the acidity or alkalinity of the soil was naturally very meagre. Some 'fertilizers', which were tried, were useless—for example, sea sand, salt and broken shells. Organic fertilizers were equally diverse—for example, woodashes, seaweed, and vegetable composts. The wilder shores of experiment reveal the lack of scientific knowledge involved. Many important innovations, like liming, were hit upon virtually by accident. The seventeenth century seems to have been as inquisitive in this respect as the age of Arthur Young, although the extent of the application of new ideas is difficult to discover because farmers as a whole were not articulate.

The management of permanent grass—meadow and pasture—changed rather less than that of temporary grassland or tillage. In the long term the most significant element was the chronic competition for grassland which resulted in so much inclosure and in the spread of ley-farming. The shortage was most evident in old, settled, open-field districts, and many of the farmers who began increasingly to exploit the market for meat products from the late sixteenth century were compelled to find grazing land in other parishes. The rich marshlands in particular attracted the attention of stock-raisers and butcher-graziers all the way down the east coast from Yorkshire to Kent. London butchers were especially numerous in the Thames marshes, where they fattened the half-finished livestock brought in on the hoof from elsewhere. Further north, it was inland farmers who appropriated a good deal of the better marsh grass for their use in the seventeenth century. Another consequence of pressure upon permanent pasture in the Midland counties was the growing custom of 'stinting' the commons (i.e. limiting the number of livestock which could be grazed at particular times). Socially this move probably enhanced the power of the well-to-do farmers in 'stinted' villages. It was always apparently an attempt to deal with the problem of overgrazing. Village 'byelaws' regulating communal arrangements for meadows, common pastures and fallow-grass proliferated in late sixteenth- and seventeenth-century England. The custom of distributing meadow-plots by lot, for instance, was frequently reinforced by these regulations, presumably intended as some kind of conservation measure. To produce more grass, especially for hay, was the mainspring of another important innovation in southern and western England—the floating of water meadows. Meadows lying near streams could be irrigated in such a way that valuable deposits of silt were left behind to improve soil quality. By means of channels and sluices water meadows could be controlled by discerning farmers to produce much better supplies of grass. They were not uncommon in Hertfordshire and around London before 1600, but their greatest expansion occurred in the next century in southern England as far west as Devon and the Welsh marshes. The use of silt to increase yields was quite widespread in England by 1700, for apart from the reclamation of salt marshes and the floating of water meadows, the technique of 'warping'—usually for arable husbandry—in which

silt, diverted from the Humber-Trent river complex onto the neighbouring farm land, was used to provide some of the richest soil in the
country.

Innovations in what we may call the techniques of agriculture were
very diverse but also remarkably coherent. The problem of supplying
a developing, and growing, demand especially for pastoral products
was married to the equally urgent problem of preserving the output of
corn without reducing the fertility of the arable land. Market specialization was a profound influence, but so also was the growing awareness of
soil characteristics and geological diversity. By 1700, English agriculture
was already fully in a market economy, and indeed was a leading
element in the general transformation. Most authorities now accept
that the so-called Agricultural Revolution in Britain occurred at some
time between 1560 and 1760, but so far there is no full agreement as to
the dating within this long period.

The Achievement of the Agricultural Sector 1550–1750. The extent of
specialization in seventeenth-century agriculture owed a great deal to
the demand of London for an immense quantity and variety of foodstuffs. Long before 1650 particular regions were well known for the cash
products they supplied to the London market. Before the death of
Elizabeth, indeed, the demand for meat in the capital had extended the
range of supplies into the south Midlands and beyond. Watling Street
was already a great drove road linking the Home Counties with the
pastoral north-west, and in the newly inclosed pastures of Northamptonshire or Leicestershire cattle and sheep were fattened for the Leadenhall
market. Oxfordshire provides a good example of market specialization
around 1600. The Chiltern district was sheep-and-corn country. On the
clay plains of the middle Thames the cash crop was corn, wheat and
barley, which was shipped down the river from Oxford, Wallingford,
Abingdon or Henley. The fields were managed by folding sheep or
running cattle on them to manure the land. Further north, around
Banbury, a good deal of the arable produce was fed to the livestock
which was walked up to London when fat. Mutton and beef were
becoming as important for farmers' incomes as wool and hides; even
princely woolmasters like the Spencers of Wormleighton, who often
possessed as many as 14,000 sheep, were already turning part of their
attention to the meat market by 1600. Droving from the Cotswolds was
in full swing by the 1620s and from the north Midlands and Yorkshire

by the 1670s if not before. By the end of the century the long-range trade of Scottish Highland and Welsh cattle, headed in stages for the metropolis, was not unimportant, and the pastures and fold-yards of Yorkshire, Lincolnshire and Norfolk were already fattening as many as 30,000 Scotch beasts a year. In the woodland pastures of Shropshire, Suffolk, Devon, north Wiltshire and Cheshire, dairying developed to supply butter and cheese for the London market. In the same areas, swine- and calf-fattening, in which surplus buttermilk was used, resulted in the production and sale of cured pig-meat and veal.

Even in cereal-growing, market specialization and changing demands altered the balance between spring and winter grains. There was a widespread tendency to increase the acreage under wheat at the expense of rye, barley and oats. Farmers' inventories in the seventeenth century indicate an increasing concentration upon wheat growing, although there were naturally many local variations. Wheat output is supposed to have expanded by about 70 per cent in the eighteenth century, by comparison with an aggregate increase in all grain output of about 50 per cent. During the period when malt was excised after 1697, there is little evidence of any significant increase in output. On the other hand, horse-rearing required more oats to be grown in the seventeenth and eighteenth century, which perhaps reduced the acreage under barley. Nevertheless, in some districts within communication with the larger towns, especially in Kent and East Anglia, farmers who were in contact with London-based malt factors continued to specialize in barley-growing. By 1720–50, Kentish or East Anglian malting barley even found a ready sale across the Channel, and one of the great Dutch commercial houses, Hopes of Amsterdam, originated in the malt trade with England. The general changeover to wheat production for sale, however, was no less stimulated by the corn bounties offered upon exports after 1675; by far the largest quantity of grain exported from 1715 to 1770 was wheat. Wheat too was encouraged by the fall in rye consumption in eastern and southern England after 1600. Wheat was not a crop suitable for the whole of England, but on the heavier, relatively dry soils of eastern and southern England it had become the arable staple of both large and middle-sized farmers, their 'rent-payer'. In the 'smiling forties' (1740s) when grain prices ruled too low to satisfy either farmers or landlords, a fair amount of wheat, as well as oats and barley, was fed to Midlanders' cattle.

The permeation of market specialization as a consequence of urban demand affected virtually the whole of British agriculture by 1700, although not every farmer was necessarily enlisted into the system of commercial production. A subsistent peasantry was in retreat by the seventeenth century not only because farms were being consolidated into larger units, but also because even their small surpluses were absorbed into the distributive system of the middlemen. It is a fair reflection of the commercial role of agriculture that so many factors and brokers in agricultural products should have been active in rural England by the seventeenth century in order to service the London and other provincial markets. But enterprising farmers with more than half an eye open to market opportunities had to weigh the advantages of a good many potentially competing demands for their attention.

The balance between consumption and production for industrial use in agricultural output tilted towards the former after 1550 but not exclusively, since so much manufacturing depended upon wool or flax, hides, tallow or dye-crops. The space reserved for industrial crops was not sufficient to reduce arable food output after 1550. The leather and tallow trades hardly suffered from the increase of livestock for meat, for the two were essentially complementary. The problem of wool was rather different. Very little raw wool was imported into England before 1750, so that both the growth and the change in the textile trades had to be encompassed in the domestic production of fleeces. Wool-growing probably lost its competitive lead over other products by the late sixteenth century and a hundred years later the returns upon wool-production were almost always lower than upon any other agricultural enterprise. Sheep, however, could be used for both meat and wool, although the woolmaster, by requiring three shearings per head before discarding the animal, usually missed the best of the fatstock trade. Moreover, the best wool came from sheep on thin, aromatic uplands like the Cotswolds, where fattening was difficult. Better feeding helped the meat trade but apparently coarsened and lengthened the staple of the fleece. Such wool was fit for worsteds but not for high-grade heavy woollens. Local breeds of sheep intermingled on the strong 'feeding' pastures and this reduced their special characteristics. Furthermore, deliberate breeding after 1650 seems to have been concerned more with carcase weight or quality rather than with the fineness of the wool. A regiment of unknown local breeders thus foreshadowed the celebrated work of Robert Bakewell and his contemporaries in the middle and late eighteenth century.

A new attention to breed-characteristics seems to have been a significant consequence of the various improvements made to grassland after 1500. Horse-breeding became a widespread fashion of the gentry by the late seventeenth century and the techniques learnt in producing thoroughbreds were probably applied to cattle and other stock before Bakewell publicized his 'new' breeds in the 1760s. Shorthorn cattle, widespread in the Eastern Lowlands from the sixteenth century, had begun the displacement of western longhorn breeds before 1700–50. Certain specialist dairy breeds in various 'cheese districts' had also emerged by the same period. The process by which cross-breeding or the selective improvement of locally indigenous breeds was carried out is obscure, but we can say that the great breeders of 1750–1850 stood at the end, or pinnacle, of a protracted development. The effects may not have been impressive as far as the ordinary livestock of the peasantry is concerned, but the 'gene stock' of the improved animals was sufficient to support the great diffusion of their progeny across the agricultural landscape of nineteenth-century England. Horses, oxen, dairy cattle, sheep, swine and poultry were all improved in quality in the two centuries before 1750. The data of milk yields or carcase weight before 1750 are scanty in the extreme, not the least because the examples quoted usually referred to exceptional animals. Many seventeenth-century cattle were sold 'prime fat' from poor pastures at 4 cwt., but more typical perhaps were the beeves required by the Navy at 5·5 cwt. in 1683. A century later the same contractors stipulated a weight of 6·7 cwt. 'Fat ware' probably increased in weight by about 20 per cent between the seventeenth and eighteenth centuries, not least because fatstock was more standardized by 1750–1800 than in 1600–50. Milk yields probably increased on average by no more than about 25 per cent between 1600 and 1800.

The increase in the size of the national herds and flocks can only be guessed. According to Gregory King in 1695 there were about 11,000,000 sheep and 4,500,000 cattle in England and Wales. By 1750 the number of sheep had probably reached 17,000,000, but for cattle, Arthur Young's estimate in 1779 suggests a total of only 3,500,000. A decline is improbable, but there may well have been little or no increase. The number of fat cattle passing through Smithfield scarcely increased between 1736–45 and 1766–75, and the recorded output of hides and skins expanded only by 10 per cent between 1726–45 and 1756–75. Local studies, based on accounts and probate inventories, suggest that a good deal of stock specialization was active after 1600 in England, but, overall, they probably do indicate that the greater concentration upon sheep for meat and folding on productive arable land was very widespread.

Underlying trends in livestock farming rested not a little upon an absolute increase in the area permanently or temporarily under grass. The same is true of cereal production. It has, for example, been suggested that the increase in corn production during the eighteenth century (43 per cent) was accounted for by a 25 per cent increase in the acreage in cultivation and by a mere 10 per cent increase in productivity. The yields of grain certainly became larger in the early modern period. Medieval wheat output probably varied between 8 and 12 bushels per acre in average years. Productivity almost certainly increased quite substantially during the early modern period. Thus Deane and Cole, in *British Economic Growth, 1688–1959*, assume 20 bushels per acre in 1700 but only about 22 bushels in 1800, and their figures seem soundly based on contemporary evidence. But as far back as 1577 William Harrison recorded wheat yields from 16 to 21 bushels. For yield ratios (the return of corn produced from corn sown) the difficulties are equally complex. There is a reasonable consensus that English wheat output in relation to the seedcorn used increased from about 1:3 or 1:4 to 1:8 or 1:10 between the thirteenth and eighteenth centuries. But at Hurdwick, Devon, in 1504–37 the yield ratio of wheat was already 6·6 and at Cuxham, Oxfordshire, in 1571–80, 8, which were the averages quoted in 1655 for England as a whole. Arthur Young's averages in 1768–71 suggest ratios for wheat between 8 and 12. Some Continental scholars have used the evidence to suggest that a decline in the productivity of all grains occurred in England, as in many Continental countries, between 1500–49 and 1700–49—for wheat the fall is alleged to have exceeded 20 per cent. A decline in the productivity of grain output is unlikely in early modern England, but the timing of the improvement between the high Middle Ages and the era of Arthur Young and the Board of Agriculture is still very much in dispute.

The broad diffusion and the slow progress of innovation—the evolutionary nature of agricultural improvement—before the nineteenth century make a discussion of the chronology of agricultural change exceedingly difficult. Increments of productivity and the contribution of agriculture directly or indirectly to the process of economic diversification are the issues most usefully taken in attempts to isolate the diverse elements of growth. But there are at least three clearly differentiated hypotheses described as The Agricultural Revolution. E. J. Kerridge describes an Agricultural Revolution 'starting about 1560 and receiving its finishing touches from the hands of Robert Bakewell before 1767'.[1] In the process of his argument Kerridge rejects both those who believe in significant basework being laid before 1550 and the notion of multiple successive revolutions in British agriculture. A. H. John, E. J. Jones and a growing number of their disciples set the turning point in the years from 1660 to 1760, while G. E. Mingay continues stoutly to maintain that the Agricultural Revolution was deferred until after 1750. The thrust of controversy depends very much upon interpretations of insufficient data or of the impact upon aggregate production of particular innovations. The essential elements in the scheme, convertible husbandry, the introduction of new crops, the development of special-ized mixed farming especially for meat, the progress of inclosure and reclamation, the creation of grain surpluses and the inception of im-proved techniques of land management, are accepted as crucial by all parties, but the precise terms of their influence are not.

The middle period, from 1660 to 1760, is increasingly preferred by non-partisans in the debate as the critical turning-point. This is partly because the progress of innovation across the spectrum of agricultural change seems to have increased in tempo after the Restoration, partly because demand schedules for agricultural products became more variable in a period of industrial diversification and apparently rising real wages. From the farmers' point of view the deficiencies of the period may often have seemed to outweigh its advantages. H. J. Habakkuk has stated that 'the low or stationary agricultural prices of the earlier decades of the century had a depressing effect on agricultural investment and indirectly on the demand for industrial goods'.[2] On the Continent, falling or stagnant prices for agricultural commodities, from 1650 to 1750, precipitated just such a long-term depression, and most scholars assume that the century before 1740–60 was one of stagnation, recession or decay.

It was to combat this view that Professors John and Jones re-examined the sources of agricultural innovation and its effects before the tradi-tional period of the Agricultural Revolution after 1750. The main-spring of change was indeed the lowness of prices, especially when land

---

[1] E. Kerridge, 'The Agricultural Revolution Reconsidered', *Agricultural History*, 43, 1969, p. 463; cf. his *The Agricultural Revolution* (Allen and Unwin, 1967), p. 15.

[2] H. J. Habakkuk, 'The Eighteenth Century', *Econ. History Review* VIII, 1956, p. 437.

rents did not follow the same trend. Enterprising farmers were faced with the need to increase their profit margins by greater specialization, by a more intensive use of the land and by increasing total yield per acre. The goad pricked harder because labour costs did not fall to the same extent as commodity prices. Moreover, periods of acute depression seem to have encouraged landlords' investment in their agricultural estates. Necessity was the spur of innovation. Jones suggested that in the earlier period, before 1640, the profitability of almost all kinds of agriculture actually inhibited productive investment.[1] The farmers' surpluses were diverted into conspicuous consumption. We have seen that this is misleading, for innovation depended upon much more than the ratio between costs and receipts. But even if we assume a very long process of evolution, the level of activity from 1660 to 1760, in a period of low prices and very slow population growth, is still remarkable. Was it the turning-point? Until we can date the improvement in the yields (and yield ratios) of grain or the increase in carcase weight of average animals—until we can actually measure changes in agricultural productivity in the pre-industrial world—the question must remain open. Circumstantial evidence, the volume of publications recording or extolling progressive techniques (especially original works) or the interest aroused by the efforts of improving gentry or landowners, for example, suggests that the period between Sir Richard Weston's *Discourse on the Husbandrie of Brabant and Flanders* (1645) or Walter Blith's *The English Improver* (1649) and Defoe's tour of Britain in the early 1720s was especially significant. The performance of agriculture in the seventeenth and eighteenth centuries was obviously impressive in comparison with the deficiencies of medieval agriculture. The fact that after 1600 the fear of famine receded in England in itself is testimony to the achievement of countless unknown farmers. Compared with nineteenth- and twentieth-century progress in temperate agriculture, the improvements before 1750 look more modest, but they were at least appropriate to the occasion of an economy passing through the early stages of industrialization.

HOLDINGS, TENURES AND RENTS

The feudal customs of medieval England had been broken into many fragments by 1500. Personal unfreedom—the status of villeinage—had

[1] E. L. Jones, 'Agriculture and Economic Growth in England 1660–1750', in Jones ed. *Agriculture and Economic Growth in England, 1650–1815* (Methuen, 1967), p. 156.

long been in decay and was eradicated by 1640. As for the holding of land, many ancient customs were locally retained, but in law most servile tenures had been converted to copyholds by 1500. By the sixteenth century all land was held to be either freehold or copyhold. The distinction was that copyhold was subject to residual manorial dues, small annual rents and heriots or fines of admission (upon inheritance or sale), while freehold was only charged with ancient military dues like socage or knight service. Copyhold titles depended for proof upon an extract from the court rolls of the manor (the copy), which was not necessarily valid in perpetuity. Thus copyholds of inheritance *by fines certain*, very widespread in eastern and southern England, were little different in practice from freeholds, having security of inheritance and insignificant obligations. But copyholds could be granted by the lord for one or more lives (often named in the deed) or for a term of years, after the termination of which they fell into the manor again. Indeed copyhold tenures were complex both as a matter of law and in their great diversity before 1650. By 1750, the practical differences between freehold and copyhold were negligible, although the two were still clearly distinguished in law (and politics).

This simplifying process was an issue of changing attitudes to 'property'. In 1750, possession was generally synonymous with property. Medieval notions of possession were very different. Occupancy at that time was an aspect of 'use', and almost all real estate constituted merely a *right* enjoyed in return for various customary obligations, especially military service. The difference between rights in, and ownership of, property was crucially important, and its breakdown between 1300 and 1700 marked a profound change in the social organization of the land. In a transitional stage this resulted in a two-tier system of possession, in which residual rights of feudal lordship (i.e. the survival of the manor) represented a form of indirect ownership, while freeholders and many copyholders had by use of the land virtually obtained direct ownership. The decay of seigniorial control was often less complete than appears on the surface, for the manor retained much of its vitality into the seventeenth century, and many copyholders found that their relations with sixteenth-century lords were as unsatisfactory as their forebears' had been in the thirteenth.

By 1600 two-thirds of the land was already classed as freehold and much of it was owned in large *rentier* estates. From the standpoint of 1750 the great bulk of English agricultural land was let for a money rent to men who owned little or none of the fixed capital which they employed. The characteristic contractual relationship between landowners and farmers was already well in evidence all over the country at the end of our period. Rent had become a sum of money more or less to be regarded as a return upon the hire of fixed capital, and occupancy was a fixed term of years renewable by agreement, but of variable length. The growth of farm leases marks the most significant element in the history of English landholding from 1400 to 1750. It reflects the triumph of the concept of ownership as well as the reconstruction of a chain of tenurial deference based upon terminable contracts. These contracts originated in medieval leases of manorial demesnes (the former seigniorial 'home farms'). They were extended in part by the substitution of leasehold contracts for copyhold tenures, often by compulsion, sometimes by consent. How much copyhold was extinguished before 1650 is unknown but it was certainly a considerable quantity. Copyholds *by fines certain* were not profitable to ground landlords in the inflationary pressures of the sixteenth century, because the fines had generally been fixed well before prices began to rise. Such copyholds had often become as secure as freeholds, but the temptation to landlords to try to change the arrangement in their own favour was very strong. The simplest method was to convert the fixed fines into arbitrary fines, though the pressures by landlords to enlarge their rentrolls was probably counterbalanced by the efforts of manorial tenants to change the custom in the opposite direction. Moreover, by no means all the decay of copyhold was brought about by greedy landlords expropriating a wretched peasantry. Some resulted from the demise of manors, from attempts by gentlemen or rich yeomen who occupied copyhold to convert it into freehold for their own use or from amicable arrangements between landlord and tenant, often to increase the latter's working capital. Copies were thus surrendered for leases or crop-sharing contracts to improve the landholder's financial position.

The letting of freehold estates by owners to cultivators took many forms. Long leases, in excess of thirty years, had predominated in the fifteenth century. For ordinary farm leases the terms were steadily reduced before 1650, when very few leases exceeded 21 years and most ran from three to fourteen years. In addition, a great many annual leases or 'gentlemen's agreements' (lease-paroles) were in existence at the end of the sixteenth century, for a variety of tenants from smallholders to gentlemen farmers. Moreover, the majority of rural cottages and many farms were let at the lord's will, generally from year to year. There were also leases for lives, as with copyholds, which were usually determined upon one or three lives, in vogue especially in western England, where they survived in considerable numbers until after 1750. One other kind of lease is important. Institutions, especially in the church, often preferred much longer leases in order to secure a stable, if increasingly uneconomic, income. These 'beneficial leases' often ran for 99 years and were taken by wealthy men who employed them as an investment by subletting the land at a higher rent.

Subletting indeed was a widespread practice often disguised in the estate and manorial records. At Walkeringham, Nottinghamshire, for example, seven freeholders of the manor had 53 under-tenants among them in the late sixteenth century. Farmers often let cottages to labourers who worked for them. Very large leases of all kinds were frequently broken up into smaller parcels by leaseholders such as Edward Ernle of Urchfont Manor Farm in Wiltshire, who in the 1630s sublet all his arable lands to a number of separate cultivators. Parts of very large farms were often let to others for temporary summer grazing for livestock and in share-cropping arrangements. Robert Loder of Harwell, Berkshire, for example, once let part of his farm 'to halves' (cropsharing on a half-and-half basis) in the 1610s. Even copyholds were widely sublet to other tenants. At Keevil, Wiltshire, in 1623, all the 35 copyholders of the manor had about 56 under-tenants of various kinds, and at Burgh, Lincolnshire, under-tenants comprised three-quarters of the individuals named in the manor in the mid-seventeenth century.

Subletting and seasonal hiring of land complicates the profile of rural social organization especially before 1640 when population pressure brought many poor men and a number of acquisitive rich men into the market for any kind of land. Landletting before 1640 was very much in a seller's market. Some landlords were able to force less eligible terms upon their tenantry, exchanging leases for copyholds by inheritance and exploiting their position by imposing arbitrary fines upon inheritance. At Barrow-upon-Humber, Lincolnshire, for example, in the seventeenth century, rents were significantly increased when leasehold was introduced. Arbitrary fines were not uncontrolled, but, like farm rents, they were particularly sensitive to general price movements. The ability of landlords to charge economic rents or to levy substantial fines may well have distinguished those who succeeded as rural landowners, between

1540 and 1640, from those who failed fully to exploit the boom of prices. Much contemporary opinion echoed Sir Thomas More's complaint against gentlemen who 'polle and shave [their tenants] to the quycke by reysing their rentes'. Reports made towards the end of the period suggest that what men paid for the use of the land had risen variously from twofold to sixfold since 1520–40. In Wiltshire, where a detailed modern study has been undertaken, the increase between 1510 and 1630–50 was as much as eight- or tenfold (Fig. 2). The cutting edge was the entry fines, where the landlords' power to obtain a greater income was most evident. Farm rents in the modern sense were adjusted upwards, but since fines were calculated upon an extended period of use, what the tenant paid in one or more lump sums covered his expected profits for a term of years yet to come. The beauty of entry fines for the landlord was the fact that, at a change of tenant, charges for admission could often be bid up by applicants for the holding.

The fixing of rent was never a matter simply of economic returns upon investment. In a period of land hunger, would-be tenants sometimes offered more than they could afford for the privilege of a farm. Moreover, William Harrison in the 1570s believed that, 'Landlords . . . use to value their leases at a secret estimation given of the wealth and credit of the taker.' Rent was fixed as much by social as by merely economic considerations. Landlords who valued particular tenants, even in the harsh economic climate from 1580 to 1630, would moderate their demands at particular times, remitting some money payments and excusing dues in kind. Payment in kind indeed was very widespread until after 1750. Vestiges of ancient customary dues—ploughing boons or capon-rents, etc.—survived everywhere, though in money terms they were not important. Rents upon produce, especially corn rents (in theory payable in kind), were much more significant, and in some areas they were used to enlarge the landlord's revenue from his tenantry. How much the tenant obtained from his agreement is open to question. Some lords gave little for what they took out of the system, although landlords had a theoretical responsibility for maintaining the fixed capital of their estates. But in the sixteenth and early seventeenth centuries the pattern of monetary allowances for repairs and improvements by the owner, or of surcharges upon the tenantry for the use of new equipment installed by the owner, had not fully developed. Scarcely any estates before 1650 accepted any consistent duty for capital improvements. A widespread rebuilding of English farm-houses in the

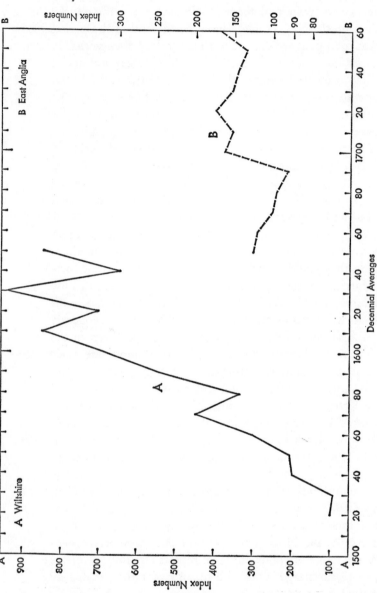

Fig. 2. (A) Rents per acre upon new takings (tenancies) on the Wiltshire estates of the Herbert family of Wilton (earls of Pembroke), from Eric Kerridge, 'The Movement of Rent, 1510–19', *Economic History Review*, 2nd series, VI, 1953, Table II. Index based in 1510–19.

(B) A composite index of rental changes—new tenancies and adjustments agreed during occupation—for a sample of landed estates in eastern England from Lincolnshire to Essex. Different estates have perforce been employed in deriving the date, but all were situated on heavier land and were as like in general characteristics as possible. Adjustments and interpolations have been made where necessary to maintain continuity, especially in 1615–1630 and 1700–15. The data, not published, have been collected by the author. That et al....

sixteenth and seventeenth centuries was carried out by the farmers themselves. But as annual money rents gained ground at the expense of corn rents or periodic fines so the economic relationship between land-owners and land-users was more formalized. The increase of rents in general continued into the eighteenth century despite the slackening of population growth and of the general price-level. Two periods of very low prices and rent abatements in 1670–90 and 1730–50 probably brought home to many landlords a new sense of their responsibility. Keeping tenants was more important than oppressing them, and several incentives, including new buildings, were provided to attract them. However, out of the doldrums landlords continued to exploit the buoyant demand for farms and farm land all over England.

The relationship between farmers and landlords was never entirely easy before 1750, however much it improved after the Civil War, but the connection or symbiosis of the two bore more and more fruit in the aftermath of the two recessions just mentioned. The dynamic of long-term agricultural improvement after 1660 depended increasingly upon a high degree of co-operation between progressive farmers and far-sighted landowners.

FURTHER READING

W. H. Hoskins   *The Midland Peasant* (Macmillan, 1957).

E. L. Jones, ed.   *Agriculture and Economic Growth in England, 1660–1815* (Methuen, 1967) especially Introduction and articles by Havinden, Jones and John).

E. Kerridge   *Agrarian Problems in the Sixteenth Century and After* (Allen and Unwin, 1969).

E. Kerridge   *The Agricultural Revolution* (Allen and Unwin, 1967).

J. Thirsk, ed.   *Agrarian History of England and Wales*, vol. iv, 1540–1640 (C.U.P., 1967).

J. Thirsk   *English Peasant Farming* (Routledge, 1957).

J. Thirsk   *Tudor Enclosures* (Historical Association, 1959).

E. L. Jones   'The Agricultural Origins of Industry', *Past and Present*, 40, 1968.

E. L. Jones   'The Condition of English Agriculture 1500–1640', *Economic History Review*, XXI, 1968.

E. M. Leonard 'Inclosure of the Common Fields in the Seventeenth Century', *Trans. Royal Historical Society*, new series, XIX, 1905.

G. E. Mingay 'The Agricultural Depression', *Economic History Review*, VIII, 1956.

J. Thirsk 'Seventeenth Century Agriculture and Social Change', *Agricultural History Review*, vol. xviii, supplement, 1970.

4

Industry

LOCATION AND OUTPUT OF MANUFACTURING AND MINING TRADES

Although we find it very useful, the term 'industry' is misleading for
the period before 1800. It was a word little used at the time, for men
preferred the ambiguous 'trades' to describe virtually all kinds of
employment other than agriculture and domestic service. There were
significant innovations in technology and organization, but industry
was almost as much craft-based in 1700 as in 1300. The contribution of
self-employed masters, including those with apprentices and journeymen, who produced everything from cloth to metalware to beer, jewellery and shoes, was perhaps greater than that of the more spectacular
capitalist concerns. Taken together, the mining and manufacturing
trades may have employed between a quarter and a third of the whole
adult population by 1700, and the value of their output, though essentially incalculable, possibly equalled that of agriculture by the early
eighteenth century.

Much of the product was directly consumed, since many of the self-
employed masters were jobbing artisans who owned little plant or
working capital and made up material brought in by their neighbours
or acquired stock-in-trade in very small quantities. This village-centred
division of labour of purely local importance was declining in the later
seventeenth and in the eighteenth centuries. Indeed, in some of the so-
called agricultural counties like Lincolnshire, the number of weavers or
dyers had become negligible by 1780. A process of 'disindustrializa-
tion', following from a *regional* division of labour between increasingly
specialized products for the market, was clearly apparent in the last
century of the pre-industrial period. Nevertheless, the village craftsman
remained a figure of social and economic importance, even though his
product can hardly be described as 'industrial'. But the word 'in-

dustrial' can be applied to trades expanding under pressure of growing market specialization. To some extent this concentration of production depended upon the resources of particular districts which made inter-regional trade essential. This is obvious in the case of coal and iron, but it applied also to textiles, although the geography of the pre-industrial woollen and linen trades is much more complicated. Important trades which employed large numbers of Englishmen before 1750, like building and leather-working, were much more widely dispersed throughout the country. Even when they were organized on capitalist lines, they contrasted sharply with other trades subject to market forces, like cannon-founding or silk-weaving, which were tightly concentrated in a few localities. Despite these variations, manufacturing industry in England consisted chiefly in the processing of native raw materials. Wool, hides, timber, malt, tin, lead, iron, hemp, flax were the most important in the sixteenth century, and with a few additions, which included some imports like silk-yarn, pine-wood deals, cotton and tobacco, they remained pre-eminent at the end of the period. The centuries before 1500 had seen the basic technology of manufacturing adopted and developed on English soil. Wool, which before 1300 had largely been exported in a raw state, formed only about 10 per cent of English exports two centuries later; its place had been taken by cloth as the staple of overseas merchants trading to or from England. Weaving, iron-making, stone-dressing, tanning, currying (i.e. leather-dressing) and brewing were almost as advanced in England by 1550 as on the Continent. Yet in spite of the slow rate of technical development before the eighteenth century, manufacturing processes were subject to a number of changes in the early modern period.

No less significant, however, was the reception of what may fairly be called 'new industries' between 1550 and 1720, mostly based upon skills and often upon enterprise derived from across the Channel. These new industries partly replaced older trades, but also extensively supplemented them. In the first instance, they added to the self-sufficiency of the English economy, since most continued to draw raw materials from domestic sources. Later, however, they became centrally important in both the expansion and diversification of the export trades and in the changing composition of domestic demand during the century after 1650. They included paper and printing, glass and soap making, oil-crushing, alum-refining, gun-founding and other sophisticated metallurgy, silk- and linen-weaving, sugar-boiling and the so-called

New Draperies which profoundly altered the woollen textile trades. They formed the basis not only for a new range of consumer products but for the chemical, metal-founding and engineering industries of the late eighteenth century.

There was an underlying pattern of continuity in manufacturing and mining between 1500 and 1750, but, despite immense difficulties and several setbacks, English industry managed to lay some of the track upon which in the eighteenth century ran the portentous engine we still call the Industrial Revolution. In this respect, manufacturing industry followed a course broadly like that of foreign trade. It is a mistake to look upon the whole era from, say, 1250, as one of steady evolution towards the industrialized society of nineteenth-century Britain. Change did not occur in a process of linear development, nor even within successive and clearly marked stages, not least because industrial activity was not homogeneous. The history of the various manufacturing trades suggests that their differences were at least as significant as their common experience. At some point in the eighteenth century there occurred what has variously been called the 'turning-point', 'great spurt' or 'take-off', to describe the phenomenon of the Industrial Revolution. Before about 1720, the rate of technical change was insufficient to negotiate this turn or to create the necessary cross-links between different manufacturing and mining industries to support a rapid acceleration. Nevertheless, obtrusive as the watershed between the pre-industrial and 'industrialized' economy seems to be, we should sell the period before 1750 short if we did not recognize how much of the essential foundations, of consumer demand and social attitudes, of agricultural surpluses and political stability, had been laid after the Restoration. Indeed, economic evolutionists have some reason to regard the years from 1660 to about 1870 as an entity, as an era of steady and creative change in agriculture and industry, commerce and financial institutions. Professor Nef, indeed, discovered many signs of industrial progress before the Civil War, but his period from 1540 to 1640 fits less easily into any scheme of historical development.[1] There were certainly two distinct periods before 1640: the first began about 1470 with the late medieval expansion of broadcloth production and ended in the slump which followed the inflationary export boom of the 1540s; the

[1] J. U. Nef, 'The Progress of Technology and the Growth of Large-Scale Industry in Britain, 1540–1640', *Econ. History Review*, V, 1934; idem, 'The Industrial Revolution Reconsidered', *Journal of Economic History*, III, 1943.

second was a period of painful and only partly successful adjustment to new demands and improved techniques, which was characterized by government interference and grandiose 'adventures'. A Neffian Industrial Revolution was certainly not one of the achievements of the Elizabethan Golden Age.

From its position in the export trade, even in the early eighteenth century, woollen manufacturing obviously retained its paramount position throughout the early modern period. By 1500, the basic structure of the industry during the next two centuries had already been established. The boom in exports under the early Tudors reinforced trends in the domestic organization of the woollen cloth industry which enriched a great many individual clothiers and put at least a temporary strain upon the supply of labour needed to produce for the export trade. The sequence of boom and recession between the 1510s and 1640s profoundly affected the shape of the industry. The long period of stagnation and crisis between the 1580s and 1620s, in particular, enforced major changes upon entrepreneurs and workmen, but it remains true that cloth-making in the time of John Leland (*c.* 1540) had a good deal in common with that of Celia Fiennes (1695) and Daniel Defoe (*c.* 1720).

The chief aspect of this continuity was geographical. The same or similar regions often produced quite different fabrics in 1540 and 1700, and by the latter date woollen textile production was rather more concentrated, but the same regions, more or less, were outstanding in the early eighteenth century as in Leland's day. There were three major districts and a number of minor centres of production. The first region roughly comprised the Cotswolds, in which every town and large village from Gloucester to Salisbury and Taunton was engaged chiefly in producing the heavy white broadcloth which bulked so large in the export trade. Some of the outlying places in Somerset and North Devon produced lighter 'kerseys' in the sixteenth century, but the western region's reputation depended upon cloth made from short-staple, carded wool of exquisite fineness. The short-wool sheep of the limestone uplands and the thin 'rye-lands' of the West were renowned in the medieval period and after for the quality of their fleeces. Elsewhere the fine wools were less plentiful and often mixed with longer or coarser fleeces. The high-grade broadcloth industry was therefore concentrated in or near the downlands of the south of England. In East Anglia, the second great growth area of the late medieval economy, production was based more on the lighter and less durable kerseys or worsteds made out of combed long wool. A whole string of villages in the East of England gave their names to more or less indistinguishable worsted-type fabrics in the early sixteenth century. A third area, growing fast even in Leland's day, bestrode the middle Pennines in Lancashire and the West Riding. It produced fabrics of mixed quality, some heavy broadcloths but many more 'Yorkshire dozens' or fustians, most of which were consumed at home. Districts of secondary importance in the sixteenth century included the middle Thames Valley, the Kentish Weald, parts of Surrey and Hampshire, Kendal, Coventry and, above all, Shrewsbury and the Welsh marches where a good deal of Welsh yarn was woven and Welsh cloth dressed for sale in England and abroad. John Leland noticed many casualties in the mid-sixteenth century. The textile trades of many of the old corporate towns which had once dominated production in their regions, Lincoln, Stamford, Leicester, Oxford, York, Newcastle, were decayed or in decline, soon to be followed by others, Salisbury, Reading, Shrewsbury, Winchester. With few exceptions the chief developments in the English cloth trades after 1400 occurred in rural districts, in villages or expanding market towns like Stroud, Lavenham, Worstead, Halifax and Bolton. The worsted, or combed wool, fabrics were probably gaining ground before 1600, partly because of the stagnation in broadcloth exports after 1550, and partly because the quality of English fleeces was becoming coarser and suitable only for combing. The extension of sheep-grazing into richer pastures, the improvement of English grasslands in the two centuries after 1550 and the greater interest in the carcase than the fleece contributed to this change. The New Draperies were largely based upon such combed wool, but the change, especially in East Anglia, to similar textiles, 'worsteds', 'kerseys', 'melfords', 'lanhams', preceded their introduction into the region by several generations.

Cloth-finishing, especially the process of dyeing, was backward in England in Leland's day. In this respect, a significant change had occurred by 1720. Dressing cloth had of course been practised in England since medieval times but almost entirely for domestic consumption, and it was heavily concentrated in the lighter-textile trades. The heavy broadcloths of Gloucestershire and Wiltshire were sold 'white' to drapers in the Low Countries and north Germany where the techniques of fast dyeing had been perfected before 1500. Combed wool fabrics required little or no fulling, and dyeing was relatively simple. Hence the bulk of East Anglian cloth even in 1540 was coloured, and much the

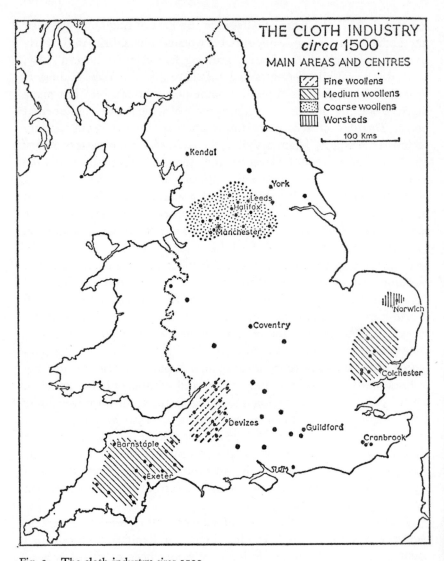

THE CLOTH INDUSTRY
circa 1500

MAIN AREAS AND CENTRES

- ▨ Fine woollens
- ▧ Medium woollens
- ▦ Coarse woollens
- ▥ Worsteds

100 Kms

Kendal · York · Leeds · Halifax · Manchester · Norwich · Coventry · Colchester · Devizes · Guildford · Cranbrook · Barnstaple · Exeter

Fig. 3.   The cloth industry *circa* 1500.
Based on P. J. Bowden, *The wool trade in Tudor and Stuart England* (London, 1962), 46.
From H. C. Darby, ed. *New Historical Geography of England* (C.U.P. 1973), 224.

same was true of the coarser textiles of the west Midlands and the north. The dyestuffs—woad, madder, woodwax, weld—were still largely imported, because the quality of the dyes of Continental plants was better, and almost all the oil used in dressing the cloth came from France

88

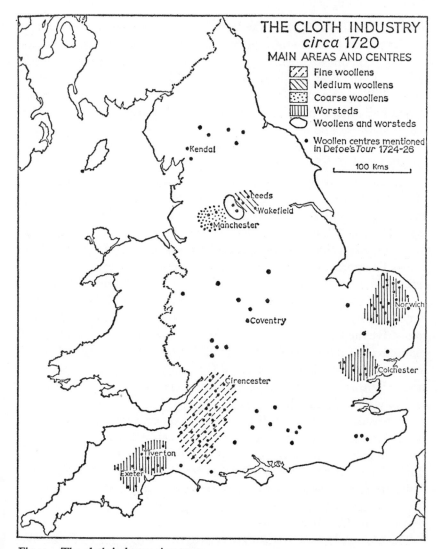

THE CLOTH INDUSTRY
circa 1720
MAIN AREAS AND CENTRES

Fine woollens
Medium woollens
Coarse woollens
Worsteds
Woollens and worsteds

• Woollen centres mentioned
in Defoe's *Tour* 1724-26

100 Kms

•Kendal

•Leeds
•Wakefield
•Manchester

•Norwich

•Coventry

•Colchester

•Cirencester

•Tiverton
•Exeter

Fig. 4. The cloth industry *circa* 1720.
Based on: (1) Daniel Defoe, *A tour through the whole island of Great Britain* (London, 1724-7); (2) P. J. Bowden, *The wool trade in Tudor and Stuart England* (London, 1962), 49. From H. C. Darby, ed. *New Historical Geography of England* (C.U.P. 1973), 359.

or Flanders. Nearly all the advantages therefore lay with the cloth-dressers of the Continent. But the profits to be derived from the finishing processes, in which perhaps two-thirds of the value added in manufacture originated, were great enough to attract English envy before the

89

death of Elizabeth. It was calculated in the early seventeenth century that 47 per cent of the profits of manufacturing wool was earned by the dyers. Dye-plants are mentioned with increasing frequency in the fields of Kent, Essex, East Anglia and Gloucestershire in the sixty years before the Civil War, and some farmers even sowed them with their corn crops. A few individuals experimented with methods of producing oil from native sources. The most successful was the early seventeenth-century Gloucestershire clothier, Benedict Webb, who grew large quantities of coleseed in the Severn valley for the purpose.

But the crucial issue of such technical backwardness was the bold attempt in the reign of James I to promote English industry by banning the export of undressed broadcloths. The project, named after Alderman Cokayne, a London merchant of large ideas and insatiable appetite for profit, was a characteristic mixture of fraud and farsightedness. Even James I's approval seems to have been compounded of both national interest and the financial necessity of the Crown. The proposal was to reorganize cloth production so that native dyers could derive the full benefits of foreign demand for the English fabrics and at the same time to deprive the Dutch of their profits. It was, however, also a commercial manœuvre to dispossess the Merchant Adventurers of their monopoly and especially to allow the Eastland Company into the European cloth trade. By this means Cokayne and his circle could enrich themselves and pay a handsome dividend to the Crown. The scheme, floated in 1614, was an unmitigated disaster. The English were defeated by the resistance of the Dutch, since they could compete neither technically nor commercially with their rivals, and the chaos of 1614–17 was profoundly disturbing in all the clothing districts, even in areas little affected by the Cokayne project itself. In the end, James I was forced to restore the Merchant Adventurers' monopoly and permit, even encourage, the resumption of white cloth exports.

The Cokayne project was destructive, but it did not cause all the severe problems of the English woollen industry in the early seventeenth century. The English obsession with the profits of broadcloth production was understandable in view of the current structure of the textile industry in 1600–20, but by that time a change in the pattern of European trade, and in the technology which supported it, was already beginning to influence the market for heavy broadcloths wherever they were dressed. The future lay increasingly with improved fabrics made of combed wool. These New Draperies had been developed in sixteenth-century Flanders, but, with the disruptions caused by war in the 1560s and 1570s, they had been taken by refugees to Leiden in Holland, to the Rhineland and East Anglia. In England they put roots down slowly and were scarcely important before the Civil War, but they grew spectacularly in the next eighty years, around Norwich, in the Stour and Brett valleys of Suffolk (Sudbury, Lavenham, Hadleigh) and around Colchester and Braintree in Essex. By 1660–80 they had replaced the old textile industry of Devon, where the trade was centred upon Exeter and South Devon, and by 1700–20 had been adopted in the West Riding woollen district. In Lancashire a parallel change occurred with the growth of the cotton trade, since until the middle of the eighteenth century the cotton yarn was mixed with other textiles to give the fabric the necessary durability. An emphasis upon mixed fabrics was one characteristic of the New Draperies. In Devon, serges made of mixed short-wool and long-wool were the speciality of Exeter; in Norfolk, by 1720, we find Norwich stuffs or bombazines (silk and wool); and in several places fabrics composed of linen and wool were also made. But the New Draperies were essentially improved 'kerseys' or 'worsteds', renowned by 1650 for their durability and for the ease with which they could be dyed. They often bore exotic names, such as 'perpetuanas', 'calimancoes', 'bays' and 'says', were striped, patterned or plain, and always highly coloured. Their durability was complemented by comparative lightness of texture, so that they were especially suitable for Mediterranean conditions. Above all, they were relatively cheap. The Dutch, and later the English, controlled almost all the world trade in the new textiles in the seventeenth century. The Italian cloth industry decayed disastrously under their competition after 1600, and in England, with the stagnant export trade in broadcloths, many of the older centres equally declined. But this was not true of centres which adapted themselves to the new fabrics, nor of the heartland of the old Cotswold region, around Stroud and Trowbridge, where, by 1660–1700, the techniques of finishing planned by Cokayne had at last been perfected. And the superb cloth of that district, then as now, contrived to find markets among the rich and ostentatious of the whole of Europe. Stroudwater cloth, like silk, satin or brocade, was a textile of aristocratic pretensions in the eighteenth century. By the late seventeenth century the European, and therefore above all, the English woollen textile industry was quite well adapted to the broad spectrum of demand for cloth of different qualities. It was affected by competition from Oriental 'calicoes', from 'cottons', linen, and to a much lesser extent from silk, but its pivotal position was nowhere challenged before 1750.

One major development remains to be mentioned. Parallel with the growth of the New Draperies was the expansion of the hosiery trade. It had been chiefly an urban, even a London-centred, trade before the seventeenth century and was closely controlled by a gild organization. Knitting for the market grew up as a handicraft in some rural areas like the Pennine Dales probably because it was easy to adopt and required little or no capital, but before 1700–20 the chief growth-points had been in the east Midlands north of the Trent, based on Nottingham, and around Norwich in Norfolk. One of the few significant inventions of the period, William Lee's stocking-frame of 1589, was extensively applied in the next century in the rural industry of Nottinghamshire. By 1750 the bulk of English-made hosiery came from the middle Trent valley, and the trade was quickly spreading into rural Leicestershire, reaching out to join with the ancient drapery trades of Coventry.

There were numerous other trades of importance to the development of the economy. An exhaustive list is unnecessary, but we must include the relatively large, old-established industries such as iron-working, tin- and lead-mining, linen-weaving, building and leather production, and others which underwent rather more technical or organizational changes between 1500 and 1700—brewing, shipbuilding or brick-making. In addition, there were essentially 'new' trades, introduced or modified by skilled immigrants, before 1700, papermaking, soap-boiling, glass, alum, copper, silver and gold, sugar-refining, tobacco-curing and many small, specialist crafts.

The first group changed least and probably grew least in size. The leather industry was one of the largest urban employers in the reign of Henry VIII and in towns like York or Northampton it may have been the biggest industrial trade by 1600. It was, however, also one of the more important rural industries, and some of the richest tanners or curriers were to be found in small towns like Horncastle in Lincolnshire, or Easingwold in Yorkshire. But because leather was so widely available and its products were so much in demand—like saddles, buckets, shoes, gloves, bellows, etc.—its dispersion over England is not surprising. London, however, was much more important in the leather trades than it was in textile production, especially in the production of high-quality goods.

The industry was moderately specialized, although there was a fundamental distinction between a tanning branch, for heavy leathers including shoes, and a 'dressing' branch for gloves and clothing. The tanners were sometimes able to control the leather trades in their neighbourhood as capitalist 'putting-out' merchants, and in the 'dressing' trades especially in London, capitalist leather-sellers (wholesalers) usually managed to perform the same role. Some of these leaders of the trades were very wealthy, and at least one, St John Wells in Lincolnshire, amassed a fortune large enough to be able to serve the office of High Sheriff in 1738. The abundance of home-produced, and therefore unquantified, hides and the lack of any interest in 'promoting' the industry by Crown, courtiers or other adventurers make it impossible to calculate the real size and the growth of the leather trades before 1750, but changes within these were in no way spectacular.

Much the same is probably true of the building trades, although the so-called Great Rebuilding of rural England, 1540–1700, and the continued expansion of the towns must have provided a good deal of work for masons, carpenters, plasterers, plumbers, glaziers and their labourers. The trades were fragmented into a myriad of small firms—man, apprentice and labourer as often as not—and some of the labourers were probably casualized to the extent that they could get work only if masters required temporarily to expand their work force. A handful of contractors employing a number of men of different grades existed in the bigger towns after 1660, but most of the domestic building labour before 1700 was not done by capitalist entrepreneurs. Some kinds of building labour were probably still scarce in rural districts in the seventeenth century. The Lincolnshire landowner, Drayner Massingberd, not only sent to Hull for materials in the 1670s and 1680s, but brought in plumbers and glaziers from the town to do his repair work. The market towns, however, increasingly supplied most of the countryman's building requirements by 1700, although not always to the satisfaction of men who knew the tradesmen of the urban centres, where training was sounder and competition more vigorous.

The greatest change which occurred between 1550 and 1750 was in the materials employed. The Great Rebuilding had been achieved in vernacular styles, using timber-frames covered with plaster, weatherboarding or cob. After 1600 brick or squared stone came more and more into use, and by 1700 the vernacular styles were moribund in England, although their death was unduly protracted. Brick-making, limeburning and stone-dressing, therefore, were rural trades which expanded rapidly in the century before 1750. Although the techniques of building altered before 1750 the occupational structure of the industry was recognizably similar in both 1500 and 1700. It was founded upon crafts slowly learnt and restrictively protected, and upon a high degree of labour intensity, in which, however, a chief characteristic was the uncertainty of regular employment for individual labourers.

The industry which grew most rapidly before 1750 to match woollen textiles in importance was coal-mining. The development of coalfields in the north-east, the Midlands, Yorkshire and south Wales between 1500 and 1700 was little short of phenomenal. According to Professor Nef total output of coal in south Britain rose from perhaps 170,000 tons in the 1550s to about 2,500,000 tons in the 1680s.[1] By 1760 the annual output seems to have reached 6,000,000 or 7,000,000 tons. In a short span from 1586 to 1606 known coal imports into London rose from 24,000 tons to 74,000. In spite of this increase, it is evident that the bulk of the coal hewn in England and Wales was consumed locally in the early seventeenth century. This is easy to understand, because of the cost of transporting coal overland. Only coastal fields, and especially that of the north-east, had any substantial long-range trade before 1700. Newcastle became the centre of the London (and foreign) coal trade in the reign of Elizabeth and its merchant oligarchy, called the Hostmen, sat firmly in control of the regional economy so long as the seaborne trade remained dominant. It was reckoned in 1675 that the land transport of coal was twenty times as expensive as sea carriage. Yet with minor exceptions, most of the great nineteenth-century coalfields were already in production by 1600–50, and the growth of the land-locked northern and midlands fields grew almost as fast as the Tyne and Wear field before 1700. We know that consumers near the pit-heads turned to using coal at the same time as or even earlier than Londoners, but off the coalfields and away from the seaports the acceptance of coal as a fuel was much slower.

Coal was used at first, and chiefly before 1700, as a domestic fuel. Householders in London, confronted with an inflation of firewood prices before 1620–30 which was unprecedented, turned reluctantly to the new mineral fuel, and by the 1650s were largely dependent upon it. The scarcity of firewood by 1600 was the consequence of a rapid denuda-tion of the woodlands after 1500, partly for fuel supplies but chiefly for farming and building. Metal-smelting, brewing, soap-boiling, sugar-

[1] J. U. Nef, *The Rise of the British Coal Industry* (Routledge 1932), vol. I, page 19.

refining, indeed some process in almost all the trades of pre-industrial England, were heavy consumers of firewood. The building trades also put an increasing strain upon timber supplies. What was serious in Elizabethan England became critical by the later seventeenth century. Thus the use of coal as a substitute was therefore not only attractive but in the long run essential. There were, however, technical difficulties in its application to trade. In brewing, for example, house-coal tainted the beer, and only in Derbyshire was the problem solved before 1660 by the employment of a gas-free coke in malting. As pressure of fuel scarcity upon other trades mounted, so attempts to discover the means of adapting furnaces to consume coal increased, but with mixed success. In metal-smelting a good deal of ingenuity was brought to bear on the problem in the seventeenth century, notably in the west Midlands, but success proved elusive until Abraham Darby's celebrated discovery in 1709. Even so, the Darby invention required more than a generation to gain acceptance outside Coalbrookdale in Shropshire. The story of coke-smelting belongs to the period after 1750, for the 'pitmen' had hardly at all challenged the livelihood of the charcoal-burners—even for the title 'collier'—in the greater part of England during the early eighteenth century.

It used to be held that the iron industry was the trade most seriously affected by the rising costs of fuel. Recent research, however, has raised certain objections to this opinion. In the Middle Ages, ironmaking was a rural process, based upon simple 'bloomery' techniques which produced small quantities of malleable iron suitable for working by blacksmiths. The dependence upon charcoal was offset by the peripatetic character of the furnace-masters and their plant—*forgiae errantes*. Even so the industry was chiefly located in the Weald, in the Forest of Dean and Cleveland long before 1500. But the introduction of the blast furnace and the refining hearth, water-driven bellows and hammers, etc., forced entrepreneurs to make a larger and more permanent fixed capital investment. By 1542 there were eight blast furnaces in operation in the Weald, a figure which had increased to at least 51 by 1574. Coppicing of trees was then practised to conserve timber supplies and in the two centuries after 1550 these new techniques of woodland management prevented the worst consequences of deforestation from chronically inhibiting the development of the English iron industry.

The demand for ordnance in the dangerous sixteenth century was at least partly responsible for the expansion of the industry from 1540 to

Fig. 5.   Charcoal blast furnaces *circa* 1600.
Based on H. R. Schubert, *History of the British iron and steel industry from c. 450 B.C. to A.D. 1775* (London, 1957), 354–92.
From H. C. Darby, ed. *New Historical Geography of England* (C.U.P. 1973), 282.

1590 and it is obviously no mere coincidence that the munitions industry of the period was located in Kent and Sussex. Much of the iron produced, however, was used in tool or smallware manufacture, and in the

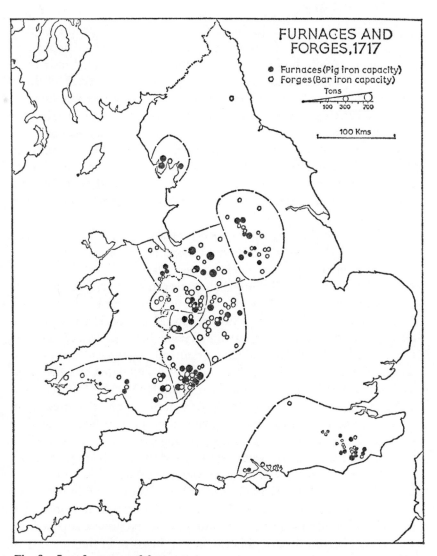

Fig. 6. Iron furnaces and forges, 1717.
Based on: (1) E. W. Hulme, 'Statistical history of the iron trade of England and Wales, 1717–1750', *Trans. Newcomen Soc.*, IX (1930), 12–35; (2) B. L. C. Johnson, 'The charcoal iron industry in the early eighteenth century', *Geog. Jour.*, CXVII (1951), 168. From H. C. Darby, *New Historical Geography of England* (C.U.P. 1973), 364.

fifteenth and sixteenth centuries many of the smiths who made up English forged iron were situated in the large towns or in rural communities near the point of consumption. But some specialized concentration was already apparent in John Leland's day. Sheffield even then bore a great reputation for edge-tools, and many small bloomeries and, after about 1575, a number of blast furnaces, were located near by to service the town's metal trades. The peasant ironmasters of Dean shipped much of their product upstream to supply the metallurgical trades of Birmingham in 1540, although a century later west Midland supplies of iron were much more important for the locksmiths, nail-makers, toolmakers and hollow-ware manufacturers of the region than those of Gloucestershire. By 1640 Bristol and Newcastle as well as London obtained iron for manufacture locally, by inland trade or from overseas, as need arose, to keep their smiths and greater ironmasters employed.

The casual wandering of the medieval iron industry was replaced after about 1580, when the need to move again became urgent, by permanent migration from depleted districts. The Wealden industry survived quite successfully into the eighteenth century, but the centre of gravity shifted in the seventeenth century into the West, stretching from South Wales into Shropshire, Staffordshire and Derbyshire. The Severn provided a link of great importance between Bristol and Birmingham, Coalbrookdale and Glamorgan, and by the end of the seventeenth century production in that region was dominated by a coterie of ironmasters headed by Benjamin Foley. Another centre of great significance by 1680 was the southern and eastern Pennines centred upon Sheffield, and a third the middle Tyne valley around Newcastle. The same problem, of increasing timber shortage, recurred in each of the growth areas of the seventeenth century, and the search for ore supplies in combination with sufficient copsewood led ironmasters into Westmorland, North Wales, Lanarkshire, and even into Argyll in the eighteenth century. However, as Dr Hammersley has recently demonstrated, the old centres did not fall into decline as new regions were opened up. The years after the Restoration saw a vast increase in the quantity of pig-iron imported, from Sweden and Spain, Danzig and eventually from Russia, but despite the air of desperation which sometimes entered into contemporary English comment after 1660, the English iron industry as a whole continued to supply a large part of domestic demand until coke-smelting became commonplace about 1760. Blast furnace production in 1600, when 73 furnaces were known to be in use, probably did not exceed 10,000 tons per annum. (Total output, however, was larger because 'bloomeries' remained important in some areas such as Dean.) Little decline apparently occurred from this peak, in the first two-thirds of the seventeenth century, and after 1670 the growth of output began again with new vigour, despite the attractions of imported bar and pig-iron. By 1717 known output perhaps exceeded 20,000 tons, almost certainly well in excess of the early seventeenth-century high-point. The annual output in England and Wales had possibly passed 40,000 tons by 1750, although the greatest growth during the eighteenth century was largely reserved for the period after 1760. As for consumption, it has been suggested that about two-thirds of the iron used in mid-eighteenth-century England was employed in agriculture, chiefly for tools and horseshoes.

Two other industries of old standing require comment. Brewing was still extensively a household occupation even in the eighteenth century, and many families, not only those of farmers, brewed ale for their ordinary use. In the towns, however, especially as the taste for beer rather than ale spread, common brewers, who sold their product whole-sale to innkeepers and householders, became a typical feature of the urban economy. Some in London were already substantial capitalists before 1640, although the greatest period of growth and the concentration of brewing in very large establishments like Whitbread's took place in the next century. Even so, one of the main filaments in the web of London's food supply, 1540–1640, was the long-range trade in malting barley. Brewing, in the later seventeenth and eighteenth centuries, provided one of the most important links in the diversification of the domestic economy, exploiting and creating consumer demand, influencing, and being influenced by, the rate of technological change, drawing out several connections with the agricultural sector which produced the hops and malt, not least by making available the spent grains as fodder for livestock. These influences, well established for the mid-eighteenth century, were rooted in the economic development of London at least as far back in time as 1600.

Shipbuilding, as befitted a people 'doing business in great waters', increased notably in the sixteenth and seventeenth centuries. The expansion of shipping, in river transport and coasting as well as at sea, was substantial. Known tonnage perhaps doubled in the century after the Armada and again from about 1680 to 1750, reaching 400,000 tons at the latter date. How much of this was built at home is uncertain. Prizes taken in war were generally added to the ships employed at home, but such windfall accessions were often counterbalanced by an equivalent loss to the enemy. Moreover, English shipowners sometimes acquired their new vessels abroad—in the seventeenth century from the Dutch, in the eighteenth quite often from the North American colonists. The English shipbuilding industry was hampered by the domestic cost of timber and by the scarcity of good oakwood near the seaports which possessed shipyards. A certain amount of ship-timber was therefore necessarily imported by the seventeenth century, as indeed it was into Holland. In the seventeenth century the competitiveness of English shipyards gave rise to much unease, chiefly because the Dutch had developed a superior all-round merchantman suitable for the European trade, which was not only much cheaper to operate, but cheaper and easier to construct. The English industry was hindered both by a degree of technical backwardness and by a continuing strategic requirement for a large proportion of the general merchant fleet—excluding fishing-boats and colliers—to be convertible into men-of-war in emergencies. Hence both the high operating costs of Elizabethan merchant ships and the diseconomies of English shipping which tried to compete in the low-value bulk cargo trade of the Baltic and the North Sea. Ironically, the resemblance of the English merchant ship to a warship came in for most comment just when the principal ships of the line were themselves becoming more specialized, before 1660. In the technology of naval shipbuilding the royal dockyards were in advance of all rivals; the general shipyards along the Thames and the east coast, however, could not independently produce an equivalent of the Dutch 'fluit' or flyboat for the mercantile marine until the second half of the seventeenth century, when, as a result of imitating captured Dutch ships in the 1650s and 1660s, and under the guidance of Sir George Downing who gained the ear of government at the Restoration, the Blackwall ship-wrights learned the trick of constructing bulk-freighters. Unfortunately, the bulk trades grew much more slowly after 1650 than before, and the deep-water or 'rich trades' of the Mediterranean, the Atlantic and the Orient were better suited to ordinary English ships. Even so, by 1700 the shipyards of England were at least as efficient, as technically advanced and as flexible as Dutch yards, although sixty years later the formidable development of American shipbuilding was again beginning to cause disquiet in the mother country. However, it is probably fair to assume that English shipbuilding at least kept pace with the growth of shipping in the century after 1650.

In addition to these basic trades in early modern England there were several new, or virtually new, industries introduced generally by wealthy entrepreneurs or by immigrant craftsmen from more highly developed regions of Europe. A few were immediately successful; others put down roots slowly but steadily; and some had to be given more than one start. The 'new industries' of the period 1550–1700 can be roughly assorted into two categories. The first included industries of a sumptuary nature, silk, paper, precious metals, pewter, glazed earthenware, glass, soap, which grew rapidly in the context of expanding urban consumer-demand. The impulse was often import-saving. The second group was of industries basically related to the supply or processing of producer-goods, the mining and smelting of non-ferrous metals, alum, oil-crushing (for cloth-dressing), brick-making. Some of these trades were older than the Tudors, but all derived great impetus and relied upon technical changes introduced, usually from abroad, after 1500.

Thus the mining of tin in Cornwall and of lead in Derbyshire was among the oldest of non-agricultural occupations, which was improved by a combination of German skills and of new capitalist enterprise. Seams of copper, calamine (zinc ore), silver, and in Scotland gold, as well as new sources of tin and lead were discovered and exploited in the century before the Civil War. Non-ferrous metal-mining was to be found in almost all the highland regions of England and Wales by 1600 —lead in the Pennines, copper in the Lakeland Fells, silver in north Devon and Cardiganshire, zinc in the Mendips and so forth.

Men bearing names like Höchstetter, Kranich, Schütz, Speydell, were to be found as leaseholders or engineers in various projects. They were German immigrants who brought with them the skills of West-phalia, the Harz or the Erzgebirge, where mining technology had undergone significant improvements in the later Middle Ages. Their contribution, both to extraction and processing of the ore, was substan-tial, especially in the newer areas of Cumbria, Wales and Scotland, but may perhaps have been overstated by writers who have seen in their influence a release from conservative practices and technical blockages, chiefly in the refining process, which prevented English miners from exploiting the new opportunities of the sixteenth century to the full. Many Germans were birds of passage, and some apparently were less technically advanced than their English promoters hoped. On the other hand, the Höchstetter family, from the time that Joachim Höch-stetter was appointed as principal surveyor of mines by Henry VIII, played a part in revolutionizing English metallurgy which in their case is difficult to exaggerate. Some Germans, especially those who acted for famous firms at home, were substantial investors in the mining industry. The company of Haug and Langnauer was drawn into mineral investment as a result of their attempt to expand cloth sales in England in the reign of Elizabeth.

The great capitalists, however, were mostly native landowners such as the earls of Cumberland and Shrewsbury, courtiers with an eye upon monopoly privileges, like Sir Walter Raleigh, or men of intermediate status as landowners or speculators, William Humfrey, Thomas 'Customer' Smythe, Bevis Bulmer, Hugh Myddelton, who made, and sometimes lost, fortunes in their entrepreneurial activities in the exploitation of non-ferrous metals. The Crown, from the time of Henry VIII to that of Charles I, was also interested, not least because of the fiscal possibilities in encouraging mining. Elizabeth incorporated two companies, The Mines Royal, and the Mineral and Battery Company in 1568, to provide interested parties with royal protection in their search for copper ore, if necessary against private landowners. Although they were the first joint-stock enterprises in England for industrial purposes, neither company was as successful as could have been expected, not least because of the vigour of entrepreneurs outside the charmed circle, but as a means of acquiring capital to promote the relatively expensive processes of copper extraction the two companies served a useful purpose in the sixteenth century. In older mining regions such as Cornwall or Derbyshire, the medieval system of mining was partly reorganized in the reign of Elizabeth without really touching the complex body of laws governing those ancient institutions which regulated the production of tin and lead in Cornwall and Derbyshire, known as the Stannaries and the Wirksworth Barmote court.

By the seventeenth century, however, tin production was stagnant at about 500 tons a year, partly because of the higher costs of getting the ore but chiefly because of inelastic demand for the product. Pewter and bronze (alloys containing tin) were suffering from the competition of brass, glass, or earthenware and from imports of German tinware. Lead output expanded greatly in areas free of medieval regulations, often under the aegis of firms like the London Lead Company. In Derbyshire the continued growth depended not a little upon the influence of Hull, Sheffield or Gainsborough, as well as of London merchants, who handled the pig-lead for internal distribution or for export to central and northern Europe. Copper and zinc were in less plentiful supply, at least until the opening up of Parys mountain in Anglesey in 1762, and by the late seventeenth century part of the English requirement of the two metals, as of gold and silver, had to be imported. Brass retained its popularity in many areas of life until after 1750 and, to some extent, copper was substituted for lead, as in brewing vessels. Non-ferrous metal-working added substantially to the stock of English technical skills in the early modern period. Its output was never large by modern standards but the far from prodigal endowment of mineral resources on English soil was in general appropriate to the level of demand at home—together with a small surplus for exports before 1750.

The adoption of import-saving industries in the sixteenth and seventeenth centuries was in part the consequence of conscious planning for increased self-sufficiency and in part the result of happy accident. The influx of skilled 'mechanics' and to some extent also of capitalists from more highly developed parts of Europe was a feature of English industrial history till 1700, after which the traffic was increasingly reversed. The Flemings in the cloth industry and the Germans in metal-working were outstanding, but since most of the skills in new industries like glass-making, sugar, paper and soap-boiling passed in Europe from south to north, the impact of strangers in all these smaller trades was even more far-reaching. New techniques of glass-making were developed by artist-craftsmen in northern Italy, spread slowly north of the Alps and were brought into England in the later sixteenth century. The upshot was that in transmission the techniques often became debased, and most English glass produced before 1650 was coarse window- or bottle-glass. The finer products of the craft were still imported. However, by 1700 the industry had again begun to be transformed, under the influence of rich Huguenot refugees, like Le Blanc, who set up in England after the Revocation of the Edict of Nantes in 1685. Though most of the glass-houses in England in 1750 still produced low-grade glass, there were already a number producing plate or crystal glass which provided a suitable framework for growth and technical development on English soil in the next century.

Very much the same course of events occurred in paper-making. The largest paper-mill in sixteenth-century England was operated by a German, Johan Spilman, and until late in the seventeenth century much of the best-quality paper was still imported from France. Portal, de Vaux and other Huguenots were again instrumental in improving the quality of English paper, and the board of the new Company of White Paper

Makers, incorporated in 1686, included many French names, although it never achieved the success of the Portal family in transforming the English paper industry. Huguenot influence extended to silk-throwing, which had had an unfortunate history early in the seventeenth century, beaver-hat-making, tapestry, where, characteristically, a former Flemish works in Fulham was taken over in the 1690s, and linen-weaving, especially in Ireland and Scotland. The Huguenots were essentially the entrepreneurs of these industries. Huguenot workmen were of course employed in the various trades, but only at Spitalfields in east London was there a substantial émigré population of French craftsmen and their families which formed a distinct element in the London scene for upwards of a century.

The windfall effects of immigration reinforced the growing demands for autarky from merchants and manufacturers, some of whom gained and held the ear of government in the seventeenth century. The nature of this obsession is best left for discussion along with other mercantilist doctrines, but we should note that the basic proposition, that English resources of raw materials and manpower and of a temperate climate and fertile soil should be employed to the fullest extent possible, worked itself out gradually in the developments between 1600 and 1750. The list of trades given above indicates how much more intensive the industrial system had become by 1750. Autarky, of course, was most attractive when England seemed poor, backward and uncompetitive. Before 1640, successive governments undertook some responsibility for industrial development, but their role was rarely as regulatory or directive as in France, and the leading spirits in many royal schemes were private businessmen, landowners or aspiring monopolists, while the Crown interest was often largely financial. After 1660, central government gradually dissociated itself from any detailed concern with manufacturing or mining. The overall consequences of promotional intervention are difficult to assess, but have probably been exaggerated by those who see in the mercantilist era a lesson for the role of the state in a modern mixed economy.

THE ORGANIZATION OF INDUSTRY

The old foundations of trade and manufacturing had rested upon the gild system. Gilds, which were largely concentrated within the towns, were remarkably diverse and changeable, at least until the Civil War. Many gilds especially in the richer towns were often dominated by an oligarchy of merchants who held nearly all the effective offices and the power which they conferred. Many gilds, too, were dominated from outside by the wealthy élites of neighbouring gilds or livery-companies, as the leather sellers in London were the masters of many of the leather craft-gilds, or the Haberdashers of several minor textile gilds. Many gilds were required to open their society to wealthy townsmen irrespective of their occupation, and the merchant-gilds in particular recruited some part of their ruling élites in this way. The instability of gilds as organizing units of trade is illustrated by their tendency to amalgamate, as in Gloucester in 1607, when nearly all the metal trades were incorporated into a Company of Metalworkers, and to dissolve or break up into parts, for example, when the London glovers hived off from the leather sellers in the sixteenth century.

Gild rivalries were often bitter and protracted. A good deal of legislation followed from the disputes between the Cordwainers and Curriers in the London leather industry in 1548–55. Where a single gild gained effective control over a whole segment of productive activity, the power of the merchant oligarchs, who also often served as mayors and aldermen of corporate towns, was not infrequently paralysing. The power of certain York gilds went a good way to bring that city low in the fifteenth century and sixteenth century as rural townships like Wakefield and Leeds grew. Gilds, by their nature, were restrictive. Their function was partly to protect the consumer by maintaining standards of craftsmanship, and partly to protect the producer-member by banning the activity of outsiders in the town, by regulating recruitment into the occupation by apprenticeship and a graduated system of membership. The social welfare of gildsmen was also supplied by a common fund, to which the members contributed and which the wealthiest were expected to support. Hence gilds were seen by successive governments before 1640 as powerful forces of social and economic stability. Tudor and early Stuart governments legislated over a wide field of industrial activity mostly in the context of supporting or arbitrating between gilds. New gilds, especially in London, were formed in considerable numbers before 1520, and again, with overt government approval, after 1560. Many organized new trades like pin-making, stationery or gardening. A particularly sensitive area, in which it was difficult to pass laws throughout our period, was the relationship between natives and strangers, especially those like the Flemings, Walloons, Germans and Huguenots who came from overseas.

Of the reorganization which was imposed upon the gild system the most important contribution was probably that of the so-called Statute of Artificers of 1563. This Act, a remarkable attempt to hold the *status quo* in a period of social turmoil, was not a great success, but its standardizing impulse was carried on less formally, by the spread of seven-year terms of apprenticeship first throughout London trades, and then elsewhere in the country, and by the action of magistrates in Quarter Sessions in imposing judicial maxima of wages and, occasionally, standards of reputable workmanship. The gilds, however, were becoming increasingly irrelevant both to industrial development and to the Crown by 1660. Oliver Cromwell had allowed demobilized soldiers into protected trades without apprenticeship, and by the 1670s there were said to be 'thousands of unlawful men' or 'interlopers' in nearly all the English crafts under gild control. By that time, indeed, the gilds, whose restrictive practices had evoked little public protest before the Civil War, were often seen as an affront to industrial efficiency and business freedom. That this was largely sentiment catching up with long-term realities is obvious. The gilds had been in decay, so far as they had controlled the whole manufacturing and mercantile structure of the economy, for centuries. The chief element in their decay was the rural migration of industry, since in the country districts gild organization either did not develop or was very weak. Entrepreneurs, both medieval and post-medieval, sought advantages of freedom and of cheaper labour outside the boroughs. The thirteenth-century businessmen of Lincoln, York or Oxford, like the putting-out merchants of later dates, who sent work out into the villages, shamelessly circumvented the gilds in their towns. In addition, as Clapham said, 'water-power had been a solvent of gild power from the days of the first fulling mill'.[1] This was partly because so much industry employing large plant was country-based, partly because it was very much under the control of capitalist entrepreneurs. Moreover, since the stimulus for rural industrialization came at least as much from peasants and landlords whose only gilds were not craft-based, the organization of industrial production outside the towns often assumed the character of an activity subsidiary to agriculture.

Gilds naturally foresaw the danger and attempted to escape some of its consequences by the exercise of their political authority, not least by gaining the ear of a sympathetic government. Even so, the most success-

[1] J. H. Clapham, *A Concise Economic History of Great Britain to 1750* (C.U.P., 1949), p. 253.

ful gilds in the seventeenth century were those found in a lively urban environment. Those of London, Norwich and Bristol in particular retained a good deal of their effectiveness until the eighteenth century. A few new gilds, like the Norwich Worsted Weavers, were still being established in the 1650s and 1660s. Even in the bigger cities, however, the problems began to multiply in the Stuart period. Trade depression, internal quarrels among gilds or among the merchants or courtiers who sought to dominate the economic life of the metropolis, the increasing fiscal obsessions of the Crown, added to their difficulties, but the real problem was the suburban migration of many business concerns. Although the physical boundaries of the cities were extended, the constituency of the gilds often remained tied to their medieval limits. Some gilds were permitted, in renewed incorporations, to include outlying parts within their competence, but few even kept pace with metropolitan expansion. The advantages of setting up in the suburbs for city-based trades were the same as for the rural entrepreneurs. Moreover, in the new urban agglomerations like Manchester and Birmingham, gilds gained no more of a footing than in the industrialized villages. After 1680, the future lay with these new places.

Few gilds had been democratic associations of equals, but they often seemed to stand in contrast to and constraint of the freedom of capitalist merchants to control the means of production and distribution. It is, however, too simple to say that gild power was replaced by pre-industrial capitalism in the early modern period. Independence of the gilds often meant the opportunity for small 'interlopers' to find a niche in any one of scores of trades, and the peasant entrepreneur all over Europe was at least as common as the nobleman or great putting-out merchant. The putting-out system was certainly a form of industrial organization very widespread in European manufacturing by 1600, and its roots lay far back in the Middle Ages. In its most complete form, putting-out was a form of vertical integration controlled by a single capitalist. Generally a merchant rather than a craftsman, he supplied the raw materials, pre-empted the product and distributed the finished commodity in the market. Sometimes his control over the material employed extended over several processes. In woollen textiles, for example, the putter-out might buy the raw wool, have it carded, spun, woven and perhaps fulled and dyed before taking in hand the 'draping', or merchanting of the cloth. Putting-out extended into almost all the trades which supplied a product for wholesale distribution, but it was variable in character even within a single industry. Common features included not only the handling of the material, but also the dependence upon a merchant of a body of more or less self-employed craftsmen and their families, and often a credit nexus between capitalist and producer. Not only was the stock-in-trade, the working capital, of the producer-artisan found by the putter-out, but sometimes also the tools and fixed capital as well. The self-employed character of many men within the system was therefore essentially fictitious, because housing, equipment and livelihood belonged to their merchants.

The alternative name for the system is the 'domestic system', which indicates that it was still essentially based in the cottages of the producers. A workman in his own home was subject to less work discipline than his successor in a factory, and there were many complaints of erratic behaviour by labourers in the seventeenth and eighteenth centuries. In other respects, however, the cottagers who produced the cloths, nails, leather goods, knives, or hand tools in the most capitalistically organized districts like Gloucestershire, Norfolk or Sheffield were only marginally better off than day-labourers. Labourers who worked only for wages were indeed numerous in the same areas, employed about the furnaces, forges, fulling mills or as journeymen in the cottages of the small masters.

There is also some evidence for what have recently if inelegantly been called 'proto-factories', that is for large, centralized workshops without benefit of mechanization. Some, like the almost legendary textile 'factory' of John Winchcombe at Newbury or the converted premises of Malmesbury Abbey used by William Stumpe for his cloth-workers, were remarkably precocious (before 1550), but the number of successful large, concentrated enterprises in England before 1700 was very limited. Professor Nef's celebrated catalogue of 'industrial' plants before the Civil War mostly included exceptional examples of what generally proved to be false starts—Johan Spilman's unique paper factory, the great 'alum houses' at Whitby, the cannon factory at Brenchley in Kent, and a few superior forges in the Weald and the West Midlands. Even when technology required fairly expensive capital installations—watermills, blast furnaces, slitting mills, deep coal-pits—the number of employees seldom exceeded a dozen. A good deal of the necessary work was contracted out to small masters, as for example in the shipyards of the time. The plantowner, like the putting-out merchant, often imposed his will upon a substantial clientèle of jobbing artisans rather than upon a proletariat. The concept of the factory, even of one without mechanical power, is scarcely expressed until after 1750. The few genuine exceptions, like the alum works of the 1630s, were very specialized, but included such harbingers of the future as Ambrose Crowley's integrated iron-works at Winlaton-on-Tyne in the early eighteenth century, a few of the largest common breweries in London, and above all perhaps the naval dockyards. That is not to say that many labourers did not work away from home, for many did, even in the textile and light metallurgical trades; but they spent their lives beside the master or in small workshops with few companions. It may even be true to state that the typical firm of the seventeenth century consisted of a self-employed master, his apprentice and one or two journeymen assistants. At the same time also, the whole family might be expected to contribute something to the householder's employment. In the more industrialized trades such as clothing or coal-mining, the family unit was the pivot of the system of production.

This was especially the case when payment was based on piece-work, as in the putting-out system it generally was; or when the family retained its independence of the greater capitalists. In the West Riding, for example, the heavy concentration of the woollen industry in the hands of the merchants was slow to develop, and in Defoe's day a good deal of the cloth was made by yeomen-weavers who sold it personally in one or other of the local cloth markets. Spinning was still the wife's domain; weaving that of the husband and his eldest son or apprentice. Even the dressing of cloth was not infrequently undertaken by such families of the self-employed. Family labour imposed special demands upon the household and the rhythm of work naturally differed considerably from modern practice in Bradford or Huddersfield. The work was hard but it was scarcely unremitting. Family labour, indeed, was almost synonymous with casualization, and may be taken to exemplify one of the most important and widespread elements of the 'pre-industrial' economy throughout the world.

TECHNOLOGY AND THE RATE OF INNOVATION

The progress of technology before the middle third of the eighteenth century has been one of the most controversial issues in the economic history of the pre-industrial period since J. U. Nef published his detailed research on the subject in the 1930s. There is good evidence of significant inventions between 1400 and 1700, but the extent to which they were widely applied in routine manufacturing is doubtful. The Middle Ages bequeathed to posterity such important basic principles as the mill, press, winch, still, sluice, and loom, upon which later innovations could be based. The mill, which proved to have a multitude of uses, had already by 1400 been harnessed to horses, wind and water. The ubiquity of the watermill in the pre-industrial world must not be allowed to detract from the novelty of the late eighteenth-century water-driven factory in northern England. The technical limitations of power transmission in a mill in which most of the working parts were wooden, and in which the mill-wheel was often inefficiently mounted, were so great that output seldom exceeded five horse-power before 1750. The techniques of lifting, pressing, hammering and grinding, however, comprised a good deal of the necessary processes in which human strength had been supplemented or replaced by mechanical power. The output of such machines perhaps doubled or at most trebled between 1200 and 1700, which is not an adequate basis for a major technological revolution.

Yet in an intellectually fertile age, like the sixteenth and seventeenth centuries, new ideas flowed in a steady stream. Many of them were misbegotten or could not be applied to existing methods of production, but one result of the spread of printing—in itself a significant new invention—was an increasing volume of handbooks on various industrial arts with woodblock engravings depicting the latest processes. Book-learning certainly influenced the educated entrepreneur or public official, as the numerous translations of the more important texts of the period indicate. A good example is Joseph Moxon's *Mechanick Exercises* of 1686, which came in the middle of a long tradition of didactic literature in Europe. But printing merely added a dimension to the age-long exchange of craftsmen and their tools and 'engines' in Europe, through which innovations were diffused. Printing brings us into the realm of what is sometimes called The Scientific Revolution. We cannot simply say that Renaissance man was equipped with a new scientific curiosity, in the manner of Leonardo da Vinci or Sir Isaac Newton. There was, it is true, a new emphasis upon empiricism in scientific inquiry. Da Vinci described himself as 'unlettered', that is to say pragmatic or non-academic in his approach, and Robert Boyle, the chemist, subordinated speculation to experience in his method of research. Many natural philosophers were interested in technical problems: Huygens, Newton and Hooke saw no effective distinction between pure and applied science. The Royal Society and its European counterparts were concerned with inventions and their application, to the extent that the developing interest in current or improved technology before 1750 was parcel of a complex relationship between government, science and economic growth which was patent in autocratic, Continental states, and not unknown in England and Holland.

Nevertheless, the great majority of practicable new inventions was the product of research by trial and error. The inventors, like the entrepreneurs, were men closely in touch with the requirements of the trade in question, or were 'curious' amateurs without scientific training, like the Rev. William Lee of Calverton, Nottinghamshire. They learned to solve problems, important for the industrial future, from experience of building blast furnaces, sluices, mills, organs, even bridges, coal-pits and dockyard installations. The thermometer, telescope and chronometer were indeed significant for the growth of crafts employing more refined skills and certainly influenced the development of a sophisticated artisanate of engineers, millwrights and instrument-makers in eighteenth-century England. We know how important clock-makers were in the industrial technology of the mid-eighteenth century, but it is still true that the breakthrough was not dependent upon the scientific rationalism of the age of Newton and Descartes. Few inventions other than the Jacquard loom or Cugnot's steam engine were founded upon a proper understanding of the scientific principles involved before 1800.

The greatest changes in technology before 1700 occurred in mining and metallurgy. Several innovations were applied to the mineral industries in late medieval Germany and spread gradually throughout Europe by 1600. In England, the blast furnace, slitting mill and tilt-hammer had been widely introduced by 1570, at which date the Sussex Weald was one of the most advanced and important iron-making centres in Europe. A tool for boring cannon barrels and a machine for stamping coins also added greatly to the efficiency of the metallurgical trades. The blast furnace, which produced pig-iron full of impurities, superseded older furnaces chiefly because it was more efficient in the use of charcoal, but since the 'make' could immediately be used for cast-iron the new demand for non-malleable iron after 1500 also contributed to its diffusion. Wrought iron, and the best steel, were often produced by first smelting the ore in another medieval innovation, the shaft furnace. In addition, the great heat required in these processes of iron-making had usually to be supplied by mechanical bellows, horse- or water-driven. Innovation certainly improved the fuel economy of smelting and forging all kinds of metal, but the burgeoning demand for all but tin maintained the pressure upon the woodlands. Improved labour productivity, which was so often a cause of complaint in the period, was also achieved. Bohemian figures suggest that the output per man perhaps doubled between 1570 and 1750, which may be a reasonable estimate for pre-industrial Europe as a whole.

In mining and the related operations of dressing the ore or the coal, the largest changes took place in the deeper pits which were being sunk as the seams became less accessible. Mine-engineering improved significantly from the tin 'wheals' of Cornwall to the coal pits of Northumberland. The biggest problems were ventilation and drainage, but it was necessary also to improve the lifting gear and eventually the transport system within the mine complex. Drainage was improved by pumping even before the steam engine was applied to the same purpose. Newcomen's atmospheric engine of 1708 was almost exclusively harnessed to pitshaft pumps in the eighteenth century. Yet the most impressive mines of the seventeenth century remained primitive, dangerous and cramped, and the technical aids to the pitman inefficient and fragile, even by nineteenth-century standards.

It is unnecessary to give here a catalogue of all the technical innovations applied in west European industry between 1500 and 1750, because the information is easy to find elsewhere.[1] The major role of innovation in the metal-working and mining industries was certainly something of an exception. Many trades contrived to use the same tools in the same operations in 1750 as in 1500 and in a majority the rate of change was slow and small in scale. In the textile trades, neither the New Draperies nor the English acquisition of new skills in dyeing added much to the stock of techniques employed by the craftsmen in the industry. On the other hand, there was a kind of fugal relationship between the spinning and weaving branches before 1700 as in the celebrated period after 1730. First, the spinning wheel was improved by the addition of a flyer and treadle (before 1600); then a comparable range of improvements to the late medieval horizontal loom slowly spread

[1] See, for example, H. Kellenbenz, 'Technology in the Age of the Scientific Revolution, 1500–1750', *Fontana Economic History of Europe*, vol. II (Collins, 1974), pp. 177–267; A. R. Hall, *The Scientific Revolution 1500–1800* (Longman, 1964); T. P. Hughes, ed. *The Development of Western Technology Since 1500* (Collier-Macmillan, 1964); S. Lilley, *Men, Machines and History* (Lawrence & Wishart, 1965); A. P. Usher, *A History of Mechanical Inventions* (Harvard U.P., 1964); J. U. Nef, *The Conquest of the Material World* (Chicago U.P., 1964).

from Italy, Germany and France to the rest of Europe. A much improved broadloom, the famous Dutch ribbon loom, and a loom on which complicated patterns could be woven, appeared and were adopted in many places before 1700, despite gild resistance and 'Luddite' turbulence from time to time. Technological development was European, not solely English, and a good deal of the impetus for change came from the silk industry in which England was laggard until after 1660. Mechanical fulling became almost universal by 1600; carding, combing, dyeing, bleaching were all improved. The gigmill, used in teasing cloth, was banned in England in 1551, but was fully established two centuries later; the calender, employed to give a lustrous finish to cloth, came into use in England and France almost simultaneously in the 1680s. Some inventions were intended to save labour; others to improve the finish; yet others to increase the range of patterns, styles or qualities of goods available in the market. Many inventions made with a particular fabric in mind could be transferred to others with little adaptation. The most important English contribution to the stock of European textile technology before 1700, William Lee's stocking-frame of 1589, however, was much more specialized. Lee was spurned by Elizabeth I who saw the invention as a threat to employment, and his frame was not widely adopted in England and southern France for at least a generation after his death.

So many of the textile inventions of the period raised productivity without increasing the demand for labour that the resentment of the people and the caution of governments is understandable. This partly explains the slow diffusion of the inventions outside the metallurgical industries, but the ability to resist change was always limited by the counterpoise of foreign competition or of the broadening and changing pattern of consumer demand in determining the entrepreneur's attitude to innovation. One of the most significant stimuli was the production of a better, more fashionable or more costly good as a result of the innovation. In paper and glass, for example, the chief motive for technical change seems to have been the improvement of the products for wealthy consumers at home. Sometimes the influence of the market was less direct. The discovery of cobalt blue glazes in the earthenware trade of Holland had the effect of creating a new market throughout Europe for Delft pottery as a substitute for pewter. By 1750 English potters, already centred upon Stoke-on-Trent, had learned the Continental arts of glazing and had built up a substantial market for their products right across the social spectrum. The parallel rediscovery of Chinese hard-paste porcelain-making in Europe spread from Germany to France and England in the early eighteenth century and in turn satisfied a growing upper-class demand for fine-ware, long before Wedgwood and Spode transformed the industry in England. The growth of a fairly broad-based market for consumer goods of this kind in England after 1660 was perhaps not matched on the Continent, but the ostentation and fashion-consciousness of the rich all over Europe were sufficient to keep inventors active in the trades serving wealthy consumers.

FURTHER READING

D. C. Coleman   *Industry in Tudor and Stuart England* (Macmillan, 1975).

J. W. Gough   *The Rise of the Entrepreneur* (Batsford, 1969).

N. B. Harte and K. Ponting (eds.)   *Textile History and Economic History* (Manchester University Press, 1974).

S. Lilley   *Men, Machines and History* (2nd ed., Lawrence and Wishart, 1965).

J. U. Nef   *The Rise of the British Coal Industry* (Routledge, 1932).

G. Unwin   *Industrial Organisation in the Sixteenth and Seventeenth Centuries* (O.U.P., 1904).

C. Cipolla   'Diffusion of Innovations in Early Modern Europe', *Comparative Studies in Society and History*, 14, 1972.

D. C. Coleman   'An Innovation and its Diffusion: the "New Draperies"', *Economic History Review*, XXII, 1969.

D. C. Coleman   'Technology and Economic History, 1500–1750', *Economic History Review*, XII, 1959.

M. W. Flinn   'Growth of the English Iron Industry 1660–1760', *Economic History Review*, XI, 1958.

G. Hammersley   'Charcoal Iron Industry and its Fuel, 1540–1760', *Economic History Review*, XXVI, 1973.

E. L. Jones   'The Agricultural Origins of Industry', *Past and Present*, 40, 1968.

J. R. Kellett   'The Breakdown of Gild and Corporation Control over Handicraft and Retail Trade in London', *Economic History Review*, XI, 1958.

J. U. Nef   'Progress of Technology and the Growth of Large-Scale Industry in Britain 1540–1640', *Economic History Review*, V, 1934.

J. Thirsk   'Industries in the Countryside', F. J. Fisher, ed. *Essays in the Economic and Social History of Tudor and Stuart England* (C.U.P., 1961).

C. Wilson   'Cloth Production and International Competition in 17th Century', *Economic History Review*, XIII, 1960.

5

Trade and Commercial Organization

OVERSEAS TRADE

A metaphor frequently employed in the early modern period was to describe overseas trade as the Great Wheel which drove the mills of society. Foreign trade certainly played a disproportionately large role in the pre-industrial economy. The number of people employed directly in this most rewarding branch of commerce was small by comparison with agriculture, domestic service, inland commerce or many manufacturing trades. Moreover, exports seem to have taken up somewhat less than one-third of total product of the country by the late seventeenth century, while many of the imports still supplied luxury goods for the wealthy end of the spectrum of consumers. Indeed, the obsession with foreign trade which was central of so many economic doctrines in early modern Europe was somewhat double-edged. Mercantilists believed firmly in the wealth-creating virtues of overseas commerce, but many of them also advocated the superior advantages of self-sufficiency. The apparent contradiction will be explained later.

At a practical level, it is obvious that foreign trade, and its related sectors of shipping and mercantile finance, were fundamentally important in supplying most of the government's recurrent revenue, in creating many of the great personal fortunes in the two centuries between Sir Thomas Gresham and Sir Sampson Gideon and, possibly, in employing a large portion of the national capital, of ships and warehouses as well as stock in trade. Trade had always been an innovating force in economic life. The expansion of an exchange system based upon money and credit has been traced far back into medieval Europe, and the instruments devised by Italian and Flemish merchants to speed their turnover, facilitate payment, raise capital and to circumvent the usury laws were common currency by the seventeenth century. Professor Gras long ago suggested that a major watershed in the development of capitalism was passed when European merchants turned from a wandering to a sedentary life.[1] Thus from being a glorified pedlar the European 'merchant' became the manager of a widespread network of credit and merchandise, employing agents in all the main commercial centres of Europe but scarcely setting foot outside Florence, Genoa or Venice. However, few overseas merchants of sixteenth-century England were sedentary entrepreneurs increasingly reliant upon the specialized services of other parties. The growth of ship-broking, insurance and exchange banking is characteristic of the period after 1600 in England, if not in Italy, but throughout our period some merchants, perhaps a majority, could still expect to go abroad, first to Antwerp, later to Amsterdam, for most of the more sophisticated services in trade.

A Commercial Revolution is sometimes invoked to precede the Industrial Revolution. The argument has been based on the assumption, first, that commerce alone provided the necessary surplus to invest in, as well as to consume the products of, industrialization, and secondly that the technical innovations of the merchants, the sleeping partnership, the insurance 'policy', double-entry book-keeping, and the mechanism of foreign exchange, provided the only stable foundation for entrepreneurial decision-making in the field of industrial production. The connection between overseas trade and industrial enterprise, however, is often indirect or diffuse, and too much of the returns upon commercial ventures were ploughed into land ownership and political activities. Nevertheless, foreign trade was still regarded as the quarter from which capital for investment was most likely to come, and we can at least accept the premise that much of the surpluses generated in the pre-industrial economy originated in that quarter.

In English foreign trade there was a period of unprecedented expansion from 1470 to 1550, followed by an equally long period of fluctuating growth which was interspersed with lengthy stretches of recession or stagnation, until the 1620s. Between about 1630 and 1690 was another period of great growth and change, sometimes called the Commercial Revolution, during which the structure of trade was modified by a number of new elements, especially the American and Asiatic trades.

[1] N. S. B. Gras, *Business and Capitalism* (New York, Crofts, 1939), pp. 67–81.

What happened after 1690 was not a recession, but the attainment of a high, undulating plateau, from which a renewed expansion in the middle decades of the eighteenth century naturally sprang, and upon which the 'foreign trade element' in the Industrial Revolution was founded. War, plague, foreign competition and politics often intervened to upset settled patterns of mercantile relations, and one could, by using a different set of criteria—the influence of Antwerp or Amsterdam, for instance—set rather different dates to the 'long phases' of English commercial activity. More important, however, than the changes implied in these different periods was the almost total export dependence upon wool or woollen textiles of English foreign trade before 1660. As late as 1640, 80–90 per cent of London's exports still consisted of woollen cloth, and even in 1699–1701 woollens still constituted 47 per cent of English exports (or 74 per cent if re-exports of 'tropical' goods are excluded). No less striking is the consistent element in the import trades of textiles, woollen or linen yarn, flax, hemp, dyestuffs, alum, etc., which in 1621 comprised at least 40 per cent of what was brought into London.

If we add to the imports a medley of luxury consumer goods, headed by wine and spices, we have a summary of English foreign trade before the Civil War. In practice, the pattern was not so changeless as the data imply. The components under each heading of merchandise, the regions from or to which they were brought, and the emerging capacity of English manufacturing and agriculture to make import savings or produce new surpluses for export modified the detailed structure of commerce, but did not really affect the immense commitment of foreign trade to textiles and textile materials until the 1660s. The English knew well, and feared equally, that fluctuations in demand for woollen fabrics determined the prosperity of English foreign trade and its capacity to accumulate earnings overseas. That these earnings were then spent on imported consumer goods worried not a few writers from the time of John Hales (in 1548) onwards, but it was the profits of the wool trade that supported the widespread comfort and ostentation which impressed even Italian visitors in the sixteenth century. It is worth pointing out, for example, that the English drove a lucrative business in cast-off clothing to northern France before 1600, an ironic return for the French luxuries they avidly consumed. Even after 1670, when textiles assumed a less critical role in the 'balance of trade', men were still concerned with the success of the export trade in woollens, since it remained crucial for employment when a large section of the new trades was in the form of re-exported tropical produce.

The old trades which reached a peak in the 1540s remained significant for the next hundred years. They consisted classically in the export of undressed heavy cloth, tin, fish, wool and lead, and in the import of Bilbao iron, wine and salt from the Bay of Biscay, Toulouse woad, linen, silk, madder, alum from central or southern Europe, pepper, nutmeg, mace, and cloves from the Near East via Venice. The medieval pattern had thus been set by regular sea voyages to Gascony and the Iberian peninsula on the one hand, and by short-haul shipping across the Channel to ports between the Scheldt and the Seine, followed by overland distribution into France, Germany and even the Mediterranean on the other hand. The North Sea and Baltic trades were substantially under the control of a German association of commercial cities, the Hanse, which possessed ancient privileges in English ports like Hull and Boston. Shipping in the Narrow Seas was in the hands of many peoples, of whom the English, even in their own trade, did not play a dominant role in 1500 or 1550. The Atlantic routes similarly were shared by English, French, Aragonese, Genoese and Venetians. By 1500, the last had established at Southampton an important base for importing Mediterranean goods and exporting kerseys or tin to the south-east of Europe. Piracy, however, increasingly made long sea voyages too hazardous, and between about 1520 and 1560 English overseas trade underwent a period of excessive concentration upon the two cities of London and Antwerp. English outports declined, and Continental supply routes focused more particularly upon the great Flemish entrepôt. Both the Hanse and the Venetians found trade through Antwerp too attractive to resist, and the scene was set by 1520 for a struggle between Hansards and English Merchant Adventurers for the lion's share of the English cloth trade.

Antwerp was at the heart of the principal industrial region in northern Europe. The overland route through the Alps passed along the Rhine into southern Germany, so that Flanders and Lombardy stood at the poles of the economic axis of late medieval Europe. Moreover, the Rhineland and Bavaria were also great manufacturing and mining regions, with a commercial prosperity based on the great mineral wealth of central Europe. Cologne, Nuremberg and Augsburg, dominated by opulent commercial magnates like the Fuggers, became both collection and distribution points for goods passing along the overland route as well as links in the chain of credit between north and south. Through Antwerp passed the wares and the merchants of the world known to the Europeans of the sixteenth century, including Peruvian silver, Persian carpets and Oriental silks. In the one market-place a man could sell his goods, provide himself with a return cargo, obtain or give credit and prospect future sales. The availability of so many commodities in one place enhanced the commercial position of London at the expense of so many English provincial ports, but the general influence of the entrepôt across the Channel was advantageous. The prosperity of Henrician England before 1546 owed an incalculable debt to the mercantile services of Antwerp, not least because so much of the cloths exported were finished near by in Flanders or the Rhineland.

The commercial boom before 1550 was centred upon cloth exports. The ancient dependence upon raw wool in English trade had been declining steadily since 1350 and collapsed into insignificance after 1521. The outflow of so-called 'nominal' shortcloths however, showed a consistently upward trend after 1470:

1473–82 96,000 shortcloths p.a.
1503–12 159,000   „   „
1533–42 218,000   „   „

After the great debasement of 1546 the terms of trade for English goods were so favourable that the boom reached dizzy proportions in 1549–50. Epidemics and famine in 1551, revaluation in 1551–2, and a quarrel with the Hanse in 1552–3 pricked the bubble. The prosperity before 1547, however, seems to have reflected an increase in effective demand for textiles in Europe, which may well have been founded upon a revival of population on the Continent at the same time. The downturn is less easy to explain, but on the demand side, the principal region of consumption for English broadcloths, central Europe, entered a period of economic difficulty as prosperity based on its mineral resources ebbed away.

West-country broadcloths, although easily the best of English textiles in 1520–50, were not the sum of cloth exports in the boom. Inferior textiles were used as wrappings or exported to poorer regions of the Continent. Cheaper, dressed broadcloth from East Anglia or Yorkshire was shipped by the Hanse and others to northern Europe, and the lightweight kerseys were already popular in the Mediterranean by 1535 when they formed about one-third by value of all cloth exports.

From Venice they passed into Turkey and Egypt, or were shipped direct to Spain and North Africa. Probably little more than one-half of the 'nominal shortcloths' of the customs accounts consisted of undressed broadcloths of the West between 1520 and 1550. Thus the apparently narrow orientation of English trade before 1560 was often belied by the evidence of final destination, just as the product specialization of the export trade was more varied than the Customs accounts imply.

From 1551 to 1553 the commercial climate of north-central Europe became more hostile. War or threats of war, breakdown of relations with Antwerp in 1563–4, again in 1568–72, and the sack of the city in 1576 caused immense dislocations. Antwerp's eclipse in the 1570s, the pre-occupation in war of Flemings and Hollanders, forced English merchants to widen their horizons, to look for new permanent links with Germany, the Baltic, Russia, the Levant, Africa, the Americas and the Orient. This territorial expansion of English commercial relations was dependent upon the distraction of rivals, Dutch, Spanish or Venetians, which meant that the adjustments made between 1560 and 1590 were less well-rooted than could have been hoped. However, cloth exports regained a good deal of their buoyancy in European markets in the middle years of Elizabeth's reign (1574–85). Although the period was not a commercial golden age, except for a few adventurers and a crowd of privateers, down to the catastrophe of the Cokayne project (1614–17), English merchants generally held their own in overseas trade. The rise of Amsterdam from the 1590s, upon the cold ashes of Antwerp's commercial primacy, the transfer of labour, capital and entrepreneurial skills from south to north in the Netherlands, were ominous for the self-reliance of English merchants and trading associations, although the creation of a new world entrepôt in north-west Europe still had many compensating financial advantages for the English economy. Even so, between the fall of Antwerp and the flowering of Amsterdam, the English Merchant Adventurers sought new staples for the German market, culminating in their establishment in Hamburg in 1612.

The old trades passed the shoals and rapids of the Reformation crisis and the Elizabethan war with Spain without too much permanent disruption. They had, however, contracted in relation to the total volume of trade in and out of England. The market structure for textiles in Europe was already showing noticeable signs of change by 1600, and the New Draperies in England had grown too slowly to take account of new demands. Broadcloth from the West of England was still in good demand in the Low Countries for finishing, and still found outlets in central Europe, when dressed, in much the same way as in 1550. In the import trades, concern with the balance of trade with different countries was beginning to influence policy, so that attempts to redress heavy adverse balances were reflected in the customs accounts. This was specially marked in the case of France. More wine was brought from the Rhineland or Spain than from Bordeaux, and the considerable outlay on woad from Toulouse had been reduced to nothing by 1600. The effects are not possible to calculate, but the flexibility of merchants in facing up to new circumstances was impressive.

The wider European trade which followed from the complex adjustments made in the patterns of supply and demand, but especially in the network of distribution, between 1550 and 1580, was concentrated in four zones, which had once lain at or beyond the periphery of English medieval commerce, the Baltic, the Iberian peninsula, Russia and the Levant. The Baltic trades had once been controlled by the Hanse from Lübeck, but after the Dutch pioneered the route through the Sound, English merchants, including many from Newcastle, Hull, Boston and Lynn, also set off in search of deal timber, pitch, tar, hemp (naval stores), bristles, furs and Polish rye, and for new markets in which to sell the cloth and lead from their hinterlands. The Eastland trade was never easy. Conflict with the Hanse in the sixteenth century and the growing threat of the Dutch as carriers of Baltic bulk cargoes caused serious tension and affected profits. The merchants trading to the Baltic joined forces to form a trading company in 1579 for their protection, and in the same year persuaded Elbing in East Prussia to offer them privileges in defiance of the Hanse. Thereafter they possessed a secure if small clearing-house in the Baltic for the bilateral trades that they handled. These bilateral trades grew in importance with the seventeenth century as demand for Baltic timber, naval stores and eventually for Swedish or Danzig pig and bar iron increased in England.

The Russian trade was always much smaller and was kept distinct from the Baltic trade until St Petersburg was built in the eighteenth century, although many of the products were the same. English interest in Russia began with the conviction that a north-east passage to the Far East was a practical alternative to the Portuguese route round the Cape. A failed expedition in 1553 had incidentally opened a route into the Tsar's dominions through Archangel on the White Sea. The trade which followed, especially furs and forest products, was valuable, but it suffered the disadvantage of being too much one-way, because the Russians needed comparatively little of English goods. Trade with Muscovy also suffered from political upheaval, from Dutch competition, and from the more convenient and generally rather cheaper supplies of Russia's basic commodities from Scandinavia, and later from North America. The Russia Company of 1555 was never the success it promised to be, and the great expansion in Anglo-Russian commerce did not occur until about 1720, with a notable increase in demand for Ural iron, when the company was a faint memory.

In southern Europe, English interest in the Levantine trade notably increased in the 1570s. English cloth had long been known in the Venetian Empire and Turkey before 1560, but entirely in the hands of the Venetians. When Venice went to war with the Turks in 1570 the English took the opportunity of sending their own ships, delivering cloth and lading cotton, wine, currants, figs and spices, in the Ionian islands, Crete and the Levant coast. Here, too, local politics served the strangers' interests. The Duke of Tuscany attracted English and Dutch merchants to Leghorn, which he hoped to develop into a great port in competition with Venice and Genoa. The English took little interest in, or had little success with, the Mediterranean carrying trade, but the bilateral trade between England and the eastern Mediterranean was very valuable. The Levant Company of 1581, set up by a powerful group of merchants to regulate their activities beyond the Adriatic Sea, was one of the most successful of English commercial associations in the earlier seventeenth century. The eastern Mediterranean, despite the expansion of Islam, and the increasing use of the Cape route, remained one of the more important centres of world trade, and cities at the head of Asiatic caravan routes, like Aleppo, still attracted European merchants until well into the eighteenth century. The chief drawback was the growing depredations of Barbary corsairs upon all shipping from the Elbe to the Holy Land.

Further west, the principal growth area of English commerce was the Iberian peninsula. Spain had always been important as a source of wine and iron, and as a market for fish. But by 1640 it had become one of the largest and most valuable markets for a great variety of English and Dutch products. The Dutch were dominant by the seventeenth century. They held the lion's share of the great trades in fish and grain into Spain. Their growing demands for merino wool, iron and non-ferrous ores, and the development of Amsterdam as the northern staple for

American and Oriental produce, reinforced the competitive edge of Dutch businessmen in the seventeenth century. Nevertheless, the English did remarkably well. The Newfoundland cod fishery has been described as 'the lever by which [England] wrested her share of the riches of the New World from Spain'.[1] The Dutch did not monopolize the trade in salt-fish to the Catholic south in the seventeenth century. The English, too, captured a good share of the market for lightweight cloths, first with kerseys, and after 1600, increasingly with bays, says, calimancoes and perpetuanas. The two northern peoples between them indirectly turned the two great peninsulas of Iberia and Italy into backward, agricultural economies, by dominating their markets for manufactured goods, including paper and glass which Mediterranean craftsmen had once taught to the rest of Europe. By 1720 there were in many parts of the Peninsula enclaves of British commercial capital and enterprise, organizing such major commodity trades as wine and iron, though the British penetration of Spain, but not of Portugal, did not necessarily make such spectacular headway under Bourbon domination between 1713 and the Peninsular War. Still, Spanish trade, directly to Iberia and indirectly by means of *Asiento* treaties with Spanish America, was among the most valuable to the British in the eighteenth century.

The oceanic trades were of little importance before 1630. After the Civil War, however, trade with Asia and America grew dramatically, until by 1700 it provided one-third of English imports, while the re-export of goods from remote waters in turn supplied a third (by value) of the export trade. Further expansion in the eighteenth merely consolidated the achievement of the late seventeenth century. The pivot of this commercial revolution was European (and domestic) demand for tropical and subtropical produce, tobacco, sugar, spices, indigo, logwood, rice, coffee, chocolate, mahogany and cotton, and to a less extent for commonplace or precious manufactures, calicoes, porcelain, metalware, silks, especially from India and China. There were, of course, other elements in the ocean trades between 1650 and 1750: African gold and slaves; South American silver and gold and hides; provisions and dry goods for plantation colonists in Brazil, the Caribbean and the southern colonies of North America; re-exported calicoes or beads into West Africa. Even after the Dutch had been beaten for mastery of the Atlantic in the late seventeenth century, the English (and after 1707 also the Scots) were faced with problems of competition

[1] H. A. Innis, *The Cod Fisheries* (Yale University Press, 1940), p. 53.

from the British settlers in northern North America, who took to the sea as traders and carriers in increasing numbers after 1670, dominating trade with the Atlantic Wine islands, pushing into the Mediterranean and even poaching 'English' trade in the Caribbean and Brazil. The oceanic trades created political and economic problems which drew European merchants deeper into politics at home and into the exercise of power in distant quarters of the globe. They became, as everyone knows, the stage of international power-politics between 1651 and 1783 which added a new dimension to European dynastic quarrels.

A few landmarks in the conversion of England's deep-water interests from the exploration and privateering of Elizabethan times to the settled commercial relations of the mid-eighteenth century can be noted. First was the opening in the 1580s of what became the very lucrative New-foundland cod fishery, which by 1610 had trained so many English (and Dutch) seamen in difficult North Atlantic waters. Next, and to some extent arising from the first, was the build-up of trade with Madeira, the Azores and the Canaries, an offshoot of the expanding early seven-teenth-century trade with Iberia. The colonization of Virginia after 1607 resulted remarkably soon in a great increase in American tobacco production. By 1615 England already imported 58,000 lb. and by the 1630s overproduction was already so threatening that the unit-price of tobacco collapsed. It fell from about 3*d.* per pipeful before 1610 to less than one shilling per lb. in 1626 and as low as 1*d.*–2*d.* per lb. in the early 1630s. In 1652, all domestic tobacco production—chiefly in Gloucester-shire—was legally prohibited to leave the way clear for the merchants of London and Bristol. Fourthly, the one benefit of the Cokayne project, in 1615–17, was a great increase in investment in English-Asian trades by the dispossessed Merchant Adventurers. The immediate upshot was a tense conflict with the Dutch in Ceylon and the East Indies that resulted in the massacre, in 1623, of the English merchant community on the island of Ambon. By the 1630s, however, the East India Company was beginning to find a footing in mainland India, and it became patently clear that the Atlantic and Indian Ocean trades would henceforward follow different courses. England's permanent interest in the Caribbean was increased in the 1650s when Cromwell's army conquered the island of Jamaica. The acquisition of most of the smaller sugar islands in the region provided the basis for the rapid expansion of English interests in cane-sugar production, which, with tobacco, formed the backbone of the commercial revolution after 1660.

By 1700 English imports of tobacco had risen to 38,000,000 lb.; they doubled again before 1750. Two-thirds of the imports through English ports were re-exported to the Continent, especially to Germany and Holland, where substantial processing trades had developed when the Dutch carried a larger share of the commodity direct from the Americas. The commitment of Virginia and Maryland to the growth of tobacco was reinforced by its decline elsewhere, in the Caribbean islands and Brazil, where a crisis in the 1630s had seen a shift from tobacco to sugar or other more tropical crops. It may not be quite true to describe tobacco in terms of 'high mass consumption' by 1750 but it was the commodity which came nearest to that description in the pre-industrial world. Even the poor who could not afford a pipeful at 1*d*. per lb. were persuaded to seek alternative native materials which they called 'tobacco'. Sugar, which in the sixteenth century had come in as one of the spices from the East, was imported via Portugal from Brazil until the 1640s when English settlers in Barbados turned their land to sugar production in order to profit from a great rise in prices of the Brazilian product. Thereafter, the history of sugar production is one of steady expansion in and around the tropical Caribbean, and as a commodity in world trade sugar surpassed even tobacco. Before 1670, the British had captured the sugar market in northern Europe from the Portuguese, and thirty years later, when sugar imports into London had almost doubled in value to £526,000 (which was over three times the value of tobacco imports), half was re-exported to the Continent. In spite of French competition in the eighteenth century, which had turned Bordeaux into a 'colonial' port as significant as Bristol by 1740, the British sugar trade continued to grow satisfactorily, to reach £1,300,000 in 1752-4.

Of the great range of other colonial goods, most of those which acted as substitutes for native products, like dyestuffs, cotton, mahogany or coffee, grew in a similar way to tobacco and sugar, but obviously much less spectacularly. To some extent product-substitution gives a false impression of slow growth, as with dyestuffs, where native production, together with a preference for tropical dyes like indigo or logwood, reduced the demand for imported woad or madder before 1700. American and Asistic dyestuff imports into London grew fourfold between the 1660s and 1699-1701.

As late as 1700, the list of imported commodities was still headed by textiles and wine. Textile imports from Europe and the Levant apparently doubled in value between 1621 and 1700, but the really significant development occured in the trade with India, whence immense quantities of calicoes were imported by the East India Company in the late seventeenth and early eighteenth centuries. Tropical textiles passing through London in the 1660s were valued at £211,000 per annum and in 1700 at £474,000. By 1700, two-thirds of the East India Company's imports consisted of calicoes, which were lightweight, cotton-based textiles produced by cheap labour in the territory of Gujerat near Bombay. European demand was insatiable between 1670 and 1740, but the company was bitterly unpopular both at home and in Holland for undercutting home producers. The New Draperies suffered badly; in 1701 and 1720, therefore, imports were prohibited for a time, but until the era of machine-wrought cottons, calicoes remained indispensable for cheap, hygienic wearing apparel. The calico trade was frowned upon officially in the 1690s for quite a different reason. The goods had chiefly to be paid for in silver because the Indians required so few European exports, until the technological superiority of Europe had been decisively demonstrated by the mid-eighteenth century. For a company which had been intended to tap the wealth of the Orient, prosaic involvement with cheap textiles in itself was a matter of contempt in certain mercantile circles of the Restoration period. The calico trade dated back to the beginnings of the company's establishment at Surat on the western coast of the sub-continent and its importance explains much of the heavy concentration around the old Portuguese 'factory' at Bombay (ceded to England in 1662) until well into the eighteenth century.

English demand for all these new commodities grew at least as fast as the volume of trade. There is no English equivalent of the 'long phase' of commercial stagnation and decay which reputedly afflicted Continental Europe in the century after 1650, for, despite difficulties, the atmosphere in Britain remained fairly buoyant and expansive. This was due not a little to the success of merchants, farmers and manufacturers in holding or extending markets for their goods in spite of a decline in unit-prices. The assumption must be, first, that costs were reduced, at least commensurate with prices, by increments of productivity, and secondly that the demand, even the European-wide demand for products, despite the depression, was more than merely maintained after 1660.

English (and British) performance in Europe cannot, however, be taken as representative of the health of the Continental economy, for the enormous growth of London's re-export trade really reflected a shift of the entrepôt from Amsterdam to London, and the great expansion of the colonial trades supplemented and was substituted for older trades. Also, the English had expropriated many rival colonial spheres of influence by the early eighteenth century.

The re-export trade is especially complex. It was an object of particular interest to London merchants in the seventeenth century because the clearing house system upon which is depended reflected the superiority of the Dutch carrying-trade. Its growth was stimulated in England by the expansion of colonial production, and by the legal restrictions placed upon Dutch interference in the trade of the dependencies after 1651. But the re-export trade had other concrete advantages. First, the import of raw commodities into the mother country often created employment in processing and packing trades before the goods were sent out again. Secondly, because of the multilateral complexities of many overseas trades, the entrepôt in itself often created yet more trade. The slave trade is a good example of such interlocking interests. It is customary to describe it as a triangular trade, between England and West Africa, and between West Africa and the Americas, and then between America and the mother country, but this is generally too simple. Thus the West African arm of the trade was more sophisticated and variable than the notion of exchanging trumpery for men implies. By the eighteenth century, European slave-traders needed to know the taste—for ornaments, for firearms or for Indian calicoes—of particular West African potentates in order to be able to purchase slaves. Moreover, the glass beads employed came from Venice, the textiles from the East India Company and the metal goods at times from Germany, so that Bristol or Bordeaux merchants needed wide contacts before they began to trade. However specialized slave-carrying itself had become before 1750, merchants were often compelled to accept mahogany or some other African commodity instead of slaves on the Middle Passage, and even on the third arm of the trade vessels often came home in ballast rather than laden with tobacco or sugar. In retrospect, the slave trade seems to have been morticed into the framework of the Atlantic economy with less precision and less elegance than the model suggests. The trade was both more opportunist, at least before 1750, and more extensively ramified across four Continents than could be contained in a simple triangle.

The carrying-trade, and with it the entrepôt for goods which entered multilateral trade, was never so completely under the dominance of London, or even of the English, between 1680 and 1780 as had been true of the position of Amsterdam or even of Antwerp in the earlier period. The nationalism of France and Prussia, the revival at least in part of Spain and certain Italian cities and states in the eighteenth century, and the tenacity of Amsterdam in clinging to the vestiges of its commercial, as well as to its financial, glory after the tribulations of war from 1670 to 1713, inhibited the unrestrained hegemony of London. It is of course true that the City both channelled into British public stocks a good deal of Dutch surplus investment and also received the advantages of skills and experience transplanted by the migration of merchants from Amsterdam in the eighteenth century. Nevertheless, it was not unreasonable for the Americans to believe as late as the 1770s that the London entrepôt for their tobacco was not indispensable and that they could do as well or better for themselves by diverting their primary product exports to the Netherlands where much of their consumption was concentrated.

The Americans, indeed, by exploiting loopholes in the Navigation System or by infringing the laws passed by successive Parliaments after 1651, in turn exemplified other weaknesses in the dominance of the mother country. Northern colonial merchants, denied fruitful bilateral trade in the products of their hinterlands by British law, turned to smuggling and even more seriously to the development of a rival network of Atlantic carrying trades, especially via the Wine Islands to the Mediterranean. Coupled with growing French commercial self-confidence in the mid-eighteenth century and the far from moribund efforts of the Dutch in the great Oceanic trades, colonial successes gave British merchants at home valid reasons for believing that their hold on world trade routes was insecure and incomplete. The vigour of attempts by colonists in the British West Indies to pursue illicit trades with Spanish America against a regulatory treaty between the two mother countries signed at the Utrecht Peace Conference in 1713 actually led to war in 1739 and for a time broke up the precarious but fruitful commercial exchanges which Walpole had been fostering with Spain. The problem, stated briefly, was that British success by 1740 was already provoking as much jealousy, if rather less legislative action, among would-be commercial and political competitors as the Dutch had brought down upon their heads in 1650–80. The British, however, were not dislodged

Table II(a). *English Foreign Trade 1699–1752 (£'000)*

	IMPORTS				EXPORTS AND RE-EXPORTS		
	1699–1701	1722–4	1752–4		1699–1701	1722–4	1752–4
					Exports		
Linens	903	1036	1185	Wool	3045	2986	3930
Calicoes	367	437	401	Linen	—	25	211
Silks, etc.	208	208	112	Silk	80	78	160
Metals	72	39	7	Cottons	20	18	83
Thread	79	40	11	Metals	114	181	587
Miscell.	215	123	107	Hats	45	125	248
				Miscell.	279	371	1131
Mnfs.	1844	1883	1823	Mnfs.	3583	3784	6350
Wine	536	573	378	Grain	147	592	899
Spirits	10	23	88	Fish	190	138	145
Sugar	630	928	1302	Hops	9	72	161
Tobacco	249	263	560	Miscell.	102	94	194
Fruit	174	135	117				
Pepper	103	17	31	Foods	488	886	1418
Drugs	53	60	179				
Tea	8	116	334	Lead	128	113	149
Coffee	27	127	53	Tin	97	67	129
Rice	5	52	167	Coal	35	98	177
Miscell.	174	156	191	Miscell.	102	94	194
Foods	1969	2450	3400	Raw mat.	362	372	649
					Re-exports		
Silk, raw				Calicoes	340	484	499
& thrown	346	693	671	Silks	150	354	281
Flax, hemp	194	182	397	Linens	182	232	331
Wool	200	114	74	Tobacco	421	387	953
Cotton	44	49	104	Sugar	287	211	110
Yarns	232	221	250	Pepper	93	44	104
Dyes	226	318	386	Tea	2	267	217
Iron, steel	182	212	293	Coffee	2	151	84
Timber	138	157	237	Rice	4	63	206
Oil	141	122	130				
Tallow	85	15	4	Drugs	48	30	102
Skins, hides	57	66	72	Dyes	85	83	112
Miscell.	191	276	362	Raw silk	63	39	70
				Miscell.	309	369	423
Raw mat.	2036	2425	2980				
				Re-exports	1986	2714	3492
				Exports	4433	5042	8417
Totals	5849	6758	8203	Total	6419	7756	11909

Table II(b). *Direction of English Foreign Trade 1699–1701 and 1752–4 (£'000)*

IMPORTS

	1699–1701				1752–4			
	Mnfs.	Foods	Raw Materials	Total	Mnfs.	Foods	Raw Materials	Total
N.W. Europe	1015	108	295	1418	745	117	310	1172
N. Europe	59	9	515	583	170	11	862	1043
S. Europe	111	747	697	1555	38	531	1028	1597
British Islands	107	46	277	430	360	23	238	621
America	—	925	182	1107	—	2250	434	2684
East Indies	552	134	70	756	510	468	108	1086

EXPORTS & RE-EXPORTS

	1699–1701				1752–4			
	Mnfs.	Foods	Raw Materials	Total	Mnfs.	Foods	Raw Materials	Total
N.W. Europe	1814	816	392	3022	2013	1709	349	4073
N. Europe	205	97	33	335	199	82	81	362
S. Europe	1338	249	111	1708	2395	564	205	3164
British Islands	131	167	69	367	243	705	280	1228
America	727	89	35	851	2003	249	82	2334
East Indies	114	11	11	136	640	44	64	748

SOURCE: R. Davis, 'English Foreign Trade 1700–1774', *Economic History Review*, 2nd series, XV, 1962.

from the position which they had gained by 1720, as the continuing high level of re-exports in the trade statistics shows. Re-exports, as a rough measure of multilateral trade from Britain and as a guide to the effectiveness of the entrepôt business of the mother country, rose from about 21 per cent of total exports in the 1660s, to 31 per cent in 1699–1701 and 37 per cent by 1774. Moreover, by 1750–70 most of the processing and financial services necessary to support a great entrepôt could be, and were generally, supplied in England and not from Holland as in the seventeenth century.

THE ORGANIZATION OF TRADE

Between 1500 and 1750 most of English foreign trade was conducted by merchants acting on their own account, singly or in small partnerships, unprotected by any form of limited liability. Merchants resorted together in regular trade in *ad hoc* associations for a particular voyage, but they remained accountable as individuals to their creditors. Private firms existed and sometimes even passed from one generation to the next, but because the law did not recognize sleeping partnerships, mercantile enterprise was typified by the individual. The wealth and capital of merchants obviously varied a good deal. Large accumulations of capital and extensive dealings in commodities, bullion or credit were possible in every generation down to 1750, and a long list of opulent merchants from Kytson and Carre, in the early sixteenth century onwards, could be drawn up to illustrate the point. Cities like London and Bristol, and later Hull and Liverpool, were dominated by oligopolies of this kind, although each of the leading ports provided considerable scope for the small man in business to try his fortune in foreign dealings. Many merchants resembled William Stout of Lancaster or Samuel Dawson of Bawtrey, who combined occasional forays into the Atlantic or the North Sea with a general wholesale business at home. Fitting out a ship for Norway, Ireland or Spain, or taking cargo space in the vessel of another, as often returned a loss as a profit, but it seems to have been of widespread occurrence among merchants with access to the sea. Such men, and others with a more permanent footing in overseas trade, often acted as interlopers in the commerce of merchants or merchant groups with legal privileges, for with so much casual or underhand dealing, the problem of unauthorized commerce trenching deeply into the monopolies of trading companies was always serious. There was always a degree of tension between the advocates of a regulated system

132

of foreign trade, closed to all but the privileged, and the considerable body of excluded provincial and metropolitan merchants, constantly pressing for freedom of action—a tension which waxed and waned with the vagaries of government policy.

A good proportion of all trade carried in English ships was relatively unspecialized. Before 1650 many merchants not only collected and stored the commodities involved, but owned or found for themselves the necessary shipping, discounted the risks, arranged for payment in cash, credit or in kind, and even managed the distribution of the merchandise at the other end of the line. Ship's masters were often merchants in their own right. Foreign exchange dealings had been greatly simplified by the development of the bill of exchange managed by Italian financiers, or later at Antwerp and Amsterdam, but it was the Dutch in the seventeenth century who perfected the complex division of labour in overseas commerce, in which specialists, acting on commission, began to provide the intermediate services between commodity merchant, shipper and receiving merchant. New professions of ship's husband, ship-broker, insurance underwriter, exchange-broker, appeared in Amsterdam before 1650 and in London before 1750 to smooth the course of the exporter. They formed part of a new commercial class of financiers, accountants, stockbrokers, experts in commercial law, which had existed only in an embryonic form in Venice or Antwerp. All would probably have been described as merchants in 1700, and many augmented their fees with the profits of direct trading so that their specialization was not as clear-cut as in the nineteenth century. The change between 1500–50 and 1700–50, however, was of fundamental importance. It was comparable and closely related to the growth of the re-export trade in England. The centre of activity was London, but provincial merchants could, and did, avail themselves of these new facilities, especially of insurance and foreign exchange, just as Londoners had used Amsterdam before their own city could rival the Dutch for merchants' services.

So far we have stressed the individual, and fragmented, nature of mercantile organization in pre-industrial England. But all the older textbooks make much of the great spate of company promotions between 1555 and 1670, usually in the context of a far-seeing policy of development in a poor but ambitious country. These great companies, organized to serve a particular region of trade, offered privileges to members and a kind of group solidarity in dealing with the Crown and with foreign governments or rival interests. The basic idea behind them, in an era of uncertain commercial law, piracy and seemingly endless European wars, was medieval and closely resembled the trade-gild in many characteristics, but it appealed especially to Elizabethan governments because company organization enabled them to control their subjects abroad. The grant of privileges, even of monopolies, to merchants was not confined to overseas trade, but it attracted opulent and powerful merchants, especially those of London, in sufficient numbers to turn the larger companies into important political organs in the state. The role, assigned to the trading companies by historians, of promoting an enormous expansion of English foreign trade is now seen as the result of false emphasis. Their direct effect upon commerce at best was neutral. The Merchant Adventurers possessed a monopoly upon the export of English undressed cloth, but in the great age of that trade before 1550 they played a small part in the large growth of the export trade beside foreign merchants, Italians, Flemings, Germans and even the Hansards, who turned their attention increasingly to the London-Antwerp trade after 1520. English merchants probably kept more than half of the cloth trade in the 1540s, but that serves to show the limitations of a theoretical monopoly in a competitive commercial environment. Much the same is true, with two exceptions, of all the other companies founded after 1555, although a problem of increasing importance for 'company merchants' everywhere was 'interloping', that is, unauthorized trade by Englishmen who were not members of the privileged company in question. The tension between 'insiders' and 'outsiders' had always been important, but at certain times, in the 1490s, 1610s, 1650s and after 1680, it became acute. The consequences were unpredictable, but often resulted in a more constructive expansion of opportunities than had been common in years of privileged trading, although equally the situation sometimes was too chaotic to sustain growth.

Trading companies are conventionally divided into two kinds, 'regulated' and 'joint-stock'. The regulated companies included the Merchant Adventurers and the Merchant Staplers, as well as a few of the new creations like the Eastland Company of 1579. Such companies were loose associations of merchants trading on their own account, who enjoyed the tangible benefits of privileges—often commercial or regional monopolies—defined by charter, and less direct advantages arising out of group protection and group negotiation. Joint-stock companies consisted of merchants with similar prescriptive privileges, who also chose to trade with a joint-stock, or pool of capital, each partner taking shares of the stock, earning a dividend upon the profits or discounting a share of the losses. In an era of inadequate maritime insurance such co-operation conferred many benefits, especially in difficult or dangerous regions of trade, but joint-stock enterprise did not offer a species of limited liability and participants could be called upon in law for more than their share capital in the event of foreclosure. Moreover, the degree of centralized management necessary in joint-stock trade proved irksome, and the limitations naturally imposed upon the number of active merchants who could participate in joint-stock companies caused a good deal of opposition. The Russia Company of 1555 and the Levant Company of 1581 started out as joint-stock operations but changed into regulated companies as the uncertainties and dangers of pioneering in new regions diminished into routine. The East India Company remained a joint-stock enterprise throughout its long career, as did the Hudson's Bay Company of 1670. Both had special problems of great distance, relatively valuable commodities and political difficulties with which to contend. The Bay Company was unchallenged at home, because of the hostile climate, and no less hostile French rivalry, in northern Canada. The East India Company, however, was always under threat from interloping and in 1698 it suffered a major political reversal at home. An attempt between 1698 and 1709 to allow in the large numbers of would-be traders to the Orient and to break the caucus of the Company by refounding it as a regulated company proved a disastrous failure because the Oriental trades were too risky, too complex and too expensive for individual merchants.

Although the East India Company retrieved its position after 1709, the next decade saw the virtual ending of joint-stock flotations. As a result of the tragi-comedy of the South Sea Bubble, the Act of 1720, to deal with the problems which arose from the mania, prohibited new commercial joint-stock enterprises as the best solution to the threat of fraudulent promotions. The South Sea Company, we should note, began as a normal commercial undertaking with privileges for trade in the still largely unknown southern oceans. As such, it might have resembled the small but profitable Hudson's Bay Company had it not been for the financial ambitions of its promoters. These ambitions reflected a change of emphasis towards what we may call finance capitalism in the eighteenth century. This was part and parcel of developing government finance, the extension of blind investment [1] and sleeping partnerships, increased concentration upon paper rather than real transactions, and of development of the money and capital markets in London between 1690 and 1750. To service the already large national debt by skilful financial manipulation had become an end in itself by 1711.

The increasing complexity of commercial and financial life after the Restoration added point to the struggle to free trade from regulation by the companies. Some of the smaller companies had already declined into impotence by 1680, partly through failure to compete with the Dutch in their sphere of influence, and partly because interlopers, especially from provincial ports, proved very efficient in capturing their trade. A few like the Levant Company decayed more slowly in the century after 1680. The Merchant Adventurers experienced many vicissitudes. As early as 1497 their privileges had been reduced by government, but the seesaw of official favour and opposition really began in 1614 with the Cokayne project. The Adventurers' rights were again suspended in 1621–34, and, after a period of disfavour under the Interregnum, were finally abolished in 1689. The Eastland Company was forced to open its trade in 1673, the Russia Company in 1698. Even new companies, like the Royal African Company of 1669, whose monopoly of the African slave-trade was abolished, also in 1698, suffered in the 'free trade' movement of the 1690s. This process of liberalization was aided greatly by the recovery of the provincial ports after 1640, since in practice the companies were heavily influenced by London and metropolitan merchants, but it benefited also from the prohibition of 'personal monopolies' in 1640. Both Elizabeth and the early Stuarts felt nothing amiss in granting extensive rights to individuals in the field of foreign trade as in the domestic economy, which, like the Earl of Cumberland's monopoly in the cloth trade or the notorious Courteen franchise in the East India trade in the 1630s, often caused chaos in established patterns of commerce.

The extraordinary concentration of English foreign trade in London by 1540 was due chiefly to the influence of Antwerp and the Rhenish trade routes upon England. London, as the cynosure of wealth and fashion, the seat of government and the largest agglomeration of consumers in the kingdom, continued to control an overwhelming share of

[1] Blind investment refers to the placing of money in an enterprise by individuals not directly involved in its management, and often through the service of an intermediary, attorney or stock-broker.

overseas trade until the Civil War. The outports which had first benefited from the revival of trade in the 1470s then entered a period of
decadence, from which they only began to emerge in the reign of Elizabeth. A century later, the tide of their revival was flowing strongly, and
by 1700 old ports like Bristol, Southampton and Hull were bustling
with great activity and new confidence, while new ports such as Liverpool and Whitehaven had already begun to develop rapidly in the Irish
and American trades. Some medieval ports like Chester, Boston or
Grimsby never regained their old importance because of siltage or
entrepreneurial backwardness—Grimsby, indeed, like so many small
places, could claim to be a seaport only because one family there, the
Claytons, still traded abroad from time to time. Nevertheless, what is
striking about a map of eighteenth-century seaports is its medieval
appearance. Among ports of at least second rank were York, Yarmouth,
Falmouth, Lancaster, Sittingbourne, Faversham, Maldon, Berwick,
Whitby, Topsham and Dartmouth. The expansion of the coasting trade
put new life into many a village wharf or roadstead in the seventeenth
and eighteenth centuries. Because seaborne traffic was relatively
unspecialized, foreign trade often benefited from this plethora of
landing places in its turn. A port like Newcastle, depending heavily
upon the coal trade, surpassed its medieval position early in the seventeenth century. Hull, long a major entrepôt for the north Midlands and
Yorkshire, shook itself free of the Hanse in the sixteenth century and
rapidly revived, by exploiting the coasting trade, by carrying Yorkshire
cloth into northern Europe and by opening up new interests in the
Baltic, which, two centuries later, still formed the backbone of Hull's
commercial concerns in Europe. The regeneration of the moribund
fishing industry after 1580 had the same effect upon ports which
specialized in deep-sea trawling around the coast.

   The history of many outports in other words was unique, but there
are three general points which applied to several different communities.
First, the increased contact with Ireland, particularly the exchange of
coal and manufactures for primary produce, in the seventeenth century,
lay at the foundation of prosperity for many Western ports from Whitehaven to Bridgwater. The vagaries of the Irish trade were supplemented by the even more lucrative, if more dangerous, trades to the
New World. Small ports as well as Bristol and Liverpool were interested
in exporting provisions and dry goods to British America and in
importing sugar, molasses, dyestuffs, or tobacco. Ironically, however,

competition in foodstuffs to the southern plantations or the West Indies was particularly keen from Ireland and Scotland, and from the northern colonies, so that the trade was often difficult, even unprofitable. In the east, direct trade to the Baltic, in commodities where the comparative advantage was not with London, played a similar role, but the real motor of growth in North Sea ports seems to have been the grain trade of the eighteenth century. Ports like Berwick, Lynn, Yarmouth, Ipswich, Mistley and Faversham grew as seaports first by exporting corn to London. The increasing agricultural surpluses after 1715 allowed more and more of England's wheat (and barley) to be exported abroad. Kent, East Anglia, Northumberland and Yorkshire regularly produced the greatest surpluses, so the east coast ports from Berwick to Dover handled the bulk (but not all) of the grain exports out of England. They lost ground only after the 1770s when Britain became a net importer of grain, since imports naturally went directly to the areas of greatest consumption.

The third element in the great expansion of the provincial ports was the congestion of London as a centre of commodity trade in the late seventeenth century. The open Thames had offered one of the largest and safest harbours along the east coast, and by 1650 wharves and landing-places lined both banks from Lambeth to Greenwich. For the relatively small vessels employed in most seventeenth-century trades, the depth and breadth of the river up to London Bridge were sufficient to support very dense traffic. Larger vessels, even those bearing valuable tropical or Mediterranean cargoes, had greater difficulties and were increasingly forced to unload into lighters in mid-stream, or go elsewhere. No dock was built on the Thames before 1660 (the Howland dock), and even in the century after the Restoration, new port installations were less extensive and less successful than in rival harbours like Liverpool, Hull or Bristol. By 1760, London's dominance as a centre of commodity trade had been eroded. To some extent it had been replaced by the growth of financial and intermediary functions in imitation of Amsterdam, but the discontent of so many London-based merchants, both before and after the port's political climacteric of 1763, indicates that the substitution was not universally approved. Between 1702 and 1763 the tonnage of ships owned in London did not increase, while that of the outports together almost doubled. In 1701, London possessed 45 per cent of English shipping; in 1763, 28 per cent. As for clearances of ships outward bound, London handled less (in tonnage) than the three

chief Western ports together in 1750. The upshot was a massive investment in dock building from the mid-eighteenth century, which did
much to restore the place of London in the vanguard of British ports.

INTERNAL TRADE

The development of inland trade between 1500 and 1750, although
much less spectacular than foreign commerce, was no less far-reaching.
It has been less well researched, but its component elements are not
difficult to identify. First, the growth of London into what was often
thought to be 'a head too great for the body' not only imposed
demands upon an ever-widening section of the country, but, by setting
standards among the rich and well-to-do, the metropolis in turn stimulated changes in local patterns of demand and supply. Secondly, the
accumulation of imported merchandise, tobacco, sugar, calicoes, silks,
linen, spices, eventually brought about the establishment of retail outlets throughout the provinces. The 'retailing revolution' is rightly
located in time no earlier than about 1860, but the mercer's shop,
dealing almost exclusively in ready-made goods, had made its appearance
in country towns and in some villages at least two centuries before.
These shops acted as filters through which imported and domestic
goods percolated to the 'middling sort' of provincial households. On the
other hand, they supplemented older forms of marketing, the travelling
chapman's business and fairs and markets, which together seem to have
expanded notably in the century before the Restoration. The third
element was improvement and extension of the transport system. The
changes were seldom outstanding, but modifications in river and road
transport and in the coasting trade stretched the medieval framework
of communications. The effect upon commerce, at least after 1600, was
quantitative rather than innovatory. What was noteworthy about transport in 1750 by comparison with 1500 was its enlarged volume, not its
type. Fourthly, the increasing specialization of industrial and agricultural production before 1750 in itself necessarily involved new
arrangements for the exchange of goods. The internal movement of
wool, yarn, hides, iron, lead and tin, always considerable, was reorganized in the hands of putting-out merchants, whose agents were employed
in gathering raw materials and distributing the finished products. The
vertical or lateral integration of many pre-industrial enterprises thus
often increased the volume and range of trade as networks of communication were constructed and strengthened by use. At the same time,

urban patterns of consumption began to invade the countryside, when bakers, common brewers, butchers, retail ironmongers, made their appearance as suppliers to rural society. A chain of supply between farmer or miner and retail customer had been fully developed in many products by the early eighteenth century.

A major component in all these developments was the adaptation to internal commerce of negotiable instruments of credit devised for use in overseas dealings. Sales credits, or the use by merchants or consumers of loan capital, were long-standing amenities of commercial life in 1500, but it is a matter of some doubt how large the element of pure subsistence remained in the peasant economy even of Elizabethan England. The use of money and credit had certainly penetrated deeply into the activities of those with surpluses to sell. Cash, or credit sales, especially at a distance, had obvious disadvantages which were not dispelled until the inland bill of exchange was introduced. Flexible, negotiable bills suited well the middleman who managed the protracted chains of supply in English domestic trade after the Restoration. They could be used, by post-dating, either to give or take credit upon a deal, and by assignment, to make payment without an exchange of cash in multiple transactions. Bills thus often moved around the country with a velocity greater than that of individual merchants participating in trade. They underpinned much of the financial structure of industrialization in the eighteenth century, but their importance ranged much wider. Farmers, for example, were constrained to take bills, and occasionally to assign them against rent, for the products they sold upon contract at least by the last quarter of the seventeenth century. Fifty years later it was commonplace to conduct almost all long-range business by bills drawn upon bankers or strange merchants. Their use did much to confirm the power of merchant middlemen or 'industrial' entrepreneurs in the trade of the kingdom.

London's influence on the course of commercial expansion in Britain, from before the time of John Leland to the point where its uniqueness was eclipsed by the growth of new urban centres, has been extensively discussed by Fisher and Wrigley. As its population grew, as it became more and more a cynosure of fashion and luxury, so the hinterland required to feed, clothe and service this population expanded. The comparatively easy navigation of the Thames at least up to Henley, the medieval system of roads which focused upon the capital, and the richness and fertility of the Home Counties, especially Kent and the Lea

Valley, formed the basis for London's food and forage supplies, perhaps until 1600. Thereafter growing regional specialization resulted in the complex web of provisioning; droves of cattle and sheep from Gloucestershire and Northamptonshire by 1630, from Norfolk, Lincolnshire and Yorkshire by 1650, indirectly from Wales and Scotland by 1660; butter and cheese from Suffolk, Banbury, Gloucester, the Fenlands, Cornwall and Cheshire; malt from Kent and Norfolk; bread grain from the Thames valley and Kent, East Anglia, Yorkshire and Northumberland. Coal came from Newcastle; building stone from Oxford; firewood and timber from wherever it could still be found in Caroline England, but chiefly from the Weald and Waltham Forest; even beer was brought from the Trent. Raw materials and manufactures from all parts of the country were sucked into the metropolis by packhorse, waggon, barge or coaster. London seemed dangerously parasitic to many men throughout the period. It was blamed for the decay of 'hospitality', for the spending of income earned in the provinces, for encouraging luxury, idleness and excessive imports. Yet John Houghton in 1681 saw the positive side to London's inexorable growth: 'The bigness and great consumption of London doth not only encourage the breeders of provisions and higglers thirty miles off, but even to four score miles. Wherefore I think it will necessarily follow that if London should consume as much again country for eighty miles around would have greater employment, or else those that are further off would have some of it.' Thus had James I's rueful comment, 'Soon London will be all England', come to pass in the seventeenth century.

London's needs stimulated wide-ranging attempts to improve both river navigation and the road system. In the plan of communications, however, other influences played an increasingly important role. The need to improve lateral communications, linking river systems or trunk roads fanning out from the metropolis, was the subject of repeated proposals from the 1650s. Projects like a canal joining Thames and Severn or an elaborate scheme to connect East Anglia with Yorkshire were not put into effect, but they illustrate the renewed concern with the economy of the provinces in the seventeenth century. At the same time local interests, in Exeter, Norwich or Leeds, for example, also were very active in promoting improvements as in the late eighteenth century. The long battle between Exeter and Topsham over the Exe canal, or the construction of the Aire navigation up to Leeds, in order to open up the expanding West Riding textile and mining districts to the Humber network of rivers and to the open sea, had little reference to the influence of London.

River improvement all over the country was very active in the 150 years after 1580. Medieval rivers had been impeded by weirs and mill-wheels, rapids and shallows or by flash floods. From Elizabethan times onwards, a great deal of effort was put into cleansing watercourses and removing obstacles, often in the teeth of local opposition from fishermen and millers. But by 1680 all the great rivers had been made navigable far up their courses: the Thames above Oxford, the Severn to Welsh-pool, the Trent to Nottingham, the Ouse to Bedford. Fifty years later barge traffic could also reach Leominster, Salisbury, Cricklade, Stratford upon Avon, Bury St Edmunds, Exeter, Maidstone, Beverley, Leeds, Bawtrey, Lincoln (via the Fossdike), Stamford, Cockermouth, Boroughbridge, Peterborough and Thetford. Some rivers, like the Ouse, Aire, Weaver, Wye and Kennet, had been notably improved with embankments and sluices by Defoe's time in the 1720s, when river traffic everywhere had become commonplace. The river-borne trade of towns like Bedford, Wisbech, Reading, Shrewsbury and Maidstone created opulent merchant communities, while the ports of trans-ship-ment, Lynn, Liverpool and Hull, derived much benefit from the elaboration of waterways in their hinterlands. In 1750, before the dawn of the Canal Age, there were already about 700 miles of 'natural' waterways and over 600 miles of canalized or improved rivers in use in England. It remained to connect the different river systems and to give access by canal to landlocked centres of production like Birmingham or the Potteries.

The road system underwent a parallel series of modifications after 1600. Attention had been paid to the needs of wheeled traffic as of pack-horses and pedlars in medieval times. The main trunk roads to London already existed before 1500, and there seems little doubt that such famous road-books as that of John Ogilby in 1675 revealed a network of communications at least three centuries old. Cross-country routes were less well developed. Journeys from Norwich to Bristol or from York to Shrewsbury were more difficult than from London to anywhere in the provinces, but we must not exaggerate the bad state of road communi-cations by the seventeenth century, since men and goods contrived to move about the country fairly regularly. After about 1620, it is true, many more complaints were aired about the damage caused by wheeled traffic on well-used stretches of road, which may indicate either that maintenance of roads was deteriorating or that cartage was greatly increasing in frequency in the early seventeenth century. Indeed probate inventories tend to suggest that the number of carts and wains owned by villagers was much greater in the seventeenth than in the sixteenth century. On impermeable clay soils, especially in the Midlands, parish roads, including stretches of trunk routes, were evidently very bad in many cases by the 1630s. Attempts were made to lighten the burden of maintenance upon parishes especially badly afflicted, or to compel the inert into action, by giving justices of the peace powers of enforcement, or by placing important roads, like bridges, under the care of the county Quarter Sessions, although the results were not satisfactory. During the Interregnum a Surveyor of the Highways was appointed to co-ordinate highway maintenance, and parochial administration was put on a more systematic footing. The outcome, however, was not the creation of a national system of well-made highways, as in France, for almost all still depended upon the zeal of parish surveyors and upon the willingness of parishioners to levy and pay highway rates. One important change was the introduction of turnpike management on a few roads from the middle third of the seventeenth century onwards, but it was not until the 1750s and 1760s that turnpike construction paid significant dividends to the economy at large, because the hostility of vested interests to the payment of tolls hindered their development.

The increasing volume of road transport is indicated by the construction of inns on major routes, by the appearance of livery stables and the introduction of carriage services on selected highroads. The great age of road transport in England was during the fifty years before the railways disturbed settled patterns of communication, but what was familiar to the young Dickens originated at least two centuries before. The road towns of the eighteenth century possessed many of the characteristics and wealth of the river ports. Most of the famous ones had already been singled out by the authors of Restoration commercial itineraries as lively centres of trade and transport services. Great roads like Watling Street generated trade. It is interesting to note how farmsteads, villages, even towns, were relocated or re-oriented near arterial roads, to obtain the benefits of business carried along the highway, in the early modern period. By the new opulence of their premises, and by their stock-in-trade, innkeepers, at least, showed the positive advantages of more frequent travel in the seventeenth century. An inn, purpose-built for the highway trade like the Scole Inn of 1655, near Diss in Norfolk, or the Bell at Stilton (1642), exemplified the new era in inland communications which opened in the early seventeenth century.

The coasting trade was closely related both to foreign trade and river transport. There was a good deal of trans-shipment handled in the bigger ports like Lynn, Hull and Newcastle, and many of the commodities traded coastwise resembled the goods ferried across the North Sea and from Ireland. As one would expect, the chief commodities in the coastal trade were bulky—coal, grain, cheese, lead, tin and iron. Cornish kaolin or tin were shipped out to places of manufacture in several parts of England. The same was true of Pennine lead, Cheshire salt and Wealden timber. Many imports were distributed by coasting vessels: wine, cloverseed, deals, etc. There were therefore many cross-links, although it remains clear that the drawing power of London was a profound influence upon the development of inshore shipping in England. The great expansion of the Newcastle coal trade after 1550 depended largely upon the demand generated in London and to a lesser extent in the hinterland of other south and east coast ports. The fleet of colliers reached 78,000 tons in 1702 and 125,000 tons by 1773, having perhaps quadrupled in little more than 150 years. By 1700, after a century of steady expansion, ports like Berwick, Alnmouth, Hull, Lynn, Yarmouth and Faversham handled substantial quantities of grain for the London market; Falmouth, Chester, Lancaster, Boston, dealt especially in livestock produce, wool, butter, cheese and hides. There were countless wharves or jetties handling goods in local demand and on occasion shipping out local surpluses. Farmers, gentry and mercers often turned their hands to seaborne trade in many rural districts with access to a landing-stage. In Lincolnshire, for example, coal, timber, wine, glass, seeds and contraband were landed on the open shore between Grimsby and the Witham in the seventeenth and eighteenth centuries. The entrepreneurs were unspecialized, often local farmers or gentry who distributed their shiploads among subscribers to their ventures, and sold any surplus to the highest bidders.

In some sections of inland trade there was already a high degree of specialization by the Restoration. This was obviously true of trade controlled by industrial capitalists in the putting-out system, who were moving towards control of both raw materials and wholesale outlets in the seventeenth century. By 1700 many graziers sold their wool or hides directly to agents of the manufacturers who passed through the countryside seeking contracts with producers, at least in buoyant years, and in agricultural counties such as Lincolnshire resident wool-merchants or hide-dealers had virtually disappeared by the early eighteenth century. The wool trade is fairly typical of the growing elaboration of inland trade between primary producing and manufacturing regions. Clothiers, linen drapers, manufacturing ironmongers, lead merchants, brewers, raff-dealers, often controlled a web of contacts and agencies over a wide expanse of country and even abroad.

The second area in which substantial specialization occurred was in handling the long-range trade in consumables. Superimposed upon an ancient pattern of marketing, in which producers and consumers were brought together directly and in which middlemen played a minor role, grew up a small army of 'caterpillars', cheese-mongers, corn-factors, malt-dealers, sheep-jobbers, higglers and forage-merchants. They organized supplies of the goods in regular demand in London, and quite frrquently travelled over great distances to arrange contracts with producers, or bought up stocks at local fairs and markets for transmission to one of the larger cities. Sheep-jobbers, for example, were graziers or butchers who made up droves of fatstock for the Smithfield market at local fairs or by buying direct from farmers. Their trade, hardly begun in 1640, had expanded steadily before 1752, when Parliament commissioned a report on their activities. Poultry-dealers, higglers or hucksters, likewise scoured much of southern and midland England in the interests of London consumers.

The volume of inland traffic in England increased greatly between 1500 and 1750 although we have no means of quantifying it. The 'cherishing veines' of trade, however, nourished both the heart and head of the kingdom. They did so because the whole distribution network became more elaborate and more routine. Trade was still slow, and the tempo of business leisurely, by comparison even with the railway age, but the establishment of sedentary wholesale merchants at key points in the geography of England underpinned not only the development of retail shopkeeping but assisted in the survival of markets, by servicing the traders with stall rights as they supplied the shopkeepers. Many wholesalers, like William Stout of Lancaster, themselves kept shops as well as warehouses. Others, like Robert Harrison of Spilsby, Lincolnshire, also maintained branch shops and stall-rights in neighbouring market towns before the end of the seventeenth century. Richard Popplewell, in the Isle of Axholme, was so powerful a figure that he was not only among the richest of local inhabitants, but controlled nearly all the trade of the district in the 1690s, including the disposal of many of the farmers' surpluses, and also dominated his clients as landowner and estate agent. All kept an extensive stock-in-trade of imported fabrics, even silks and satins, tea, coffee and spices, ironmongery and stationery, drugs, herbs and some chemicals, haberdashery, trinkets and so forth. The capital tied up in stock ran into hundreds, even thousands of pounds, since the wholesale merchant had to maintain a circulating capital large enough to support his market, at least until the railway age.

Before the later seventeenth century, these sedentary wholesale merchants were rare birds outside the larger towns. The part, in their hands after 1700, was still played by the great general fairs, which had survived the Middle Ages and prospered in the sixteenth century. The extraordinary number of markets and fairs which nominally still existed in 1600 is misleading because many were already moribund. Moreover, much of the vitality of those which did well was derived from the booming sales of livestock, corn and cheese after 1550, since the largest stock fairs and many markets were attended by farmers and merchants from great distances. Cowlinge sheep fair in Suffolk, for example, was a great meeting-place for all the graziers of East Anglia, and the fatstock fairs attracted butchers from far and wide even in the sixteenth century. Fairs (or markets) specializing in the sale of particular products, which included woollen or linen yarn, cloth, hay and metal ware, remained indispensable to internal trade until the nineteenth century. But fairs dealing in a wide range of commodities, like the famous Sturbridge fair at Cambridge, lost a good deal of their *raison d'être* except as stock fairs after 1660. In 1600, however, buyers and sellers (and middlemen) came to Cambridge to stock up for the winter, to spend the profits of trade or lay out harvest earnings on a variety of wares, including saltfish from the North Sea. The great fairs remained features of local life throughout the early modern period even when their importance had declined. Provision markets and the smaller fairs retained their vitality in spite of the growth of shops because they appear to have catered to a rather different clientèle, and because they remained useful for the disposal of local produce put up for sale directly by farmers or craftsmen.

FURTHER READING

R. Davis   *English Overseas Trade 1500–1700* (Macmillan 1973).

G. D. Ramsey   *English Overseas Trade during the Centuries of Emergence* (Macmillan, 1957).

B. Supple   *Commercial Crisis and Change in England 1600–42* (C.U.P., 1959).

T. S. Willan   *River Navigation in England, 1600–1750* (O.U.P., 1936).

T. S. Willan   *The English Coasting Trade 1600–1750* (Manchester University Press, 1938).

R. Davis   'English Foreign Trade 1660–1700', *Economic History Review*, VII, 1954.

R. Davis   'English Foreign Trade 1700–74', *Economic History Review*, XV, 1962.

F. J. Fisher   'Commercial Trends and Policy in Sixteenth-Century England', *Economic History Review*, X, 1940.

F. J. Fisher   'Development of the London Food Market, 1540–1640', *Economic History Review*, V, 1935.

F. J. Fisher   'London's Export Trade in the Early Seventeenth Century', *Economic History Review*, III, 1950.

A. H. John   'Aspects of English Economic Growth in the First Half of the Eighteenth Century, *Economica*, 1961.

E. A. Wrigley   'A Simple Model of London's Importance . . .', *Past and Present*, 37, 1967.

6

The Sources of Enterprise

The extent to which social mobility and materialist aspirations were translated directly into economic action poses a question of great importance for the social bearings of early industrialization. This resource, which most economists identify as enterprise or entrepreneurship, has acquired a vast theoretical apparatus, economic, sociological and psychological, in which common elements of behaviour and attitude in the personality of entrepreneurs have been selected as the salient features of enterprise, business initiative or capitalism. Before considering the relevance of entrepreneurial theory to the economic history of England, 1500–1750, we must examine the role of the men whom contemporaries tended to call 'projectors', 'adventurers' or 'undertakers'.

The period when Arkwright, Wedgwood and the Duke of Bridgewater were heroized in the later eighteenth century is a turning-point in the history of innovation. A great many of the individuals who carried through technical or organizational innovations or opened up new markets before 1700 remain anonymous, and few have ever attained the celebrity of business leaders in the century after 1770. Moreover, a number of the innovations effected before 1750 were abortive or seem in retrospect to have been small in scale and localized in significance. Thus the temptation to belittle achievements in the pre-industrial period is readily understandable. But the roots of entrepreneurship (and the sources of enterprise) in the period after 1770 reach deep into the past, and it is unreasonable to discuss the career of Wedgwood or Bridgewater without reference to the willingness of their forerunners to take similar risks or to the broad base for recruitment into business avocations of all kinds. Most theorists of entrepreneurial activity regard it as a special facility, from which the majority of

148

businessmen are excluded by temperament or ability. This is probably correct, but it is no less true that the significant innovations which were the contribution of English industrialization and urban growth in the seventeenth and eighteenth centuries arose because the business community as a whole was receptive to new talent, social diversity and new ideas.

The men who described themselves in general as merchants, tradesmen or undertakers were drawn from almost every social group except the very poorest. This was made possible by the breakdown of gild restrictions, at least in dynamic regions of the country, so that in most trades and in most towns it was possible to purchase one's way into a business, at the level of apprentice or even of master, without difficulty. Moreover, as more and more commercial and industrial activity was carried on in towns or in the countryside where gilds were inoperative in the seventeenth and eighteenth centuries, traditional restraints upon occupational mobility were unimportant. At the same time, the awareness of opportunities in trade among landowners and farmers and their younger sons, even among the clergy and other professional men, especially lawyers, reinforced the openness of English society to the fertilizing influences of money and ensured that no attempt to belittle commerce within the gentry could hope to be successful. Indeed until the Church offered material rewards as substantial as those of the counting-house or the law—from about 1770—it was generally passed over by younger sons or by gentlemen in the toils who hoped to restore their family fortunes. All over England, from London, Bristol or Norwich to small provincial towns or developing country districts, younger sons or the heads of families joined the ranks of businessmen. The nobly born, who did not concentrate upon exploiting the resources of their estates, were recruited into the higher reaches of commerce, especially into the overseas trade of London or Bristol where there were not only always many merchants of 'good family' at any particular time, but also sufficient masters of breeding and probity to whom aristocratic families could entrust their sons as 'apprentices'. The nobility and gentry in business formed complex, interlocking patterns. Families of seventeenth-century gentry like the Whichcotes or Nelthorpes in Lincolnshire retained many connections with their commercial origins in different branches of their families after setting up as country squires. Another family in the county, the Doughtys, were rescued, if only briefly, when one of them, a London merchant, bought the patrimonial estates from his bankrupt elder brother in 1714. A third Lincolnshire example is of a small landowner who sold his family estates, purchased a niche in the London hosiery trade and eventually acquired a small landed estate elsewhere out of the profits. These are quite typical examples of the link between trade and landownership in the country as a whole.

The chief contribution of the nobility and gentry to economic development, however, lay in the exploitation of their estates. Landed gentlemen were particularly active in mining and metallurgy, because minerals provided their most obviously valuable non-agricultural asset. Between 1500 and 1750 the techniques of leasing sub-surface resources, ore, coal, building stone, alum, brick-earth, rock-salt, etc., were developed in the same way as farm leases were perfected by the fruitful dialogue between landlords and tenants. Tenants could rent mineral seams and even plant and machinery from their landlords, and many a yeoman or 'artificer' began his career as industrialist by taking a mining lease. The great majority of landed gentlemen who invested in industrial or commercial ventures in order to increase their revenue did so thus indirectly as ground-landlords or sleeping partners. But in the extractive and mineral processing trades the gentry and nobility played a more positive role in their development. In the Wealden iron industry, for example, the landed plutarchy, from the Duke of Norfolk and Lord Abergavenny down to the Sidneys, Ashburnhams and Robertses, owned and operated furnaces and forges from the early sixteenth century. Ironmasters came both from the old-established aristocracy and from among the families who had bought up monastic property after 1540. The Sidneys of Robertsbridge were especially notable, and their concerns in Sussex were increasingly supplemented by interests and family connections in the west Midlands and south Wales. In south Wales the Sidneys were joined by other men of good birth from Kent or Sussex before 1600, Menyfee, Relfe, Hanbury, who found the excellent timber supply between the Severn and the Towey a better prospect than the Weald. In the west, too, Lord Pembroke was partly responsible for modernizing the iron industry in the 'free mining' region of the Forest of Dean from 1611 onwards, although, typically, he relied upon lessees and other skilled operators for most of the exploitation. Other important landed families interested in ironmaking in the western region, the Winters, Scudamores, Pagets, Dudleys, Gerards and Talbots, enjoyed a varied degree of success, but after 1660 the efforts of individual landowners were overshadowed by the great consortia which increasingly dominated the region of the Severn. Before 1640, however, George Talbot, sixth earl of Shrewsbury, was not only the largest demesne farmer, but also the greatest (and most diverse) industrialist of his generation, with interests in iron, coal, timber and lead, in Derbyshire, Yorkshire, Staffordshire and Shropshire.

His only rival was Sir Francis Willoughby of Wollaton in Nottinghamshire, whose projects, and those of his successor, Sir Percival, were even more varied—but not always successful—extending beyond mining and iron-working into glass, fancy cloth, dyeing and quarrying. Willoughby's interests depended largely upon an immense enterprise in coal, some from his own land and some mined upon lease. Many of his adventures arose from his need to stimulate demand for this primary product. Around 1600 the Willoughbys were sinking £20,000 a year in their coalpits, so that outlets for the material were matters of major concern. As it happened most of the gentlemen ironmasters after 1550 were also substantial coalowners, because the two products often lay together and could be jointly exploited.

In the mining districts, indeed, many gentry families obtained the larger part of their income from mining and mineral leases. Around Nottingham, Sheffield, Leeds, and in Warwickshire, Staffordshire and Lancashire almost all the gentry with land on the coal measures profited in this way, but very few, the Beaumonts of Coleorton for example, could vie with the Willoughbys. A younger son of the latter family, Huntingdon Beaumont, became one of the most ambitious of British entrepreneurs, working coalpits in Nottinghamshire, Warwickshire and Northumberland. Part of the venture he shared with a kinsman by marriage, Sir John Ashburnham of Sussex. Beaumont's plans involved too elaborate capital equipment, notably railway carriage at the pit head, and his vast borrowing eventually bankrupted him in 1618. Most of the leading estates which were committed to coal mining in the Midlands and Yorkshire after 1550 continued to be interested until the nineteenth century, and in some cases, Willoughby of Wollaton, Beaumont of Coleorton, Byron of Hucknall, the Wentworths, Savills and Spencers in south Yorkshire, within the same family. Only a few like James Clifford of Broseley, Salop, were celebrated for their innovations before 1660, and the largest number of gentry mining enterprises in coal or ore differed little if at all from the shallow pits or outcrop workings of the local peasantry until the eighteenth century.

151

By 1750 the mines of Lord Gower, the Duke of Bridgewater, Lord Byron, Lord Middleton, the Marquess of Rockingham or the Duke of Norfolk were as deep and well equipped as any in the country. Even so, much of the initiative rested with the lessees or tenants of such aristocratic coalowners, not with their agents or managers who were sometimes not even mining specialists.

In the northern coalfields a similar pattern of ownership and exploitation is revealed. In Cumberland, peasant-miners, although numerous, were always overshadowed by a handful of great families. Before the Civil War the dominant family was that of the Cliffords, Earls of Cumberland, whose interest in multifarious industrial undertakings in the region was pervasive until the third earl lost his fortune in privateering. In the next century gentry like the Senhouses and Curwens played an important role, but the great figure in the region was Lowther, who rose from merchant to magnate on the strength of Whitehaven's growth and by 1750 already dominated society, politics and trade. In the Tyne-Wear field, the situation was somewhat more complicated since the connection between the merchant community in Newcastle and the landed interest, and between trade and landownership had long been close and fruitful. Several of the great magnate or established gentry families like the Earl of Newcastle and Lord Lumley, the Surtees, Lambton, Delaval, Gascoigne and Grey families were very active in coalmining. The first-named had a very large ironworks on the Tyne which produced £1,000 a year in about 1640. Among the greatest owners of mining leases in the north were the Bishop and the Chapter of Durham and many of the cathedral prebends were rendered valuable by coal-rents. Lumley's practice of exploiting the large pits himself and letting out his small ones to peasant-miners is fairly typical of the region.

But the greatest fortunes in coal before 1700 were made by merchant families who, like the Lowthers in Cumberland, acquired great landed estates—the Liddells, Dobsons, Blacketts, Ridleys, Cotesworths, Brandlings. The Blacketts, who intermarried with the Beaumonts, and the Liddells, who acquired the immense Gascoigne estates in Durham, are the best examples, for both retained varied industrial interests into the nineteenth century, the Blacketts in coal, iron and especially in the Allendale lead trade, and the Liddells in many aspects of Tyneside industry. Land and industry were especially intimately connected in the north-east, and newcomers to landed property assimilated the precepts of industrial as well as land management in the country between the Tees and the Coquet. The dissolution of monastic property after 1540 and the decline and fall of bastard feudalism, which lingered long in the Border regions, released new energy which gave the quickest results in trade, mining or manufacture. The transition of Newcastle's trade from cloth to coal and iron in the sixteenth century was as much a stimulus as a response to rural investment in the hinterland. By 1750 scarcely an estate of any size within 40 miles of the town did not draw substantial receipts from mineral working. Moreover, in the north landowners were more likely to be innovative entrepreneurs than in the south, investing capital and installing plant according to the advice of expert managers or skilled mine-engineers. The landed interest even dominated a good many mining partnerships active in Durham around 1700.

As a rule, however, the nobleman or gentleman as innovators were rare birds in all the trades to which they turned attention. In the sixteenth century several gentry in mining districts are recorded consorting with German experts and from this exchange came a few important innovations. Lord Shrewsbury, for example, was much interested in a steelworks and in a technique of refining lead which owed a good deal to German example, and in Cornwall families like the Godolphins also relied upon German experts to improve their tin mining. Both we might class as innovators. Less typical, however, were genuine individualists of vision and organizing skill among the landed gentry. Peter Edgecumbe, who kept alive interest in Cornish tin during the financial crisis of 1587–94, but who could not find anyone else 'willing, much less desirous, to adventure any money with me in such a desperate and forlorn hope', is worthy to stand beside the great Sir Francis Willoughby, because of his invincible optimism. Another was Sir Edward Zouche, a good Jacobean specimen of courtier and diplomatist, speculator and 'undertaker', who was also one of the leading entrepreneurs of the early seventeenth-century glass manufacture. The Chaloners of Guisborough and the Sheffields of Mulgrave reputedly discovered and opened up the North Riding alum trade, as did the Blounts of Canford that of the Hampshire-Dorset district. Later examples include William Marbury, who found rock-salt on his estate near Winsford and greatly extended the Cheshire salt industry from the 1690s, and Robert Rigby, proprietor and entrepreneur of the Essex port of Mistley near Harwich, a man with ambitions similar to those of the Lowthers at Whitehaven. By 1700, however, the gentry as initiating entrepreneurs had been surpassed by other social groups. The catalogue of landed families with extensive business interests was still lengthy, but men like the Duke of Bridgewater were exceptions, not the rule, in the eighteenth century.

Even in the sixteenth century entrepreneurship was not confined to the larger landowners in rural industrial regions. Some of the yeomen and tenant farmers who held dual occupations in areas such as Sussex, Staffordshire or the West Riding rose from the ranks of small artificers or tradesmen to a larger enterprise in manufacturing or mining. The connection between farming and business was natural in areas of rural industrialization. The prevalence of dual occupations and complex inheritance customs was as important in setting up enterprising peasants as business leaders as in determining the location and development of the industry as a whole. From the *mêlée* of masters and labourers in rural industry emerged a small number of individuals who by their superior ability and vision reached positions of economic dominance, or, like the most successful of commercial farmers, came to acquire a greater share of local industrial capital than their neighbours. The impulse to 'make good' was apparently no less strong among the rural 'middle orders' than among the landed gentry. Necessity was often a sharp spur. Younger sons of non-gentry families found similar outlets for their talents in commerce and manufacturing, but the habit of sharing out the movable wealth in each generation, and the formal custom of partible inheritance, widespread in districts of rural industrialization, meant that for many peasant families all sons were under a similar obligation to make their own way in the world. All over Europe a class of peasant entrepreneurs appeared in the industrialized countryside between 1400 and 1850. Their success, however, was due in large measure to the flexibility which the system of dual occupations imparted to able and ambitious countrymen. The yeoman-clothier, yeoman-blacksmith, yeoman-tanner, were as much a part of the industrial scene in early modern England as the cottage-weaver, cottage-nailer or the gentleman-ironmaster or gentleman-mercer. The dualism of the rural economy in pre-industrial Europe was as stratified as the society itself. For farming families, therefore, the opportunity was readily available to rise by stages from the position of artificer to capitalist within particular trades, by marriage, inheritance or the careful husbandry of accumulated resources.

Another path by which peasants passed into trade or manufacturing was by leasing industrial plant or resources from ground landlords. Most great estates with industrial interests possessed a tenantry primarily concerned with mining or manufacturing by the seventeenth century, of whom a fair number came from local farming stock. Only the largest or most immediately profitable enterprises generally attracted outside capitalists or tempted the landlords into direct exploitation for themselves. On the other hand many farming families, having gained experience in industry by small-scale activities as part of their farms, acquired sufficient skill and experience to specialize and even to become managers of the larger plants operated by their lords or by outside investors. Sussex, for example, had become a reservoir of managerial and technical skills for the British iron and allied trades by the seventeenth century in precisely this way. None of the great entrepreneurs of the region could have expanded as they did without the support of their 'middle management', originally recruited from their tenantry or from neighbouring peasant stocks. The diffusion of entrepreneurial skills across the country, from a 'mature' to a developing industrial region, for example, was characteristic of each generation at least from the early sixteenth century, and the geographically remote origin of many business families in boom areas is at least partly explained by this kind of migration.

The rural sources of economic enterprise in the industrialization of Britain before the nineteenth century are more diverse than the older textbooks suggest. The connection between agricultural change and industrial diversification is complicated by the mobile confusion of the European rural world between 1400 and 1800. Every historian has paid his tribute to the resourceful class of yeomen farmers, who leavened the dough of any group of commercial or industrial entrepreneurs in town as well as country before 1800. The belief, however, that their presence in the vanguard of industrialization reflected the progress of inclosure and the consolidation of holdings so that agriculturists of talent and ambition were compelled to seek their fortunes in trade is now superseded by later research. Nevertheless, the old view retains much of its power to persuade. J. U. Nef observed that peasants in coal-rich districts were in fear of the deprivation which often followed from the discovery of minerals under their holdings, and Paul Mantoux, in discussing the role of yeomen in the growth of Birmingham or Manchester, intimated that their enterprise was similarly the result of rural expropriation.[1] A dispossessed peasantry was accordingly bifurcated into capitalists—i.e. the comparatively small number of rural emigrants who 'made good'—and labourers, who formed the basis of the nineteenth-century industrial proletariat. There are naturally examples of farmers who abandoned, or were driven from, the land, and ended up as merchants or industrialists, thereby repairing their fortunes. The larger towns with established mercantile connections were particularly important as magnets for rural emigration. The brief reign of so many English merchant dynasties—the recurrent pattern of two or three generations from arrival to departure of particular families—left much scope for newcomers from almost any social background to find success in urban trades. Most of the countrymen who moved into an urban environment and reached the heights came from relatively well-to-do families, and the attractions not only of town life but also of urban-centred economic opportunities were sufficiently compelling for both successful and deprived agriculturists.

But the number of the poor, forced out of the country by unemployment or loss of position, who rose above day labour or petty trade was very small. The London common brewer, Ralph Thrale, was certainly the son of a farm labourer, but he owed his start in life to his uncle's money. A good many legends of self-help were current at the time, but were often much embroidered in the telling. Dick Whittington was a potent folk symbol for the age, but his fabled success in trade eluded the hopes of nearly all ambitious poor men in pre-industrial England.

The contribution of farming families to English industrial and commercial entrepreneurship is difficult to disentangle with greater precision because of inadequate evidence. Not enough work has yet been done on the biographies of business leaders before the later eighteenth century, but because the careers of so many entrepreneurs followed a remarkably tortuous course, it is only by analysing the social origins of a substantial number of case studies that we shall obtain any greater insight into the problem. The Darby family, however, was not untypical of the yeoman's progress. The family originated in the farming and nailmaking trades of the West Midlands, passed out of this dual occupation by way of the Bristol iron trades to found the dynasty of

---

[1] See J. U. Nef, *The Rise of the British Coal Industry*, passim; P. Mantoux, *The Industrial Revolution in the Eighteenth Century* (Methuen University Paperback ed., 1964), pp. 370–3.

Coalbrookdale ironmasters in the eighteenth century.[1] It is obvious from this how significant for our understanding of the sources of enterprise is the genealogy of particular families. Amidst the ubiquity of the peasantry in mining and manufacturing, few, however, stand out as innovating entrepreneurs in the classic sense of the term. These few, however, are still often hard to distinguish in the surviving records, not least because we cannot often go back far enough to lay bare their true origins. However, it is probable that some regions at least, the Midland metal trades or the Yorkshire woollen industry, for example, benefited greatly from the *collective* contribution of local farming stocks which were drawn into their development. Individual efforts are much less easy to identify.

The landed gentry and the farming community did not naturally form a concerted interest-group in the display of entrepreneurial behaviour. Why particular gentlemen should have ventured upon mining or shipowning, manufacturing or commerce was often a matter of chance or desperation. Hoped-for profits outside agriculture or public service underpinned the life-style or conspicuous investment of European gentlemen, but we cannot assume that business enterprise was an alternative to office-holding, for the two frequently went hand in hand. This was inevitable before 1640, when so much activity in industry and commerce was related to Court favour or protected by monopolies and patents which issued from the royal prerogative. But exploitation of English economic resources, domestic or foreign, was not confined to the established nobility or gentry whose breeding recommended them to the Court. Even after the Civil War the public official as entrepreneur stands out as a distinct type of business operator in almost all branches of trade and production. The abolition of monopolies had removed one prop from the edifice in which men as diverse as Customer Smythe, Sir Walter Raleigh, William Humfrey, Sir Bevis Bulmer or Sir Robert Mansell had come to dominate large sections of the English economy. But the survival of officially approved joint-stock enterprise and the relationship of leading figures at Court, such as Sir George Downing, with the naval dockyards and government arsenals and with the developing policy of protectionism, kept in being some materially useful connection between government and enterprise at least until the age of Walpole. Sir Ambrose Crowley, for example, owed

[1] See A. Raistrick, *A Dynasty of Ironfounders. The Darbys of Coalbrookdale* (Longman, 1953).

a good deal financially, and in the formation of his ideas and the building up of his industrial empire, to the organization of the London dockyards and ordnance establishments.[1] The great period of the courtier-projector, however, barely survived the assembly of the Long Parliament in 1640.

In the century before 1640 the men who bore the risks of economic diversification or skimmed off the profits of other men's enterprise—for their motives were always mixed even when self-interest prevailed—were extremely heterogeneous. But the largest number of those who rose from routine management to make some entrepreneurial contribution to the English economy before 1650 came from the ranks of commerce. London wholesale dealers, overseas merchants or members of City gilds and livery companies, looking for a new source of investment or for a new field of domination, were drawn into provincial enterprises of great variety. Most apparently began with an interest in their own branch of trade, like the ironmongers who moved out into the Wealden iron industry or the leather sellers into the non-metropolitan leather trades where profit margins were greater. A handful in each generation from the sixteenth century sought more varied enterprises, and for them the freedom of a particular company or gild was but a stepping stone to more diverse profiteering or investment. Not only had this tendency to break the chains of corporate restraint an ancient pedigree, but it was at times forced upon astute entrepreneurs, as late as the eighteenth century, by their need to regulate supplies or co-ordinate markets. The merchant wholesaler-become-industrialist was an ancient type whose heyday was achieved with the wide diffusion of the putting-out system in the seventeenth and eighteenth centuries. There is nothing surprising in the fact that the majority of important textile entrepreneurs until the nineteenth century were drawn from the merchanting side of the industry, nor indeed that the names they commonly bore, 'draper', 'clothier', 'mercer', etc., originally referred to dealers. Perhaps half of the ironmasters whose antecedents are known, between 1600 and 1750, were ironmongers or sons of ironmongers at their beginning, including some famous names such as Roberts, Crowley, Reynolds, Baddeley, Bacon, Wilkinson. And several others came from ancillary trades: cutlery, nail-making, file-making, etc. Capitalist ironmongers in late seventeenth-century Sheffield, for example, not only controlled the local cutlery and edgetool trades, but operated their own furnaces and

[1] See M. W. Flinn, *Men of Iron* (Edinburgh U.P., 1962), chap. I.

forges, dealt in imported pig- or bar-iron and, in the case of large-scale entrepreneurs like John Fell, joined in partnership with leading rural producers, as in the South Yorkshire ironmasters' associations or even in the Midland-based Foley partnership. The collaboration of gentry, yeomen and speculative investors with ironmongers/forgemasters in the Weald dates back to 1540, when the merchant capital came out of London. As business and family connections, like those of the Sidneys, Ashburnhams, Foleys or Crowleys became more far-flung, the commingling of enterprise and capital from many sources in the iron industry was much extended.

In this context, the growth of the private firm or of a cartel of producers and merchants, like the Foley partnership after the Restoration, facilitated the broadening base of entrepreneurial decision-making. Private links, arranged upon kinship or religious affiliations as well as credit, were more important than the proliferation of joint-stock companies in manufacturing and mining before 1720, which met with little success. The London Lead Company, which opened up part of the northern Pennines to mining, was rather an exception, but even in large-scale mining the joint-stock enterprise which emanated from the London mercantile community was no more significant than private associations or landlords' ventures after 1660. Chiefly for financial reasons, group support in risk-taking became more practicable and more necessary in the last century of our period. The firm was a vehicle both for mobilizing capital on behalf of able and ambitious 'projectors' of small resources, and for allowing the same kind of personality to dominate particular trades or localities. Not even the joint-stock companies enjoyed the advantages of limited liability, but the appendage '& Co.' seems to have had an almost magical quality for the business community, especially during the eighteenth century, and it certainly concealed a good deal of sleeping-partnership investment in the pre-industrial period. But the relatively small scale of fixed capital in industrial enterprises before the 1780s meant, first, that many partnerships were unstable, and secondly, that financial arrangements to secure entrepreneurial liquidity could rest upon the deferred payment for goods or services—sales credit or rent arrears—in a way barely credible to modern industrial accounting. The instability of partnerships, therefore, scarcely affected the pattern of economic development before the nineteenth century. The significant contribution was still that of the individual, whose creditworthiness, expert knowledge and

159

initiative remained the chief determinants of entrepreneurial success or failure. But if the organizing genius of a Wedgwood or an Arkwright was a scarce commodity in all places and at all times, less outstanding entrepreneurial or managerial talents were always more plentiful.

We owe to the research of specialists in modern developing economies the conviction that economic enterprise is a universal if sometimes latent force in most human societies where trade and money are well established. The problem, it would seem, is not to divert men from non-economic patterns of behaviour into materially useful occupations, but to offer a plethora of would-be entrepreneurs adequate opportunities to display their talents in productive concerns appropriate for the economic growth of developing countries.

Most theoretical considerations of entrepreneurship stress the innovation or risk-bearing involved in carrying out managerial decisions. Not all constructive innovation was confined to technology, for the unifying element in the formation of the entrepreneur is his sense of market opportunity, his ability to grasp the import of strategic investment, of new invention or of a new market for his goods. But the genius of the few exceptional business leaders was no more important for the integration of economic development than the number and the distribution of the secondary entrepreneurs and managers who adopted, or adapted, innovations for general use, and built up a framework of support for the new patterns of production and organization. As a group, these 'imitators' have been unduly slighted. Their consolidating function is obviously not spectacular, but for a society in the throes of fairly rapid growth the 'follow-up' process may well determine the difference between success or failure. Men with the flair and vision of the great innovators are essential to initiate change, but those qualities alone in a hostile climate are likely to be insufficient. The routine functions of management may prove stultifying, and there is ample evidence of resistance to change within particular trades or processes apt to weaken them mortally in a competitive world. But the inertia of economic life without the energizing impulses of the entrepreneur can be exaggerated. A continuous, piecemeal and small-scale process of adjustment, adaptation and emulation occurred in almost every section of the English economy between 1500 and 1750, and even the most gild-ridden occupations revealed a flickering power to change successfully from time to time.

Nevertheless, theories of entrepreneurship have usually been cast in a more heroic mould. It is the great figures who have attracted the historian's interest and the theorist's preoccupation. Max Weber set the hare running with his hypothesis associating the Protestant ethic with the spirit of capitalism in Europe.[1] His premises were simple. First, Protestant theology, especially that of John Calvin, was more conducive to economic change than medieval Catholic doctrine, for ancient injunctions against usury (the taking of interest), the just price and the suspicion of trade and money were relaxed or even abandoned. Secondly, the more materialist bias of Protestant thought admirably mirrored the emphasis upon self-help, individualism and rational behaviour which characterized the new beliefs. Thirdly, the doctrine of predestination, by which men were elected for salvation by God's grace alone, implanted a severe anxiety concerning the believer's after-life. Calvinists assumed that the chosen would behave in their earthly lives as if they enjoyed grace, because they did not know their fate. In other words, predestination caused men to make a virtue of worldly, as well as spiritual, success, as a token of God's blessing. Fourthly, religious individualism, being compounded of men's need to interpret the ways of God through the medium of the Bible, placed a high premium upon education. Finally the Calvinists, who rejected the Catholic notion of salvation by good works, stressed socially useful outlets for human charity. Once the process of instilling ideals of self-justification, hard work and restraint in daily life had become established, the rational and material values could become secularized and independent of religious inspiration. Weber did not believe that Protestantism alone created modern capitalism, but it seemed to him that the development of north-western Europe after 1500 was not mere coincidence, especially when its success was compared with the failure of China or India to make the breakthrough, despite their ancient technical superiority.

One objection to his thesis, that sixteenth-century Protestant theology was no more receptive to materialist ideas than contemporary Catholic thought, was answered by R. H. Tawney,[2] who postponed the critical date until the seventeenth century, when Protestantism was more obviously friendly towards individual acquisitiveness (especially the taking of interest). This then raised another question—which came first, the fact or the thought? Did Calvinist ethics mould the capitalist, or did

[1] M. Weber, *The Protestant Ethic and the Spirit of Capitalism* (Eng. translation, 1930).
[2] R. H. Tawney, *Religion and the Rise of Capitalism* (Penguin ed., 1947).

businessmen converted to Protestantism effectively reanimate its doctrines? We do not know, but the paradox recurs frequently in discussions of the relationship between ideas and action. Predestination and salvation by grace were not necessarily applied to the principle of self-justification by success, for the strain of fatalism before the majesty of God, which derived from the same source, was hardly less potent in Protestant thought. The antipathy to profit and the indifference to worldly success of Calvin continued to influence the more zealous sects until well into the nineteenth century.

Weber's other ideas have also been criticized. Especially contentious is his application of theoretical concepts to particular case studies. Weber's opinion was that the Protestant ethic imparted a dynamic to economic development which was reflected in the success of Protestant countries by contrast with Catholic countries. There is something to be said for this point of view, but it is altogether too crude. The elements of capitalist change—banking, insurance, the growth of mercantile and industrial specialisms, the devolution of managerial authority, as well as many of the great innovations put to work in Europe before 1750— were the products of medieval, Catholic enterprise. Commercial Revolution is a term employed to describe developments in thirteenth-century Italy no less justifiably than in seventeenth-century Holland or England. And what was appropriate for Florence, Genoa or Venice, Flanders or Barcelona before 1540 was not suitable for Holland, England or France till much later. Moreover, the reasons why so many Catholic countries failed to keep up with leading Protestant countries after 1550 are multifarious: Italy, Spain, Poland and Bavaria were in decline politically, socially or economically, and others remained too deeply rural, too dependent upon subsistence farming, to achieve the necessary diversification. Weber also overlooked the fact that the second Industrial Revolution occurred in Catholic Belgium and that the economic history of France, Bohemia and Savoy-Piedmont does not support his primary contention of Catholic indifference to growth in the early modern period. The critical factors are more likely to be resource endowment, the size and composition of domestic demand, central planning, or the impact of overseas trade in relation to the supply and location of entrepreneurs.

The empirical evidence for the Weber thesis may be suspect, but even those authorities who have questioned his interpretation have tended to accept more readily his concept of the entrepreneur as outsider, as the foreign body introduced into the bloodstream of economic life which, in a state of tension, prevailed over the denizens of the system. The innovating businessman, whatever his origins, is an irritant of established routines. The most famous phrase used to describe his role is 'creative destruction' (J. A. Schumpeter).[1] In carrying through a technical invention, in opening up a new market, in making a labour-saving (or cost-saving) innovation, in reorganizing a trade or branch of industry, the entrepreneur must destroy a tenacious but outmoded way of doing things in order to create a new order. The contribution of the entrepreneur need not be so cataclysmal as to undermine a whole industry or system of commerce, for many significant innovations made only minor changes in the structure of economic life. But since, for Schumpeter and many other economists, the entrepreneur must by definition introduce fruitful changes, he must, at some level, transform investment, employment and managerial behaviour. The power loom might destroy the handweavers' living; a significant cluster of innovations like the railway might remodel the world economy; trade in Indian calicoes might threaten the prosperity of the cheap textile industry in Europe around 1700; in turn the Indian trade might be sapped by the impact of labour-saving innovation. Examples of this creative destruction are legion. For Schumpeter it was a timeless function of entrepreneurship, which distinguished his theory from those of Weber and Marx.

Against their premise of 'stages' of social organization overturned by revolution, Schumpeter posited a spiral of progress. He referred to the 'circular flow' of economic life. The entrepreneur as innovator brought about the necessary restructuring of the economic frame into which his innovation was introduced; his example was then applied generally by imitation, at which point the innovation lost its impulsion. But the cycle thus followed did not regress to the original starting-point, so that with each important innovation some movement forward took place. Hence Schumpeter's conviction that economic development was a dynamic process and the attraction of his theory for historians of the evolutionary school of economic history. This point of view is a useful corrective to the proposition of pre-Reformation stagnation, but it is too elegant, too formalized, to fit all the facts relevant to economic growth before the Industrial Revolution. Many of Schumpeter's ideas have

[1] See J. A. Schumpeter, 'The Creative Response in Economic History', *Journal of Economic History* VII, 1947, for the briefest statement of his position.

been found wanting when applied to particular case studies both in the European past and in the modern underdeveloped world.

For Schumpeter, Protestant ethics were, at most, tangential influences upon his concept of capitalist enterprise. But in almost all theoretical explanations of the human causes of economic development, particular attention is paid to those ideals of entrepreneurial behaviour, hard work, frugality, self-reliance, the inwardness of the personal impulse, which for Weber were largely religious attributes. Thus David MacClelland has generalized just such traits into a more or less universal concept of 'need achievement', the drive which affected individuals or whole societies to prove their material success. It may well be that the seed of seventeenth-century materialism lay in Protestant doctrines of self-justification by success,[1] but the psychology of the early modern capitalist, as that of his counterpart in Japan or Brazil, must needs be fixed on a broader footing. Exclusiveness, or alienation, doubtless contributed to the need of ambitious entrepreneurs to succeed, but so did the degree of parental control, their upbringing and exposure to educational persuasion and pressure. This at least is a salient feature of a complex intergenerational model of entrepreneurship produced by E. E. Hagen to qualify and extend sociological explanations of economic change like that of Weber. Hagen's thesis was founded upon a number of case studies, including a detailed examination of the background influences upon the lives of the greater entrepreneurs of the Industrial Revolution.[2] The emphasis upon the total social *milieu* of the entrepreneur is obviously sensible, but for the period before 1700 it is complicated by the lack of personal information of the kind required for the purpose.

Two impulses widely assumed to influence entrepreneurial behaviour which can usefully be discussed for the pre-industrial period are the appropriateness of the educational system and the instrumentality of alienation or exclusion from the mainstream of social life. For education, the questions we should ask are themselves far from easy to answer. Popular notions of what were suitable precepts in the formation of an aptly pragmatic character did not necessarily depend upon the diffusion of formal education. The folklore of capitalism, out of which

[1] D. A. MacClelland, *The Achieving Society* (Princeton U.P., 1961).

[2] E. E. Hagen, *On the Theory of Social Change. How Economic Growth Begins* (Tavistock Press, 1964); cf. M. W. Flinn, *The Origins of the Industrial Revolution* (Longman, 1966), chap. V.

164

Samuel Smiles fashioned his didactic Victorian biographies of entre-preneurs and engineers, possessed an oral (and often fabulous) tradition going back presumably as far as men felt it necessary to gloss their devotional texts with practical instances. It would be interesting to know the consequences of the shift in popular taste from John Foxe's *Book of Martyrs* or Bunyan's *Pilgrim's Progress* to Defoe's *Robinson Crusoe* in the common reading of literate Englishmen. Crusoe, however, is a near-perfect example of the secular, self-reliant and adaptable man of a Europe from which religious conflict had ebbed away. It was through such painless indoctrination that suitable humanist and social values and the spirit of enterprise percolated down the generations from 1650 to 1850.

On a different level, however, educational changes in the early modern period equally influenced the formal composition of the so-called 'fully possessive market society' of pre-industrial England. The ability to read and write, and even more the self-discipline necessary to encourage learning, were important attributes of economic develop-ment. Weber had been impressed by the educational differences between Protestant and Catholic regions in nineteenth-century Germany, which, he believed, exposed the greater enterprise of the former. The idea of education as an accessible if not universal facility of social and religious, as well as cultural, development, owed much to the Reformation. The Protestant belief that divine truth was revealed in the word of God placed a high premium upon education in literacy, and encouraged an immense flood of educational endowments across Protestant Europe after 1520–50. Men were required to know enough to read and interpret the Bible and to understand the sermons and lectures of learned divines. Ministers of religion, schoolmasters and other leaders of opinion had to be even better educated, so that uni-versities, training academies, etc., were no less favoured by benefactors. To the impetus generated by the Reformation was added the classical and humanizing bias of the Renaissance, which for cultured and discerning men opened vistas dimly perceived in the Middle Ages. From these premises grew virtually the whole institutional, as well as intellectual, system of European education before the late nineteenth century, since in Catholic countries the legacy of the Renaissance was added to the Counter-Reformation to set in train similar developments, if only to combat the spread of reformed doctrines. Nevertheless, the schools and universities founded in the sixteenth and seventeenth centuries supplemented or replaced medieval institutions, and the habit even among peasants in the high Middle Ages of educating younger sons to the Church reflects a ready appreciation of the material value of education long before Alberti, Erasmus or Calvin.

But the Protestant emphasis upon personal conviction rather than collective obedience and the Renaissance emphasis upon humanism resulted, often in the teeth of official persecution, in this liberation of thought from the 'godly and spiritual exercises' for which education was intended even by Calvin. The tradition of observation and experiment in the entire realm of science and philosophy is the most obvious and important heritage of the cultural efflorescence before 1700. From it there were several developments of immediate application in everyday life, notably in medicine and navigation, surveying and bookkeeping. But the scientific rationalism which flowered in the age of Newton and Leibniz was too rarefied to produce many results of direct utility to entrepreneurs, although nearly all the members of the Royal Society in Restoration England were as obsessed by the need for practical innovations as by the theoretical considerations of natural or human philosophy. This is equally true of most aspects of educational development in the sixteenth and seventeenth centuries. Educated men continued to obtain nearly all their intellectual nourishment from classical or scriptural studies, and despite the number of chairs founded in famous universities in 'scientific' or 'practical' subjects, useful studies as commercial law, book-keeping, modern languages, mechanics, etc. could only be obtained from private tutors or a handful of special academies. By the eighteenth century the superior reputation of English dissenting academies or Scottish universities chiefly depended upon their attention to 'real' or useful subjects, by contrast with the ancient grammar schools or universities in the south.

For the majority of the people, however, education merely meant the acquisition of certain basic skills in reading, writing and reckoning. The extent to which any pre-industrial society is literate (or numerate) is impossible to judge except by reference to the proportions of adults able to sign their names, for other statistics are not available. On that basis, it is evident that northern and north-western (usually but not exclusively Protestant) Europe enjoyed the highest degree of common literacy in the seventeenth- and eighteenth-century world. Perhaps 30–40 per cent of men in 1640–80 and 50 per cent in 1750 in England could sign their names, which, to judge from Elizabethan anxiety about the proficiency of even the Anglican ministry, marked a significant improvement since the sixteenth century.[1] The meaning of such basic literacy for economic development is more a matter of opinion than hard evidence, but since almost all development economists set great store by such attainments, it is probable that the relatively wide social diffusion and accessibility of education in pre-industrial England, as in Holland and the more dynamic parts of France and Germany, contributed not only to social mobility but to the inculcation of some of the principles of enterprise as well. The connection must not be exaggerated, for many very poor regions in seventeenth-century Europe, Scotland, Savoy, Denmark, had even higher educational standards, and exported their surplus scholars to teach the people of better endowed regions.

On the influence of outsiders or minority groups upon the development of entrepreneurship much has been suggested elsewhere in this book. In the case of the Germans who were imported into England to develop the techniques of mining and smelting their contribution to entrepreneurship in its specific sense is ambiguous since many were merely artificers or technicians imported to teach their skills to native businessmen and labourers. However, many of the arts involved in metallurgy, paper-making or glass-blowing were so specialized that some German immigrants necessarily had to undertake risk-bearing or innovative functions in order to achieve an acceptable degree of resource exploitation. The agents of technical diffusion from developed to backward areas were generally skilled emigrants of the type found in Elizabethan Cumberland. No less important, however, was the migration of the persecuted or war-weary, like the Flemings who brought so many new textile skills to England in the fourteenth and sixteenth centuries, or the Huguenots whose contribution to British economic development after 1690 was widespread and influential. Huguenot merchant-industrialists, by their determination to make good in their adoptive country, by their wealth, experience and technical knowledge, became entrepreneurs of so many superior trades in England, Holland, Germany, Switzerland, Ireland and Scandinavia that they precipitated the slow-acting change towards a technologically more advanced industrial economy in all the Protestant countries of Europe before 1750. Huguenot business leaders stand out as classical examples of heroic entrepreneurship. Their role in France of appropriating to

[1] L. Stone, 'Literacy and Education in England, 1640–1900', *Past and Present*, 42, 1968.

themselves many of the technical, mercantile and industrial functions of the economy in itself is held to support the Weber thesis, since their comparative exclusion from the mainstream of French political and social life reputedly drove them to achievement in other fields often despised by the 'establishment'. Abroad they were apparently driven by the same impulse. The Huguenots, however, were probably a special case; but in a general way the contribution of minorities within a society did not depend upon their being foreign.

Most communities in the pre-industrial world contained social groups alienated like the French Huguenots from ready social acceptance. The need felt by such minority groups to assert themselves 'paid off' in the efforts they put into the development of the economy. The most celebrated example in British economic history is that of the Protestant dissenters, Quakers, Presbyterians, and later the Unitarians and to a lesser extent the Methodists, in the formation of trade and industry after about 1680. Excluded from the main line of preferment, imbued with sternly Protestant values of self-help, saving, justification by outward marks of divine favour and its corollary, diligence and effort, the dissenting sects formed closely interdependent networks of relatives and co-religionists, established educational institutions for the instruction of useful subjects and created informal, and later formal, exchanges for cash and credit within the group. As an instrument for the organization of comparatively scarce resources of enterprise, capital and technical skill, these minority groups were particularly successful in the exercise of moral sanctions, supervision and the regulation of activity by members of the group. Since the problem in economic development is ever to harness the will to the means of change, the collective efficiency of Huguenots or Quakers was a matter of significance. In this respect the success of certain early members of different sects in converting, by example and leadership, humble, sometimes fanatical and often anti-materialist groups like the Quakers into respectable, affluent and essentially oligarchic organizations amenable to the requirements of a capitalist economy is outstanding. In the case of the Quakers the progress, from George Fox's revivalist enthusiasm of the 1650s and 1660s[1] to the quiescent, authoritarian and materialist leadership of a century later, can be discerned in the diary of William Stout of Lancaster, whose mixture of piety and profit-consciousness is not only typical, but can be

[1] See *The Diary of William Stout of Lancaster*, 1665–1752, ed. by J. D. Marshall (Manchester U.P., 1967).

seen as a permanent state of fruitful tension between his spiritual needs and his business sense. Stout's Quakerism was already more akin to Gurney than to George Fox.

That worldly ends eventually triumphed has been repeated so often in the history of purifying religious movements that it is not necessarily a Protestant trait. In the real world, however, the introvert coherence of minority groups may have been translated into economic action less often than theoretical explanations of the need to achieve have presumed. In England the exclusiveness from the normal attitudes of society of Huguenots or Quakers was at most a transient phase of their becoming opulent, and the old pattern of enrichment by trade followed by 'gentrification' and political and social absorption into the landed plutarchy or lesser gentry asserted itself after a generation or so of striving. Such ambitions influenced even rich London Jews by 1750, and social acceptance was quite easy for well-found Huguenots, Dutchmen or indigenous dissenters of gentlemanly demeanour. Industrialists, like merchants or lawyers, who had accumulated their fortunes, passed as readily into the squirearchy as any other new men. There were, indeed, few dynasties of entrepreneurs extending beyond two generations even among Protestant sectaries at any time in English history. In other words, the celebrated mobility of English society rather restrained the formation and persistence of self-conscious minority groups standing outside the main concourse of that society. This scarcely mattered even in the generation of Wedgwood and Arkwright because trade in all its branches, and industrial enterprise specifically, was regarded as a principal artery of material advancement and fresh recruitment was constant and open-ended in the ranks of business.

From the mass of hopeful business leaders in any generation after 1550 enough risk-taking innovators could usually be found to encompass the necessary economic changes to keep the developing economy of pre-industrial England dynamic. The medley of personal impulses and individual achievements may have resulted in a good many abortive enterprises and a certain waste of capital and other resources, which are a reproach to effective central planning, but it was precisely because England before 1750 already possessed a broad middle band of investible wealth and a widely diffused secular, materialist and rational frame of mind, receptive not only to some degree of technical change, but also to the idea of trade and industry as a respectable source of personal accumulation, that the massif of industrialization, in the complete sense of that term, could be negotiated in the eighteenth and nineteenth centuries. The combination of great Schumpeterian 'entrepreneurs', changing the course of production or distribution processes, a legion of 'imitators' or secondary entrepreneurs who built up the new superstructure, and a proficient and generally not restrictive labour force, in being in many sectors before 1750, was the most obvious consequence of the mass of changes which were active in English society in the three or four centuries before 1800.

FURTHER READING

M. W. Flinn *Men of Iron: the Crowleys in the Early Iron Industry* (Edinburgh University Press, 1962).

M. W. Flinn *The Origins of the Industrial Revolution* (Longman, 1966).

J. W. Gough *The Rise of the Entrepreneur* (Batsford, 1969).

E. E. Hagen *On the Theory of Social Change* (Tavistock Press, 1964).

D. S. Landes, ed. *The Rise of Capitalism* (Collier-Macmillan, 1966).

R. H. Tawney *Religion and the Rise of Capitalism* (Penguin, 1947).

H. R. Trevor Roper *Religion, the Reformation and Social Change* (Macmillan, 1967).

T. Bevan 'Sussex Ironmasters in Glamorgan', *Cardiff Naturalists Society Transactions*, 86, 1856.

R. B. Grassby 'English Merchant Capitalism in the late 17th Century', *Past and Present*, 46, 1970.

B. C. L. Johnson 'The Foley Partnerships', *Economic History Review*, IV, 1952.

W. E. Minchinton 'Merchants in England in the Eighteenth Century', *Explorations in Entrepreneurial History*, X, 1957.

W. C. Scoville 'Minority Migration and the Diffusion of Technology', *J. Econ. History*, 11, 1951.

R. S. Smith 'Huntingdon Beaumont. Adventurer in Coal Mines', *Renaissance and Modern Studies*, I, 1957.

L. Stone 'The Educational Revolution, 1560–1640', *Past and Present*, 28, 1964.

L. Stone 'The Nobility in Business', *Explorations in Entrepreneurial History*, X, 1957.

C. Wilson 'The Entrepreneur in the Industrial Revolution', *History*, VIII, 1957.

7

The Role of Government

Sir Thomas Smith, in his celebrated discourse on the Tudor constitution, described the composition of government in England which would serve for the whole period before the nineteenth century. After declaring that Parliament (i.e. the Crown in Parliament) is supreme in legislation, he stated that 'everie Englishman is entended [understood] to bee there present, . . . from the Prince . . . to the lowest person of England.' But 'day labourers, poore husbandmen, yea marchauntes or retailers which have no free lande, copiholders, and all artificers . . . have no voice nor authoritie in our common wealth, and no account is made of them but onelie to be ruled, not to rule others.' Since all men professed to believe in the supremacy of statute law, and few were able or willing to over-rule Parliament for any length of time, it follows that everyone of property vicariously participated in and consented to acts of government. This is reflected in the retrospective opprobrium of Henry VIII's 'tyranny' in 1532–47 and the massing of forces to defeat Charles I's personal rule in 1629–40.

Smith, however, accepted that the franchise was restricted to men of property, and his use of the term common wealth (or *res publica*) implies the consensus of a minority of subjects of the Crown. On the other hand, all constitutional writers of the period believed in the responsibility of government for the excluded poor, but in this it was not assumed that the Crown should necessarily act as judge between the disfranchised and a class of rampant capitalists who controlled the machinery of Parliament. Naturally in a period when the executive power of the Crown was increasingly involved in affairs which touched the vested interests of substantial property-owners, recurrent friction and occasional confrontation were inevitable. But unless Thomas Cromwell were an outright autocrat, there is little evidence of a coherent theory of state directed at changing the traditional belief in at least nominal consensus into a bureaucratic absolutism on the French model. J. W. Allen rightly argued that, 'Emergence . . . from the anarchic conditions of the fifteenth century brought with it an accession of faith and hope in the shaping power of government.' [1] Men simply trusted in the ability of centralized government to realize its ends. That these expectations were concentrated upon the Crown before 1640 is not surprising, because the Prince alone was entrusted with executive government by the same constitutional precepts which stressed the supremacy of statute and the rule of law. The machinery of government, from legislation to administration, the rules and tolerances which made it work, were essentially medieval. After 1660, even after 1688, these ancient and conventional ideas about the 'common wealth' which transcended the interests of particular groups were not obsolete. This is especially the case in the response of government to the 'fourth estate' of excluded poor. In spite of much short-sightedness on the part of legislators, it is a travesty to describe social policy after 1660 merely as class legislation of the well-to-do against the unprivileged. Governments perhaps lost faith in their ability to shape national development after Charles I. The legislation of 1660–1760 indicates a decline of interventionism, but not abdication of social and economic responsibility for the welfare of the State and its people. Since there had always been a swift current of pragmatism in government policy, even in the 1560s or 1630s, not a theoretically impressive combination of despotism and 'mercantilism', the change was not so much decline from omnicompetent, far-seeing statism to a ragged oligarchy of selfish interests, as a gradual, and sometimes painful, release of the leading-strings by central authority. What exercised Englishmen of property throughout the period from the fifteenth to the eighteenth century were the fundamental problems of law and order and internal security; freedom from the recurrent nightmare of civil war; freedom from invasion and excessive foreign competition; and freedom from arbitrary impositions, like forced loans, billeting of troops and monopolies. Good government, however, was felt often to mean strong government and a deal of temporary inconvenience was tolerated in the interests of security, especially in the dangerous sixteenth century.

Another element in these practical considerations of the role of the

[1] J. W. Allen, *English Political Thought*, 1603–60 (Methuen, 1938), vol. I, pp. 59–60.

Crown as government of the realm illustrates the preoccupations and the tensions of the 'common wealth' very well. This was the need of government, at least after 1550–60, to obtain sufficient revenue to conduct the affairs of state assigned to the Prince whether by consent or by usurpation. The fiscal motif in what is called mercantilism has only recently received the scholarly attention which it deserves, for it is clear that a good part of the economic activity before 1640 which we call 'state control' or 'state participation' was in reality a device to obtain money, and in the great age of indirect taxation by Parliament after 1690 the fiscal character of the tariffs or excise was at least as pronounced as the protective. After Henry VIII squandered his enormous fortune, the English Crown was financially reduced to its late medieval impotence, and a wide range of makeshifts had to be devised to avoid too great dependence upon the rising self-confidence of the House of Common. Since the expedients involved the sale of offices and monopolies as well as farming the customs, it is clear that central authority was often reduced rather than enhanced by the action of the Crown.[1]

The history of government finances before the era of Sir Robert Walpole is instructive as a guide to the vicissitudes of government activity in economic affairs. The assumption until late in the seventeenth century was that the executive should live off its own resources, which included customs, the dues of prerogative administrations like the Court of Wards, the revenue of landed estates belonging to the Crown, and whatever loans could be raised at home or abroad to meet necessary expenditure. Taxation was at the command of Parliament and normally was voted only to meet extraordinary contingencies such as war or insurrection. An acquiescent Parliament could sometimes be required to supply money to the Crown, but after the reign of Henry VIII the grant of a subsidy was generally a matter of wheedling and compromise, although increasingly impecunious governments before 1629 were forced into the dilemma of 'unconstitutional exactions' or reliance upon the Commons' generosity. After 1660, partly in reaction to the heavy taxation of the Interregnum, Parliament fixed an annual allowance to the Crown for its necessary maintenance and government which quickly proved to be too niggardly, but the principle of a Civil

[1] Revenue farming means leasing out the collection of Crown income—usually some specific branch like the Customs—to financiers (singly or in combination) who paid a lump sum in advance of collection for the privilege. It saved on the employment of a large bureaucracy.

List was established which eventually evolved into regular supplies for particular departments of state and the Court. Before 1690, however, the story of government finances is of successive expedients, many of which caused friction between Crown and people.

The management of the Crown estates caused trouble only to the head of state. The enormous accession of real property in the hands of the Crown between 1471 and 1539, of which the monastic lands formed the largest but by no means the only portion, relieved the earliest Tudors of financial anxieties, but Henry VIII's profligacy in disposing of his father's fortune and then in beginning the dispersal of Cromwell's vast bequest of the 1530s undermined the independence of royal government within a generation. The strains were apparent in 1549 when Somerset was prevailed upon to despoil the chantries, and again by 1560 when Elizabeth turned her eyes upon the still immense episcopal estates of England and Wales. Between 1536 and 1640 the Crown sold land valued in constant prices (based in 1630) at almost £6,500,000, which passed into the private property of subjects or into public institutions. After 1547 the sale of estates often became the only way to raise necessary revenue. Elizabeth more often preferred to consume the seedcorn than to accept the humiliation of parliamentary demands. By 1603 the Crown estates were already smaller than they had been in 1500. The problem, however, was made acute by the antiquated system of management practised on the royal estates. The deep suspicion of rack-renting, inclosure and other devices to raise the yield of landed property prevented the Crown from imitating the entrepreneurship of less exalted landlords, and the rent income of the royal estates signally failed to keep pace with inflation. The landed income of the King in 1509 was about £42,000 p.a. Elizabeth's total recurrent revenue at the end of her reign seldom exceeded £200,000. We can easily understand James I's attempt to reverse the process of decline. The Survey of Crown Lands in 1607 was a plan not only to assess the true value of royal property but also to investigate the extent of recent reclamation from the wastes, to which the Crown was entitled to a share. Even so, it met with little success. When the Civil War broke another spate of selling (£3,500,000 of Crown lands and £2,500,000 of Church lands) began, in order to pay for the royal cause. Thereafter there was no chance that the revenue of royal property could pay for a significant share of public administration.

After the income from the Crown estates, the Customs and Excise provided the largest share of recurrent revenue within the royal prerogative. But customs dues were difficult to collect, and had long been left to individual lessees or local municipalities. The Marquess of Winchester as Lord Treasurer had tried to impose system upon the Customs collection in the 1550s and 1560s, which resulted in 1570 in a 'general farm' of the revenues. Thomas Smythe, the 'Customer', leased the collection in 1570 for £17,500 a year, and even though when he relinquished the farm in 1588 he was paying £30,000 he still contrived to make a great fortune. Revenue farming was doubly useful to the Crown. It provided money in a lump sum monthly or even annually in advance of collection, and the responsibility for setting up machinery for assessing and gathering the customs was left to the farmer. Smythe supplied his own bureaucracy, which when direct collection by the government was attempted in 1588–98 provided a useful basis for the new system. The very considerable improvement in revenue before 1600 was due almost entirely to the organizing skill of Customer Smythe, not to the government. Indeed, revenue farming was much too valuable to be given up permanently, and after 1604 a new 'farm' of the Customs was established which lasted for a good part of the seventeenth century.

The potential value of the Customs was so great after 1604 that there were always rich financiers willing to advance the £10–45,000 needed to buy into the 'farm'. By 1625 the annual rent of the Customs had risen to £160,000 altogether. After 1604 the Crown merely drew upon the farmers by means of 'tallies', and in time they became bankers to the government, advancing money on security of the Customs. The identity of money-lending and Customs-farming became more pronounced after 1630, when the old sources of long-term credit to the Crown, the Corporation of London, 'foreign merchants', or great subjects like Sir Baptist Hickes, dried up in the withering blast of increased royal extravagance. The tax-farmers obviously lent the king his own money in advance of its collection, but they also acted as middlemen in raising other loans for assignment to the needs of the Crown, whose credit on the open market sank year by year. In 1641 the financial syndicates which competed to serve the royal interest suffered heavily at the hands of Parliament. In the next twenty years the Customs were managed by Commissioners, but for a government with a weak bureaucracy and a perennial need for ready money, revenue farming still seemed the most suitable arrangement after the Restoration. It was finally abandoned only in 1671, when a Board of Commissioners was appointed to preside over collection of the Customs. When in 1696 Edward Culliford was made Inspector-General and given administrative responsibility, the level of efficiency at least temporarily improved. Between 1688 and 1702 the Customs supplied well over one-fifth of government income, or about £1,000,000 a year.

By that time the Customs revenue was rivalled by the Excise as well as by the Land Tax. The Excise issued from emergency legislation in 1643 and because it imposed taxes upon commodities in inland trade it was always very unpopular. By 1654 it was farmed, and was not taken back into central control until 1683. In 1688–1702 the Excise yielded about as much per annum as the Customs, but by 1750 when the Customs brought in about £1,500,000, the Excise produced well over £3,000,000. Ever since 1643 the number of excisable commodities had grown steadily, much to widespread public disgust, and many producers and merchants came to despise and fear the excisemen on their rounds. Many important industrial commodities were subject to duty from the mid-seventeenth century, but in 1700 rather more than half the total yield was taken from the output of beer. The eighteenth century found indirect taxes easier to collect than direct levies, but the proliferation of dues upon output complicated the problem of administration. Walpole modified and reduced Excise duties in 1721–4, in a way which suggested that he was at least partly aware of the need not to smother commercial prosperity by fiscal demands, but his later scheme to raise the reorganized Excise in 1732 was beaten by massive popular protest.

Parliamentary taxation before 1640 was based upon the medieval subsidy, a tax upon the assessed valuation of real and movable property, which was modified from time to time but remained essentially the same in the sixteenth century as in the fourteenth. It was never intended as a permanent tax but as an irregular subvention to the Crown in emergencies. As such it became a potent political weapon in the fight between Crown and Commons, and the increasing difficulty of obtaining a vote of taxes from Parliament forced the government into numerous expedients. Henry VIII had reputedly obtained £700,000 from direct taxes, 1539–47, but his successors had no such luck. Elizabeth, despite the inflation of prices, raised only about £50,000 a year from parliamentary subsidies, or no more than one quarter of her yearly revenue at the beginning of her reign. Between 1588 and 1603 war consumed £4,000,000, less than half of which was voted by the Commons, and then at the cost of much public discontent, which spilled over into dissatisfaction with early Stuart mismanagement. The system more or less broke down in the 1620s, but from the 1640s taxation as a permanent feature of government appeared in a new light. In the Commonwealth, a vote of £1,300,000, to be collected in part out of a more realistic property assessment, was granted to the Protector. The new system of managing direct taxation, called The Assessment, survived the Restoration and eventually formed the basis of the later Land Tax. During the 1670s, under the guidance of Sir George Downing, a number of new ideas began to permeate English fiscal policy, concerning direct as well as indirect taxation, many of which were founded upon Dutch example. New direct taxes after 1660, a Hearth Tax, Window Tax and Poll Tax, and even for a period in the 1690s duties upon baptisms, burials, marriages and single people and stock-in-trade and status, were levied by Parliament, although all but the Land and Window Taxes had a short innings. Increasingly, however, in the late seventeenth century, direct taxation was accepted as a regular and recurrent feature of the government's revenue. After 1689, in the era of what the Tories called 'Dutch finance', the whole framework of English taxation was systematized and made routine. By 1700 the Land and other assessed taxes yielded about one-fifth of total public revenue, a proportion which remained about the same in the first two-thirds of the eighteenth century. Opposition to direct taxation and considerable difficulty of collection continued throughout the eighteenth century. The English professed themselves superior to all their rivals in the 1720s as in the 1570s because of the lightness of their tax burden. The regressive nature of almost all taxes worried nobody in authority until the nineteenth century, but political realities often reduced the effectiveness of the direct taxes. The Land Tax established in the 1690s was fixed in its assessment soon after, and as late as the nineteenth century the tax was paid upon rentals valued at the end of the seventeenth century.

The consequence of the English reluctance to be taxed was that the government was frequently in distress for money. Not all the expedients proposed by Tudor despots, Stuart monarchists or Parliamentarian representatives sufficed to make ends meet before the eighteenth century. Of course there were years after 1547 when government income exceeded expenditure, but they seem in retrospect to have been exceptional amid a long run of budget deficits. Even Elizabeth, who like her grandfather knew the value of money, found war or the danger of war too much for her financial resources. At the beginning of her reign her annual income barely exceeded £200,000. Her unwillingness to ask Parliament to vote subsidies approaching the taxable capacity of the nation kept her largely independent of the Commons, but forced a degree of parsimony upon her administration which other monarchs could not understand and would not imitate. Nevertheless before 1588 Burghley had amassed a war chest of £300,000, and Hawkins had supervised the construction of 25 modern or modernized warships in readiness for the awaited invasion by Spain. Elizabeth's credit stood high, and while Antwerp survived as an international money market her agent, Sir Thomas Gresham, could negotiate loans at interest rates more advantageous than those offered to any other crowned head in Europe. But Elizabeth did not live upon her credit, unlike her successors, even when the deficit became ominous in the 1590s. James I was as well served by financial agents as she, but the early Stuarts had largely exhausted the good will of all potential lenders by 1630, except those who dealt in tax-farming, through their profligacy and unsafeness. Charles I's 'fiscal experiments' in 1629–40, which compounded his unpopularity, are in themselves a measure of the depths to which his public credit had sunk. The pool of his creditors was dangerously shrunk to a band of financial opportunists.

The shaping powers of government were not strongly in evidence in the development of financial institutions before the Restoration. In constructing the pyramid of debt and credit which became a permanent feature of political economy after 1660 the role of government was more positive, but the whole panoply of 'Dutch' finance in England, the so-called Financial Revolution, was not ordered solely to service the increasing deficits of public administration. The needs of European governments for the sinews of war and justice had always put merchants on their mettle to devise suitable instruments of payment and credit, but in the seventeenth century the innovating role often passed to ministers. From Sir George Downing's 'order of payment' in 1665, which was a form of Treasury bill of credit, to the establishment of a sound sinking fund to service the National Debt, itself a concept new to the era, the fusion of mercantile credit and government finance in an institutional structure slowly emerged. The role of the Treasury, supplemented by the Bank of England but also by individual merchants or commercial syndicates, like the South Sea Company or Sir Sampson Gideon, took on a new importance in controlling national finances as the Commons acquired their supervisory powers over the government's financial affairs, and when war imposed new demands upon ministers, Parliament and people, 1689–1713.

The political basis of public credit had been transformed by the Glorious Revolution, which not only allowed a higher tax burden than had been envisaged since the last years of Elizabeth but made the many projects for banks and new instruments of credit much more plausible than in the 1660s and 1670s. A succession of determined and often able financial ministers, Edward Montagu, whose monument is the Bank of England, Sydney Godolphin and Robert Walpole did more than merely reorganize the fiscal system; they seized the initiative from merchant creditors. Hereafter the future lay with the small investor or annuitant whose funds the government was at pains to attract by presenting such security as could not be rivalled in private. The calm which surrounded so much eighteenth-century dealing in government stock was hard-won. The proliferation of bank schemes and lotteries in the 1690s was doomed to failure and the mania of 1711–20 was very disturbing to public confidence. Walpole made his national reputation by his breezy good sense in dealing with the wreckage of the South Sea Bubble, and in contrast with the comparable situation in France public credit emerged in the 1720s with no permanent damage. Indeed one of the remarkable features of the so-called Financial Revolution was the willingness of English, Scottish and Dutch investors to service the national debt. British public borrowing after the Bubble was one of the most important financial outlets for private savings in Europe. The Funds became at least as attractive as land, and many an eighteenth-century widow lived upon the dividends of a portfolio of public stocks.

THE PROFILE OF MERCANTILISM

The Mercantile State seems now largely to have been a myth of late nineteenth-century opponents of classical free-trade doctrines. Gustav Schmoller's description of mercantilism as a planned programme of 'state-making' (*Staatsbildung*) [1] may have been apt for a number of German states emerging from the chaos of the Thirty Years War, but the idea of a resolute and clear-sighted government forecasting the long-term consequences of planning in England is misleading. Before 1650 the interference of central government in economic affairs was per-

[1] G. Schmoller, *The Mercantile System and its Historical Significance* (Eng. trans. Macmillan, New York, 1896).

sistent but it depended upon traditional or pragmatic considerations—the medieval legacy of tempering the wind to the shorn lamb (policing markets, protecting the supply, price and quality of the necessaries of life, managing the diplomacy of foreign trade) and of unifying the institutions of economic activity into a national pattern: the emergency of war and international relations; the vested interests of individuals or groups whose opinions were as various as their sources of livelihood; the necessity (or inability) of compromise with Parliament for the Crown in its execution of acts of state; finally, the all-important problem of government finance as a motive of economic policy. It was with a mixture of traditional prerogative and shifting objectives that economic policy was formulated. After 1650, the emphasis changed, but even in the golden age of Adam Smith's mercantile system, the evidence of what was legislated reveals 'the influence neither of economists' theories nor ministers' long-term commercial policies, but simply of urgent fiscal needs . . . to pay for costly wars; tariffs were the response to these needs, rather than the implementation of a policy derived from [any] economic theories' (R. Davis). Even so, policy went beyond fiscalism; the same balancing act between factions inside or outside the counsels of state which had characterized Jacobean and Caroline economic policy was still practised a century or more later. The gathering momentum of economic liberalization, well in evidence before Adam Smith's *Wealth of Nations* was published, was frequently compromised by the self-seeking of the merchants who promoted it.

Nevertheless there was a body of ideas about the nature of economic forces current among merchants and officials. These ideas gained considerably in coherence in the 1620s and 1630s in England, under pressure of financial and commercial crisis, but the basic precepts were very ancient. Fundamental was the belief that foreign trade was inelastic, that while the portions of particular countries might increase or decline, the volume of world trade had little capacity for aggregate expansion. Whatever the theoretical justification for this assumption, it originated in the direct observation of merchants in medieval and post-medieval times when the difficulties of exploiting markets and defying competitors seemed inescapable. From it also developed the useful concept of a balance of trade between commercial regions. It has been suggested that this derived from the technique of double-entry book-keeping introduced into England from Italy in the sixteenth century, but earlier legislation and action reveal that the fact if not the thought of balancing trade was a working principle long before the Tudors. Thirdly, the emphasis upon treasure (precious metals), which so insulted the sense of early nineteenth-century economists, because it seemed to confound wealth with money, is so old—and by no means extirpated even now—as a necessary objective of commercial activity, that to use it even slightingly to define an economic theory is wholly misleading. Finally, another medieval belief—expressed by Aquinas— which stressed a clear commitment to economic self-sufficiency (autarky), not to destroy trade altogether but to keep out unnecessary commodities or foreign rivals, was a necessary concomitant of the theories of trade prevalent until the nineteenth century.

A milestone in the expression of these economic ideas in a coherent formula is the polemic literature of the Commonwealth faction which operated as a loose pressure-group under Protector Somerset in 1548–1550. The celebrated *Discourse of the Common Weal* (1549) contains the classic statement: 'We must alwaies take care that wee bie no more of strangers than we sell them . . . for so we sholde empoverishe our selves and enriche them.' If the commodity trade between two countries was out of balance, the difference must be made up of exports or imports of coin. The treasure thus gained or lost was useful, the author said, because precious metals are light to carry in relation to their value, go current everywhere and are easily divisible into coins or bars. Precious metals therefore simply formed instruments of exchange 'to measure all things by, most apt to be either carried far, or kept in store, or to receave [for] things whereof wee have aboundance . . .' This quite sophisticated view of bullion was certainly held by great merchants like Gresham and statesmen like Burghley, but probably not by a majority of mid-sixteenth-century Englishmen, who saw Spanish treasure as a desirable objective in itself and amassed gold, silver and jewellery for private gratification or public enrichment. A well-filled war chest was a major objective of state policy and many practical men saw that if the French or Spaniards could be made to pay out gold and silver in return for goods their power to make war was effectively diminished. Moreover, the close parallel between the *Discourse* and Thomas Mun's even more famous *England's Treasure by Fforaign Trade* should not lead us to connect the Commonwealth party to later pressure-groups. Somerset's gadflies were as likely to produce arguments attacking the commercialization of life as to justify the role of foreign trade. The pluralism of English 'government', as Sir Thomas Smith described it, left ample room for intellectual conflict whatever a handful of advanced thinkers at the centre of authority might have believed.

Thomas Mun's contribution to this ferment of ideas was to construct the conceptual framework in which traditional notions could be logically expressed. His work, probably written in 1622, but not published until 1664, arose out of crisis. To those who believe in mercantilism as a system, 1622 seems more significant than it does to those who emphasize the makeshifts of policy, since in that year the Privy Council, exercising the King's prerogative powers, appointed Commissions of Trade for the first time in order to suggest remedies for the depression. From this new kind of reliance upon experts ensued a furious debate among the men selected, Malynes, Misselden and Mun, which, on the face of it, was not very helpful. Malynes put forward the sixteenth-century view that England's currency was simply undervalued and that too much specie was flowing out. The solution was to control the rate of exchange. Misselden argued that it was the *coin* which was undervalued by comparison with the issues of other European mints. The solution was to raise the value of the silver coinage to prevent the international operation of Gresham's Law. Mun apparently began on the same track, but soon changed direction to resuscitate the theory of trade-flows. (Lionel Cranfield, whose position in the midst of affairs made him influential at Court, apparently held the same opinions.)

What Mun was at pains to demonstrate was the physical rather than monetary causes of the slump. In order to establish his case fully, he argued that what mattered was the annual casting of accounts, not the balance of individual regions of trade. Thus it was possible, though not necessarily desirable, to support an adverse balance with one country, provided that the total account was favourable. This was intended to undermine the bullionist view that any outflow of precious metals weakened the exporting country as it strengthened the receiving country, although the idea of the overall balance, inevitably at a period when statistics were inadequate, was slow to root itself in public sentiment. A great deal of ink was subsequently wasted in attacking or defending particular imbalances, with France, the Baltic or the Far East, until well into the eighteenth century. From Mun, however, it became commonplace to justify a preoccupation with trade balances by advocating policies of economic diversification in order to increase the range and quantity of exports and reduce the level of imports. The author of the *Discourse* had done just this, but two new elements in the situation by 1620–30 added to the consistency of the exposition. The Dutch had become such successful rivals, especially in the fishing and carrying trade, that the vigour of English hostility was much more thoroughgoing than the older doubts about the strength of French competition had been. To do down the Dutch was a pillar of English mercantilist thought from Mun to Defoe. The emphasis upon colonial production in the seventeenth century was only novel in the sense that English interest in sub-tropical plantations, once predatory, had recently become settled, again in the teeth of Dutch opposition. At least from Henry Robinson's *England's Safety in Trade's Increase* (1641), perhaps the ablest commercial tract before the Restoration, we find colonial expansion linked to the theme of national self-sufficiency. Colonies should supply materials which the mother country could not provide for itself, and in return should take temperate commodities and manufactures. From Mun and Robinson this body of ideas, commonplace or novel, was woven into the fabric which clothed economic literature for over a century. The question is whether the intellectual diversions of merchants really influenced policy, as they hoped.

The period from the Cokayne project to the outbreak of Civil War is conventionally taken as critical for the translation of economic ideas into acts of state. The relationship of economic planning to Stuart notions of absolutism is inescapable. The more personal the rule the greater the degree of interference. The 1622 Commission of Trade was transitory, but the active merchants, led by Mun, at least scotched the seductive proposal to rig the exchanges. In 1630, however, a permanent Commission of Trade under the Privy Council was set up, though its role was not clearly defined and its success elusive. Under the Commonwealth merchants came even more into the forefront of public debates, although the Protector's Trade Committee of 1655, with 70 members drawn from most branches of foreign trade and finance, was very unwieldy. At best these institutions can be seen as evidence of consultation between government and mercantile society; at worst as lobbies serving the narrow purpose of commercial *cliques* in imposing the 'sophistry [of men] who are always demanding a monopoly against their countrymen'.[1] Neither view is exactly true to life, but they fit the circumstances better than the portrait of a mercantile state in the seventeenth century. The years 1620–90 are part of a seamless web of government intervention, being neither a point of new departure nor an

[1] A. Smith, *The Wealth of Nations* (Everyman ed., Dent, 1910), vol. I, pages 436–7.

example of resolute economic nationalism to set anti-Stuart historians by the ears.

The driving forces of policy-making were diffuse, diverse and sometimes contradictory. The Crown possessed many prerogative powers, some immanent in the office of king, others granted or usurped to deal with particular needs. The early Tudors were especially successful in exercising their latent powers, the Stuarts much less so, but both justified their actions by precedents generally medieval. It is not possible to discuss every aspect of government intervention in economic affairs after 1500, but some things are so important that a selective treatment will serve both to illustrate the problems involved and to indicate the main areas of activity.

First is the extensive, misused and unpopular power to grant privileges by letters patent to individuals or to groups for a particular purpose. At its simplest this power resulted in the 'monopolies' which were so roundly attacked in Parliament and in the country from 1597 onwards. In origin monopolies as such were introduced from Italy in the mid-sixteenth century, but this was simply the application of old privileges to new ideas. In theory special dispensations for the regulation of trade monopolies could be used either to permit a man an exemption from statutory provisions, for example to export goods otherwise forbidden or to evade gild regulations, or to give sole rights of manufacturing or marketing particular commodities, salt or sugar for instance. The first kind was unpopular in Parliament because it threatened the authority of statute, and it was unpopular elsewhere for obvious commercial reasons. The second kind could be justified as protecting new inventions or fragile enterprise in difficult conditions. Most, however, were noxious and all too often resulted in the enrichment of courtiers or financial syndicates bent on exploiting the public by raising prices. They were not mourned when abolished by the Long Parliament.

But monopolies were the tip of a great iceberg. The same legal frame supported a superstructure of incorporations, from boroughs and gilds to trading, mining or drainage companies which were no less monopolistic but seldom encountered the same objections from the public. The common element was a privilege or franchise giving special advantages to the recipients as a group. The trading companies, whatever in detail their charters provided, all enjoyed exclusive rights to the trade of the regions they served. The Merchant Adventurers' monopoly of exporting undressed cloth across the Channel was frequently tampered with, but until 1689 they held on at least to some trace of their franchise. By 1603 all the regions of trade to which the English sailed were subject to company regulation, though the companies were not equally successful. At home the Mines Royal and Mineral and Battery Companies served the same purpose for the entrepreneurs, English and German, who sought to extract and process domestic resources of metals. The reconstruction of medieval gilds, the formation of the livery companies which increasingly came to dominate urban trade and urban politics performed a similar, though less overtly entrepreneurial, function in the regulation of the economy in the century after 1530. Company promotion continued along similar lines until the South Sea Bubble burst, after which commercial incorporations were prohibited by statute for over a century. Incorporation was not completely uniform in legal status and in practice was often merely the public sanction of established interests, but it belonged nevertheless to the same area of prerogative as the monopoly or the municipal franchise. In this sense it mattered not whether the company was regulated or joint-stock, for both depended for their powers upon a royal charter.

The effectiveness of official protection for the development of trade and industry cannot be assumed simply from the volume of incorporations or other supporting activity, since, apart from the obvious problems of enforcement in pre-industrial England, many franchises merely expressed the *status quo* or catered to the needs of wealthy merchants and speculators. George Unwin's belief that 'the feverish delusions of speculation and the selfish greed of monopoly [overshadowed] the triumph of honest enterprise',[1] has been challenged but not overthrown by subsequent research. This honest enterprise indeed usually produced its results without or in spite of government protection.

In the area of foreign trade the trading company which dominated conventional thinking from 1550 to 1670 played a useful organizing role. It was supported by government diplomacy in foreign affairs. The English negotiated a long series of commercial treaties from Henry VII's agreements with Denmark, Florence, Spain and Burgundy in 1490–6 to Macartney's Anglo-Russian treaty of 1765. The Crown had a duty to protect its subjects and an undisputed power to obtain trading benefits for English nationals by means of diplomacy whenever possible. There followed in the sixteenth century the beginnings of a consular service, in cities or states to which the English resorted, that by 1750 had

[1] C. Unwin, *Studies in Economic History* (Macmillan 1927), p. 177.

185

become a permanent and quite extensive department of government. Consuls were not always helpful to merchants, but there are few examples of gross inefficiency and self-seeking as in the French consular service. Even so, many merchants or commercial companies beyond the range of European diplomacy had to take greater responsibilities upon themselves. The 'factories' of the East India or Hudson's Bay Companies, for example, became more than mere depots of commerce, but political and military establishments of great potential significance. Although Henry VII seems to have possessed a fairly clear idea of commercial diversification in the formulation of his economic diplomacy, his efforts were premature. In general, however, treaties followed after a generation of commercial penetration into a new area of trade, and, combined with a policy of national or group exclusivity, bilateral agreements could be employed to encourage a positive readjustment of the balance of trade.

National exclusivity was crowned by the Navigation Acts of 1651–60, which lay at the foundation of colonial policy until the American Revolution. The Navigation Act and its corollary, the Staple Act of 1663, were intended to keep foreigners out of the English plantations. The Navigation Act required that all shipping to and from the colonies must be possessed by English (or colonial) subjects. The Staple Act listed commodities which must also be brought first to England before re-export in order to prevent direct trade between the colonials and their ultimate customers. The idea basically was to drive the Dutch out of the North American trade and to undermine the great entrepôt for tropical wares at Amsterdam. But the Navigation Act necessarily went further and incorporated older provisions for reserving English trade in general to English shipping, which dated back into the fourteenth century. The relative failure of earlier legislation was due to the strength of entrenched powers, especially of the Hanse, whose position had been guaranteed by special privileges in several English seaports, and of the Italians. The seventeenth-century Navigation Acts were necessarily supported by economic warfare against the Dutch and later the French, but English merchants were in a stronger position to carry their own trade in 1660 than they had been when Richard II or Henry VII attempted to protect their interests.

The three Anglo-Dutch wars of 1652–4, 1665–7 and 1672–4, followed by the intermittent but protracted struggle of the Dutch against the French, 1672–1713, undermined the economic prowess of the Republic.

By 1674 the Dutch had been driven out of North America and their wide-ranging aspirations in the Far East had been curtailed. Forty years later the dominance of Amsterdam had at least been dented. The Dutch decline of the eighteenth century was due not entirely to effective foreign competition, but also to internal weakness and excessive taxation. Much the same was true of France when, in the long series of dynastic wars before 1782, the struggle for mastery of North America and the East was refought in the context of European politics. The effects of war in England, in the century from 1689 to 1782, were almost always depressive in the short term, but many merchants were found among the vociferous advocates of aggressive policies. There was a kind of understanding between the City and Whitehall which reached its apogee in the Seven Years War, but this is not evidence of a commercial and imperialist conspiracy in British policy-making after the Restoration.

Much attention was paid, in legislation and ordinances, to growing demands for national self-sufficiency. Burghley expressed the conventional thought that the 'remedy [for imbalances of trade] is by all policies to abridge the use of such foreign commodities as be not necessary for us', which, as Lord Treasurer, he was well placed to implement. But the very considerable diversification of the English economy between 1550 and 1660 owed less to state planning than the avowals of ministers suggest. The growth of temperate industrial crops, hops, woad, weld, madder, hemp, flax, coleseed, like the introduction of new agricultural crops, owed more to working farmers and businessmen than to the agency of government. The relative cost of foreign supplies and the availability of soils suitable for rather exhausting crops were more important influences than the balance of trade. Indeed, government was necessarily rather irresolute before the 1670s because industrial cropping often reduced the food supply, and in dangerous years, 1594–7, 1619–31, or the 1650s, when a good deal of public advocacy of import-saving was expressed, poor harvests certainly diminished official enthusiasm for woad, cole or flax. Even though bounties upon corn production were offered to cereal growers after 1675, industrial crops were not so encouraged until the eighteenth century. From 1670 to 1700, indeed, official policy became ambiguous because of the growing supplies of dyestuffs, oil and fibres from colonial possessions in the subtropical zones. Tobacco-growing was banned in England in 1652, and the production of saffron, madder, weld and even woad declined gradually after the Restoration, while coleseed often became a fodder

187

crop. The Crown's manipulation of monopolies of course could help in the achievement of autarky. Well-known entrepreneurs, like the clothier Benedict Webb, obtained patents for inventions, using home-grown commodities, but he, and many similarly placed, found great difficulty in maintaining their rights against determined patent-breakers. Much the same was true of mineral production, despite the powerful monopolies of the joint-stock metal companies and the Newcastle Vend, although the government's determination to exploit England's mineral resources dated from Henry VIII's time and included some direct investment by Crown and Court in likely ventures. There is no evidence of direct state management of economic resources, such as one finds in mercantilist states on the Continent, only of participatory investment. Contrivances of doubtful utility were certainly adopted to enrich court favourites, especially between 1610 and 1640, which included ostensibly promotive joint-stock enterprises like the London Society of Soapboilers, and the cormorants who gathered around the Court in the last thirty years before the Civil War did very well out of the Crown's munificence.

SOCIAL WELFARE AND THE PROBLEM OF POVERTY

Before 1688 all governments avowed that the state rested upon an organic harmony between Crown and people living in mutual de-pendence. The instinct of Tudor and Stuart governments was deeply conservative, and their intention was to restore or to maintain the framework of social order which rising population and running inflation continuously threatened before the Civil War. Paternalism, inherent in medieval kingship, was intellectually justified by the advisers of Thomas Cromwell or Protector Somerset, who gave the initial stimulus to the debate upon welfare and social mediation by the state that still reverberated in the reign of George II. The transforming influence of economic forces was allowed to describe new patterns on the fabric of the approved social structure in the seventeenth century, when men began to distinguish between socially beneficial and deleterious changes. In practice, the necessary acts of state generally failed to match up with the theories or the plans, because ideal prescriptions were almost always unenforceable. After 1520, the chief preoccupation of the state became the problem of poverty. This was probably not the ground on which pre-industrial governments would have chosen to deploy the weapons of their social responsibility, but the evidence of disorder, underemployment and hunger could not be ignored. Even in its attempts to prevent idleness and starvation, the Tudor state, and its successors, was concerned with a great deal more than the mechanics of relief. Poor law policy in the three centuries before 1834 was informed by broad, if not always consistent, precepts of social order in which the responsibility of government for the well-being of those fit 'onelie to be ruled' was never quite buried in selfish motives.

The coincidence of the breach with Rome and two Tudor statutes concerning the poor in 1531 and 1536 is taken to represent the secularization of such religious affairs as charity with the Protestant reformation. Medieval societies had not required poor laws because of the emphasis upon alms-giving in the Catholic doctrine of good works and because local institutions such as monasteries and gilds both in villages and in urban crafts could cope with such problems as there were. This, however, is an oversimplification. Poverty in the thirteenth century was quite as bad as, and the suffering perhaps worse than, in the sixteenth. Private charity was certainly inadequate, and although we cannot judge the effectiveness of communitarian relief, it is unlikely to have been sufficient for the needs of the poor. After the Black Death the the government legislated against idleness and vagabondage. In 1501 this legislation was repeated, and the duty of punishing the sturdy beggars was entrusted to the justices of the peace. Thus many elements in the later poor laws had been foreshadowed before 1530. Moreover, in the sixteenth century a great many European states, Catholic or Protestant, autocratic or feudal, tried to provide a body of law to deal with their poor, since the problem was virtually universal. The Protestant ethic had little to do with the formulation of poor law policy. It is true that Protestants believed in discriminating charity, and especially in giving for educational purposes, so that the poor as such could hope for little in the way of direct relief from hard-line Protestants. There were of course comparatively few such in Tudor England, and the evidence of wills suggests that the medieval habit of leaving money or goods to the community, in some sense, continued until the early seventeenth century at least.

The 1531 Poor Law distinguished between the work-shy beggars and those unable to work, and entrusted the justices not only to have vagabonds whipped but also to license the impotent poor to beg. It was difficult to enforce, and was revised substantially in 1536, when it was first accepted that the state was responsible 'for the failures and victims of society'. Cromwell commissioned a detailed plan which was too far-reaching to be implemented, but the Act of 1536 embodied certain new principles—that the parish was responsible for collecting alms, employing the fit and relieving the needy. The penal clauses of necessity were kept and apparently much used, and the new emphasis upon parochial financing remained at the heart of all poor law policy until 1865. The Parliament in 1547 passed a savage Act in which the vagrants who were especially troublesome in the late 1540s were made liable to slavery. The Elizabethan Acts of 1563, 1572 and 1576 restored the old position and added the compulsory principle into the collection of poor relief. The 1572 Act also prescribed the methods of parochial collection, and that of 1576 introduced the idea of 'houses of correction' for those who would not work and of 'houses of industry' for those who would. In 1597–1601 two great codifying Acts incorporated all the useful precepts of earlier legislation and attempted to put administration on a systematic national basis.

Several English corporate towns, London, Norwich, York, Coventry, had anticipated the government by introducing their own regimes of poor relief to supplement or supersede private, ecclesiastical and gild charity. The towns, London in 1547, Norwich in 1549, first showed how the principles enunciated in Parliament could be made to work and how in practice the different categories of the needy could be treated. The detailed provisions of legislation from 1563 owed much to the municipal authorities of England. It is a mistake to assume that poverty was wholly urban, but the towns had to face up to problems of recurrent unemployment and massive immigration out of the countryside. From these experiments the position in 1597 and 1601 can be summarized as follows: parochial responsibility for the helpless, aged and sick, financed by a compulsory rate administered for the parish by elective overseers of the poor; unemployment to be relieved by the provision of tow, hemp, flax, yarn, etc., where appropriate; apprenticeship of young paupers, orphans, bastards, etc. at the cost of the parish; incorrigible rogues to be dealt with by the justices of the peace in such a way that they would be deterred from a useless life of vagrancy. The problems of administration proved to be complex and daunting, but the basic system remained in being for centuries. It seems repellent to us because it contained such a sternly religious abhorrence of idleness as well as a genuine vein of cruelty that its idea of welfare is lost upon a less stringent age. But S. T. Bindoff's comment remains true nevertheless: 'It was a notable beginning to a long journey; and an England which has just buried the unwept remains of the Poor Law may yet salute across the centuries that earlier England which cradled so long-lived and . . . so memorable a forerunner of National Insurance.' [1]

The history after 1601 is not a long slide into unimaginative impotence. The problems for the poor lost little of their severity in the seventeenth century. It is difficult to get any clear view of the amounts spent upon poor relief until the eighteenth century but it is evident that price-deflation and the slowing down of population growth after 1660 did not affect expenditure upon the poor. Eighteenth-century writers were practically unanimous in their opinion that the poor-rate had risen alarmingly since the Restoration. Various estimates of national expenditure in the late seventeenth century range from Arthur Moore's £632,000 in about 1690 to £840,000 in 1673 and £819,000 a decade or more later. None is very reliable. The parliamentary survey of 1776 produced a figure of £1,700,000 collected for maintaining the poor, which was profoundly shocking to contemporaries. Even though the figures for particular years may not represent trends, there can be no doubt of a general increase in the public outlay on the poor between 1600 and 1776. The reasons are complex, compounded in part of mismanagement and of much more generous notions about the welfare of the chargeable poor than in Elizabethan times. The eighteenth century appears repulsively hard-faced in its treatment of the poor, but the quality of the food given in workhouses before 1780, the clothing, medical care and similar needs, were often better than could be expected by the poor not in receipt of relief. To make matters worse for the ratepayers of many parishes was a kind of selective immigration, from village to town, from 'close' parish to 'open' parish, from inclosed to uninclosed village. Villages possessing surviving commons were inundated by the vagrant poor in search of squatters' rights, whilst the 'war on cottages', which reduced the population of so many 'close' parishes, also threw many families potentially chargeable into places less protected by the selfishness of rural property-owners. The worst excesses of increased poor-rates occurred in the towns and in comparatively few rural villages, noted for their squalor and overcrowding, in the eighteenth century. The problems in 1750–75, in other words, still resembled those of the Elizabethan period. Rural misery became worse after 1750, at least in the south of England, as wages once again

[1] S. Bindoff, *Tudor England* (Penguin 1950), p. 294.

signally failed to equal prices and because the industries which had underpinned the rural economies of Sussex, Devon, Wiltshire and East Anglia were unable to expand as rapidly as those in the north. That it was bad enough before 1750 is clear from the variety of men who studied the problem, from the lawyer Hale to the corrupt politician Arthur Moore, from the journalist Defoe to the philosopher Locke, and from the merchants Firmin, Cary, Child and Dunning to the clergy Josiah Tucker and John Howlett.

So much literary activity was inevitably translated into legislation. The chief developments after 1601 were the 1662 Settlement Act, which merely clarified the legal position of the pauper labourer; the 1697 Act which similarly provided enabling legislation for the use of certificates to allow labour mobility; and the 1723 Act which encouraged the founding of small workhouses and parochial work-making schemes. The 1662 Act was designed to keep wandering paupers out of places where there was 'the best stock, the largest commons and wastes and the most woods to burn and destroy'—to keep people and resources apart—and it empowered parish officers to remove people likely to become chargeable who could not claim a legal settlement in the place. The definition of settlement was modified from time to time, but for most poor men it meant the place where they were born. The 1697 Act admitted that some men must be allowed to move legally. The 1723 Act followed from a warm controversy on the merits of public work-making, which had decayed in country districts since 1601. The result was not especially encouraging, but in a pioneer scheme under the same Act, a number of Suffolk hundreds agreed to build joint workhouses for the parishes in their boundaries in 1756, which supplied the inspiration for a number of later schemes and for the 1834 New Poor Law.

In each case parliamentary sanction followed from local practices. Settlement was implicit in the parish system of the Tudors, and well before 1660 some places had begun to distinguish native-born from immigrant paupers in the giving of relief. Certification of travelling labourers was also widespread before 1697; and despite the frailty of almost all workhouse schemes, a good deal had been achieved by private act or by local initiative, particularly in the corporate towns, before 1723. Some examples, notably the workhouse at Bristol, were famous by the end of the seventeenth century. Bristol became a model for the elaborate work-and-welfare scheme of John Cary, who believed firmly in the public duty to provide employment for the able poor.

The diversity of local experiment testifies to the obsession of the period with the problem of poverty. It is less clear how effective the central government was in developing poor law policy. The influence exercised by the law over parochial administration was often very slight. Poor-rates, for instance, were only levied when necessary, and many parishes made no assessments till long after the law had made them compulsory. The settlement laws, too, had no serious influence upon labour migration. In 1788, for example, John Howlett noted that agricultural labourers 'ranged from parish to parish and from county to county unthinking of and undeterred by the law of settlement'. The law complicated the lives of people in disputed cases, but a glance at surviving constables' or overseers' accounts will indicate not only how much movement there was, but also that officials often connived at it. Local authorities also chose to farm out the maintenance of their poor to contractors, whose humanity varied enormously but who generally treated their charges less well than the parish officers, if only because their services were cheaper than direct management could hope to be. Even so, a good many of the English poor, not only those temporarily out of work, were relieved in their own homes because it seemed cheaper and more convenient to do so. Parishes frequently erected or purchased cottage accommodation for their poor families, and although the 'poors' cottages' often stood out as eyesores even in the squalid villages of pre-industrial England, they remain as examples of the long-standing commitment to social welfare. Quarter Sessions of the county justices retained a number of ambiguous powers over the poor throughout the seventeenth and eighteenth centuries. Some, like the indictment of employers and their servants for paying and receiving wages above the permitted maximum, or the licences to destroy cottages not supplied with four acres of ground, look strange and certainly could be repressive, but were intended to enforce different aspects of Tudor social policy. However important, however much it troubled the intellect, poor law policy was only part of a once-comprehensive programme of social organization, which like Banquo's ghost, still haunted the Augustan complacency of the generation of Defoe and Walpole.

As arbiter between conflicting social forces, central government itself appeared many times on the stage until the Civil War. The attitude to inclosure and depopulation has been discussed elsewhere, but it illustrates clearly the complex mixture of motives and opportunities out of which social policy was formed. The sequence of legislation after 1485 which sought to prevent or restrain inclosure, the investigations of official commissions of inquiry, and the actions of the prerogative courts and the Privy Council were less effective than governments hoped, but official attitudes changed slowly with public opinion, as it became clear that not all inclosure had the evil consequences so often ascribed to it. The simple rule that large-scale inclosure was destructive was rarely applied in the second phase of public disquiet, 1590–1640. Two reasons for this official antagonism were grounded in practical needs. The first was the Tudor need for a sturdy peasantry as the backbone of defence; the second, their recognition that employment revolved around the fundamental occupation of agriculture. The ultimate attitude, however, was often less pragmatic.

Tudor and early Stuart concern for the poor and for the small self-employed men rested upon notions of the Commonwealth, and indeed upon the political and social undesirability of change when it threatened the inherited structure of society. The great statute, known to us as the Statute of Artificers, enacted in 1563, attempted to fix the structure at the bottom of society in an earlier mould. Its immediate causes were perhaps epidemic disease and short-term labour shortage, but inflation, poverty and disorder in general were in the minds of the Parliament that framed the Act. The remedy in 1563 bore clear marks of resemblance to the 1351 Statute of Labourers, but it was more comprehensive. Men were required to stay both in the locality and in the work into which they were born. This was to be achieved by control of labour mobility, by enforcing craft apprenticeship even in agriculture, by preventing idleness and by empowering the justices of the peace to fix maximum wages. In a sense, the statute embodied a system of priorities for employment. The official mind wished to exalt agriculture and handicrafts and to deprecate commerce and the professions, because the first seemed to be basically productive, the others almost parasitical. Yet men displayed the awkward tendency to move out of the arduous and unremunerative trades of agriculture and manufacturing to the least exhausting and most rewarding of the livelihoods open to them. The ideal of the husbandman clearly inspired the statute, but more practically what was prescribed was the systematic adoption of ancient regulations and local customs in the national arena. Thus, seven-year apprenticeship, already customary in some leading gilds, was proposed as a national standard, and the rules for wage regulation were based on numerous precedents going back as far as 1351.

The results of the statute were mixed. Inasmuch as it sprang from short-term disorders, the problem sorted itself out without undue interference. But apprenticeship and wage-regulations remained features at national or county level throughout the seventeenth century. The Quarter Sessions of various counties continued to fix or amend the maximum wages for different occupational categories even into the second third of the eighteenth century, although detailed arrangements and energetic enforcement declined steadily after the Revolution of 1688. The authorities set *maximum* wages because it was their intention to prevent job mobility and migration in search of better wages. This lends weight to the view that the Statute was born in a period of acute shortage of manpower. Subsequent flurries of action in the counties perhaps also reflected sudden disturbances in the labour market which tended to force wages upwards. It is, however, still uncertain how obedient employers were to official regulation. After 1680, wages apparently exceeded the rate appointed in a large number of cases; before 1680, the position is less clear, for the relatively few cases brought before the courts can be interpreted either way, to indicate general acquiescence or too widespread evasion. Probably wage-fixing had little direct relevance in a period when wage-rates tended to remain stable or to lag behind prices. When manpower was adequate or surplus to demand, the consensus of employers and magistrates was general. When economic forces applied pressure to the labour market employers seem to have been indifferent to the voice of authority, and to have done what economic sense dictated.

FURTHER READING

M. Ashley *Financial and Commercial Policy under the Cromwellian Protectorate* (O.U.P., 1934, Cass., 1962).

R. Ashton *The Crown and the Money Market 1603–40* (O.U.P., 1960).

D. C. Coleman, ed. *Revision in Mercantilism* (Methuen, 1972).

P. G. M. Dickson *The Financial Revolution* (Macmillan 1967).

F. C. Dietz *English Public Finance 1558–1641* (New York, 1932).

D. Marshall *The English Poor in the Eighteenth Century* (2nd edn Routledge, 1969).

D. Marshall 'The Old Poor Law, 1662–1795', *Economic History Review*, VIII, 1937.

P. Slack and P. Clark, eds. *Crisis and Order in English Towns 1500–1750* (Routledge, 1972).

B. Supple *Commercial Crisis and Change in England 1600–42* (C.U.P., 1959).

S. T. Bindoff 'The Making of the Statute of Artificers', Bindoff, Hurstfield and Williams, eds., *Elizabethan Government and Society* (Athlone Press, 1961).

M. Blaug 'Economic Theory and Economic History in Great Britain, 1650–1776', *Past and Present*, 28, 1964.

R. Davis 'The rise of Protection in England 1668–1786', *Economic History Review*, XIX, 1966.

L. Stone 'State Control in Sixteenth Century England', *Economic History Review*, XVII, 1947.

C. Wilson 'Mercantilism: Some Vicissitudes of an Idea', *Economic History Review*, X, 1957.

C. Wilson 'The Other Face of Mercantilism', *Trans. Royal Historical Society*, Fifth series, IX, 1959.

D. M. Woodward 'The Assessment of Wages by Justices of the Peace, 1563–1814', *Local Historian*, VIII, 1969.

8

The Structure of Demand: Income and Expenditure

INCOME

According to Gregory King in 1688 average per capita income in England and Wales amounted to £8 or £9 per annum. By 1760 the figure had apparently risen to around £12–£13, which is equivalent to the figure in modern underdeveloped nations such as Brazil and Mexico, and far ahead of most third world countries. Before 1688 data are scarce and obscure. Even King's figures have required adjustment by Phyllis Deane.[1] But for western Europe as a whole, Simon Kuznets has estimated the possible (i.e. the maximum) increment of output per head from 1500 to 1750 at about 0·2 per cent per annum (65 per cent compound).[2] Since population only grew at about 0·17 per cent, some increase in per capita income must have occurred, if only slightly. But Kuznets used population data for England which were obviously too low. English population more than doubled and may almost have trebled between 1500 and 1750, yet all the circumstantial evidence suggests that England enjoyed an increase of income at least as great as the rest of Europe. But his figures are difficult to test. As a starting point, the lay subsidy returns of 1522–5 (i.e. the direct parliamentary tax on non-ecclesiastical estates—land, goods, wages, etc.) may with reservations provide a basis for calculating per capita income for comparison. Unfortunately, men paid the tax only upon the category of their in-

[1] P. Deane, 'The Implications of Early National Estimates for Measurement of Long-term Income Growth in U.K.', *Econ. Development and Cultural Change*, IV, 1955, p. 12.

[2] S. Kuznets, 'Capital Formation in Modern Economic Growth', *Third International Conference of Economic History*, Munich, 1965, p. 30.

come—from land, 'goods' or wages—which yielded most to the Treasury, and underassessment or incomplete returns create additional difficulties. What they suggest, however, is interesting. Those who paid on wage incomes assessed at £1 per annum averaged 20–30 per cent in the countryside and 40–50 per cent in the towns. In addition, between 5 and 20 per cent were exempt on account of poverty. Thus if we assume that 40 per cent of the employable population were wage-earners or excused poor and that about 5 per cent paid taxes upon assessments in excess of £20, the mean taxable income per taxpayer falls between £4 and £5. Hence, per capita income somewhat less than 30 shillings in the 1520s is the best approximation possible, and it lends support to the view that income growth more than kept pace with inflation and outstripped the sheer increase in population in the pre-industrial period.

King's plan also reveals a good deal of the social distribution of income and wealth, which can be interpreted either on the basis of income-groups (Table III) or of social orders (Table IV). In Table III the calculations of income per family give a clearer idea of what was available for consumption in each unit, although King's 'families' included domestic servants wherever appropriate. It is less of an abstraction than income per capita, though how King arrived at his data is still uncertain (he probably guessed). Table III also foreshortens the discrepancy of income between the richest (£3,000 p.a.) and poorest families (£6.10.0), but it does suggest how important was the middle ground between £38 and £200 p.a. Divided into what the nineteenth century called classes (Table IV) the configuration is similar, and remained surprisingly constant as late as 1803. Colquhoun's classification in 1803 added at least a score of new groupings to King's social plan, but this diversified and did not reorder the structure of English society.

The subsidy returns of 1522–5 similarly suggest a degree of long-run stability in the wealth-structure of English society. Briefly the top five per cent of the taxable population possessed at least half of the wealth assessed in the subsidy, while the lowest 60 per cent (excluding the exempt poor) shared about 20 per cent. The proposition that the income inequality of English society may have narrowed between 1436–1520 and 1688–1803 is possible, but the effect must have been very slight. It is true nevertheless that the composition, or the sources, of income, changed between the sixteenth and eighteenth centuries,

Table III. *Income Distribution in England in 1688*

Family Incomes (p.a.)	Number of Persons	Number of Families	Percent. of Total Number of Persons	Percent. of Total Number of Families	Aggregate Income £'000	Percentage of Aggregate Income per Group
over £200	209,520	23,586	4	2	8,285·8	18·6
£70–£199	440,000	65,000	8	5	7,360	16·5
£38–£69	2,026,000	412,000	37	30	19,400	43·5
£14–£37	1,495,000	449,000	27	33	6,950	15·6
under £14	1,330,000	400,000	24	30	2,600	5·8
Totals	5,500,520	1,349,586	100	100	44,596	100·0

SOURCE: M. W. Thomas, ed. *A Survey of English Economic History* (Blackie, 1957), p. 216, from Gregory King.

Table IV. *Social Distribution of Income in 1688 and 1803*

1688

	Number of Families	Percent. of Families	Aggregate Income £'000	Percentage of all Income
Aristocracy	16,586	1·2	6,285·8	14·1
Middle Ranks	435,000	31·7	26,340	59·0
Lower Orders	919,000	67·1	12,010	26·9
Totals	1,370,586	100·0	44,635·8	100·0

1803

	Number of Families	Percent. of Families	Aggregate Income £'000	Percentage of all Income
Aristocracy	27,204	1·4	32,801	15·7
Middle Ranks	634,640	31·6	124,633	59·4
Lower Orders	1,346,479	67·0	52,096	24·9
Totals	2,008,323	100·0	209,530	100·0

SOURCE: H. Perkin, *The Origins of Modern English Society, 1780–1880* (Routledge, 1969), pp. 20–1, from Gregory King and Patrick Colquhoun.

Note: The 1688 data in Tables III & IV are derived from different versions of King's original computations.

but few new types of income were introduced before the nineteenth century.

The principal sources of income before 1700 were rents, tithes, profits, fees, annuities, interest upon loans, pensions, wages and salaries.

The diversity is misleading. Property-incomes probably took the lion's share. In addition, interest upon mortgages, annuities, pensions, largely depended upon capital in land or buildings, until such times as equally secure and high-yielding investments to produce income were available. Dividends upon stocks became significant as a component of national income after the Restoration, especially after 1690. The economic primacy of landed income was certainly challenged by other forms of investment, as many prudent contemporaries realized, early in the eighteenth century, although it was not overtaken for some generations because land retained its social prestige. According to Gregory King's estimates, principal factor incomes in 1688 were arranged as follows: rents 27 per cent (£13,000,000); wages and salaries 36 per cent (£17,000,000); profits, fees, interest, etc., 30 per cent (£14,700,000). It is not unreasonable to believe that the proportions retained a similar order of magnitude throughout the early modern period, though the share of rent declined in the century after 1650.

It is probable that the full-blood *rentier* even among the aristocracy was essentially a product of two or three generations around 1700, for the majority of great landowners before 1660 obtained much income—perhaps three or four times as much as from rent—from the direct exploitation of their estates by farming, forestry, mining or manufactures. Even in 1750 many gentry were still in some sense entrepreneurs upon their own properties. Nevertheless, what happened to rents was of major importance for the English plutarchy. Everything suggests that land rents outstripped the general price rise from 1500 to 1750, rising from 5*d.*–6*d.* an acre to 4*s.*–5*s.* by 1630, about 6*s.* in 1688 and 9*s.*–12*s.* by 1750. The wealthiest *rentier* in 1524 perhaps received about £3,000 a year; in 1750 a handful of great aristocrats enjoyed rent-rolls in excess of £30,000. Part of this increase occurred as a result of changes in tenures. The concept of rent as payment for hiring land became more rational, and 'rack-renting' based on monetary valuations was often substituted for customary rents or leaseholds for life. At the same time the landlord's attitude to the upkeep of his estate became more responsible, and after 1650–1700 the relationship between lord and tenant became more recognizably businesslike.

After rents the most significant and widespread component of income was the return upon capital employed in business and agriculture. Profits, however, are notoriously difficult to discover across the whole spectrum of business activity. Gross returns may have exceeded 25–35 per cent in different branches of enterprise, but they were apparently exceptional. The median rate of profit in the whole period was nearer 10 per cent even in comparatively large concerns, and profits as little as 3 or 6 per cent were not uncommon for many independent merchants in the seventeenth century. Charles Davenant set the average rate of return on the commodity trade in the 1690s at 6 per cent. In the Wiltshire woollen industry in 1739 the net profit upon products was said to be 3 per cent. By contrast, early in the seventeenth century the profit on the production cost of woollen cloth was worked out at 13 per cent, and the return on capital in shipping averaged about 20 per cent after 1660. In all, commercial profits do not seem to have been excessive, and indeed, frequently were not greater than the prevailing rate of interest on loans. As Richard Grassby has written, 'Had the rising bourgeoisie [before 1700] depended upon trading profits, they really would have taken centuries to arrive.' [1] On the other hand, contemporary opinion was unanimous in charging middlemen with taking excess profits on their trade, and there is something to be said for the view that both wholesalers and retailers took a large 'mark-up' on the goods they handled. But since the daily turnover of small businessmen was often so little, the rate of their profit is immaterial. In 1614, for example, a small shopkeeper was assumed to turn over 5 shillings a day altogether, and if this fell to 2s. 6d. a day, 'he would be ill able to pay his rent or keep open his shop windowe'. Again, a London tavern in 1639 was reckoned to sell only 212 quarts of wine a day, at an average profit of 3½d. per quart, when the innkeepers' overheads were among the highest of small businessmen. For agriculture the evidence appears to indicate a higher rate of return, but this is very doubtful if not incredible. Robert Loder's profits in 1612–20 actually exceeded his annual expenditure, and upon two 'hypothetical' farms, one a mixed holding of 30 acres and another a 500-acre sheep farm, in 1600–2 the rate of profit upon the outlay works out at 36 per cent and 14 per cent respectively.[2] These figures almost certainly reflect potential returns rather than average levels of profit. The evidence of a massive profit inflation enriching the business community and supplying the means for capitalist develop-at the expense of labour and the landowners finds little support in

[1] R. Grassby, 'The Rate of Profit in the Seventeenth Century', *English Historical Review*, LXXXIII, 1969, p. 733.
[2] P. H. Bowden, 'Agricultural Prices, Farm Profits and Rents', J. Thirsk ed. *Agrarian History of England and Wales*, IV (C.U.P., 1967), pp. 650 ff.

surviving business accounts of the period. The men who waxed fat as merchants almost invariably accumulated their fortunes from diverse sources—landowning, money-lending, judicious marriage, as well as trade or manufacturing. A large income from trade required the employment of a large circulating capital, or an especially daring and successful enterprise which could frequently not be repeated.

In many respects, fees, the profits of office, and interest on money invested offered the highest returns for ambitious capitalists. Few economic enterprises were as profitable as legal offices such as protho-notary of the Common Pleas or even the chief justiceship, and many of the great fortunes laid out in founding families of greater gentry from Sir Christopher Wray to Sir Matthew Lamb were first accumulated in the Law. Lord Keeper Bacon, who received £1,200 a year for his office and at least £1,600 a year in fees, was able to spend almost £1,400 a year on land during twenty years around 1600. A handful of very remunerative legal and administrative offices before 1640 therefore enriched a number of new men like Bacon or Brownlow and augmented the already substantial incomes of some nobles and gentlemen. Aylmer calculated the total yearly receipts of government offices in 1640 as £500,000.[1] No wonder offices were jealously guarded by families in possession and that the pressure built up, as in France, for sale of offices among the opulent. 'Place' by 1700 was a species of property like many parliamentary seats, and even some offices of state like the Paymaster-ship of the forces were so valuable that certain families attempted to monopolize them. The first Duke of Chandos reputedly made £600,000 out of the profits of office in 1705–13.

At a lower level the fee-taking professions so expanded before 1688 that a small but clearly important 'professional middle class' is apparent in King's plan. Lawyers proliferated everywhere after 1530; medicine became a profession during the next two centuries, and a host of new agencies or consultancies developed to service commercial and social life, brokers, insurance agents, estate stewards and so forth. Although many doctors or lawyers were in fact paid in kind for their services, a fee of about £2 a visit or £30–£100 for a major transaction—drawing up a settlement, proving a will, preparing a suit—were not uncommon by 1700. Professional men not only lived but thrived upon their emolu-ments. On the other hand a major trade in offices or professional

[1] G. E. Aylmer, 'Office-holding as a Factor in English History, 1625–42', *History*, N.S. 44, 1959, p. 236.

appointments did not develop after 1650 despite the evidence of ample savings in search of fruitful investment. The explanation is that the expansion of the stock market diverted funds into blind investment. In fact, by 1750 a considerable body of fundholders or annuitants depending upon stock-holdings had grown up in England. Many were great landowners or entrepreneurs who preferred to place their private fortunes in stocks rather than land. The Duke of Chandos had £250,000 in stock and £80,000 in mortgages at his death, and in 1766 the land-owner-ironmaster, Lord Foley, died with £500,000 in stock. The bulk of investors, however, lived upon the interest or dividends of £100–£500 of debenture capital. The mixed portfolio, often composed of landed property, mortgages, other loans as well as stocks and/or shares, was not uncommon at the time. It was more secure and perhaps yielded a higher income than a single type of investment.

Wages and salaries also contributed substantially to national income in the pre-industrial period. In 1524 about 7 per cent of tax assessments were paid on wages and perhaps one-quarter to one-third of the population were classified as wage-earners. In some towns half the employable population was dependent upon wages in the sixteenth century. Both number and proportion substantially increased in the next century, so that by 1750 wage-labour, regular or casual, had become a major component in the economy of both town and country. Wage-labourers' families perhaps already accounted for 44 per cent of all families in Joseph Massie's plan of English social structure in 1760. Salaries of course were already closely connected with fee incomes in the professional status-groups. The salariat consisted of curates, land stewards, house stewards, schoolmasters (at least ushers) and other superior functionaries of the household or of institutions. Except that many of them already belonged in the middle ranks of society (both by status and wealth) they were collectively unimportant before the nineteenth century.

On the general subject of earnings, the trend between 1500 and 1750 does not suggest that any major long-run improvement took place before the Industrial Revolution. Wage-rates are misleading because they often disguise broad regional variations and also because we usually lack evidence sufficient to estimate unemployment. Earnings, which were often eked out by the provision of some food or other perquisites, by piece-work or even by overtime at higher rates of pay, probably seldom equalled or excelled the maximum possible at stated rates of payment. Winter and summer rates, at least in agriculture or in trades dependent upon the length of daylight, were often different, but it does not follow that winter unemployment was always higher than in summer. Recurrent booms and slumps also affected manufacturing wage-incomes, and a crisis like that of the early 1620s could result in a wholesale lay-off of journeymen in the export trades. Even so, the simple picture is bleak enough. It is not unlikely that real wages declined by 50–60 per cent between 1500–20 and 1590–1630, not least because many of the commodities most wanted for immediate consumption by the poor rose in price faster than the average for all goods. The improvement between 1660 and 1760 was substantial but not spectacular, and even in the 'smiling forties' of the eighteenth century real wages had almost certainly not regained the level of the late fifteenth century. By 1750 things were nevertheless notably better than in 1600. The lower rate of price inflation after 1670, a slow-down of population growth before 1750, the accumulation of agricultural (especially food) surpluses, and the revival of economic activity, especially in labour-intensive trades, were responsible for the increment to real wages before 1750 upon which an extension of the domestic market for consumer goods down to the labouring poor has been predicated by writers such as A. H. John and E. L. Jones.[1] The fact remains, however, that most wage-incomes were often at or below subsistence level except in periods exceptionally favourable to such uncertain incomes. Wages, moreover, reflected local supplies of labour, not the prevailing price of food and clothing. The further away from London one went the lower the rate was. It was only at the beginning of the eighteenth century that any spurt in areas away from the south-east of England can be discerned, and not until after 1750 that Lancashire or Yorkshire, Durham or Staffordshire overtook the 'metropolitan zone' of the south in the payment of their wage labour force.

Underemployment was certainly endemic, though its effects are difficult to estimate. For some quite large agricultural estates, however, 'regular' men were often employed on only about 150–200 days in the year towards the end of the period. What happened to the poor when wage labour was not available is unclear, but the inexorable growth of poor relief may be part of the explanation. It is possible that smallholdings contributed to the income of the labouring poor, but, even in

[1] See E. L. Jones, ed., *Agriculture and Economic Growth in England 1650–1815* (Methuen, 1967).

the countryside, there were already numerous landless families before 1580 without livestock or farm goods of any kind. At least for the towns we know how important pawnbrokers had become by 1746 in eking out the liquidity of the working poor between pay days or in periods of intermittent work, because in that year Parliament was moved to investigate their functions and activities. Temporary loans were already indispensable in 'tiding over' the casually employed in times of idleness.

By 1650–1750, England not only possessed a complex, interlocking social structure but a diverse composition of personal incomes. The great disparity of wealth was doubtless founded upon a severely unequal distribution of property, but property incomes were already extensively supplemented by money receipts from other kinds of capital investment or professional skills which eventually weakened the grip of landowning plutarchy upon the helm of society and government, but which before 1750 fundamentally provided a support, by diversification of the factor incomes of the well-to-do, for the social institutions of the pre-industrial community.

CONSUMPTION

The pattern of consumption in the pre-industrial economy was affected most by the enlargement and expansion of the market for consumer goods. Demand was stimulated by the range of choice available and by the diffusion of ideas about comfort, prestige and fashion. The growth of the market was not entirely a matter of middle- and upper-income demand, for even the poor were affected in a small degree before 1700, and much more so in the early eighteenth century. It was the rich who set the tone and who, by their consumption, created the framework of production and trade in consumption goods, but, without a deepening of demand, the trade in luxuries and semi-luxuries, in durables and semi-durables, and in 'inessential' foodstuffs would have remained so closely bound to patrician appetites—as in the high Middle Ages—that no room for growth would have been possible. We know how the market changed, but we cannot yet measure the real impact of domestic demand upon economic development before the nineteenth century. Viewed as determinants of demand, the changing organization of the domestic market, new patterns of conspicuous consumption, the rage for 'aping one's betters', and the introduction of new or improved products into the market after 1500, contributed notably to reorient the

205

economic structure of English society in preparation for Whitbread, Arkwright and Wedgwood in the generation after 1750.

Although the whole development of internal trade is important, the particular influence of London and the growth of a provincial and local network of distribution based on the mercer stand out. The substitution of regular retail outlets for intermittent fairs, and the fact that by 1650 small-town mercers and even village shopkeepers could supply most if not all the goods available for consumption on the seventeenth-century market wrought profound changes in the consumer behaviour of the provincial well-to-do, who had probably learned the new habits from direct or indirect contact with London. London as a centre of government, culture and refined education had become so popular among the 'political nation', and even among the yeomanry and professional 'middle class', that governments before the Civil War attempted to reverse the trend by ordinance. London, like Paris, became not only the depot of the foreign import trade, but the headquarters of most of the luxury trades producing metalware, silks, hosiery, furniture, tapestry, glass, paper, especially for gentry and rich merchants of the metropolis. So much had London become the centre of conspicuous consumption in England by 1600 that social reformers, bewailing the decline of hospitality in great houses, accused the capital of bleeding the country white, as rents and profits made elsewhere were consumed in London trumpery. To a much lesser extent, however, could the same charges be levelled at provincial centres, Bristol, York or Norwich, and later at the resorts of the wealthy at leisure, Tunbridge, Bath or Scarborough, where seasonal concentrations of gentry families brought together a similar body of innkeepers, retailers or craftsmen.

Conspicuous consumption was closely related to the greater variety of social and political life of the comparatively wealthy in the early modern period. It had many fantastic and wasteful aspects, but it was sanctioned increasingly by public opinion on the grounds, first, that it was a duty of the rich to consume the products or services of the labouring classes, and secondly that 'living up to one's income' had an important ceremonial function in an age of changing social landmarks. Ridicule of the rustic squire without benefit of London speech or London manners was a common theme of literature from Ben Jonson to Oliver Goldsmith. In order to encompass upward social mobility in an organic framework of authority, behaviour became a measure of social acceptability. Needless to say exorbitant ostentation also became an end in itself. The splendour of palaces such as Knole, Burghley, Chatsworth or Woburn and the life-style of grandees like Sir Francis|Willoughby, the Earl of Leicester, Sir Robert Walpole and the Duke of Newcastle were extravagant on any rational interpretation of consumption. Walpole, for example, laid out £90,000 in personal expenditure in four years from 1714 to 1718. In practice, such excess possessed a logic of its own. Eighteenth-century magnates lived like great princes, using the objects and punctilio by which contemporary society measured prestige, just as late medieval notables revealed their power in the number of their retainers and clients. The Duke of Buckingham, on Twelfth Night in 1508, entertained no less than 459 people under his roof, and in 1521 the Percy household numbered 166 individuals. The great household remained a little universe, and the income which supported it had many calls upon it, for wages, benefactions, pensions, etc., which inhibited the harmful consequences of conspicuous consumption. In addition, the emphasis upon display at the top of society filtered downwards through the gentry to the rural 'middle class' and the bourgeoisie. This rage for emulation was especially fruitful in the seventeenth century, but it affected every generation after the fourteenth century and touched most aspects of everyday life. Thus, servants were infected with the virus, at least from William Harrison's time (1570s), when they spurned bran bread and straw bedding in preference for more palatable or more comfortable items. Ralph Verney's servants (in the mid-seventeenth century), Luce and Besse, demanded meat: 'I know noe English maids will ever bee content . . . to fare as thes [French] servants fare . . .' And if we can believe Defoe or Swift, the domestic servant of the eighteenth century had come to have a very advanced notion of his material worth. It is likely that one channel through which demand for refined foods and comforts trickled down to the lower orders was the gentleman's servant.

Such 'aping' took many forms. One was straight imitation. Fashion, at least in clothes and furnishing, was already a major determinant of demand by 1500. But fashion in dress was also influenced by new customs, the sexual differentiation of costume from the late Middle Ages, the habit of wearing different clothes indoors and out, encouraged by improved house insulation and the extension of coal fires. The dress of the rich, however, passed through successive stages dominated by Italian, Spanish, French or Dutch fashions, in apparel, furniture and house design, which were essentially imitative. Moreover, we can perhaps discern a kind of primitive 'consumerism' in the frequent stylistic changes introduced into the worsted industry of East Anglia throughout the period, which were like ripples on the surface of the great transformation from broadcloth to the new draperies. Emulation was always allied to the diffusion of changed cultural standards and ideas of comfort. When yeomen and merchants adopted the dress, diet, housing and entertainment of the gentry, purchasing power rather than lineage became the chief impulse of 'high spending'. This diffusion was reflected in the great rebuilding of provincial England after 1500. The correlation of new construction and the acquisition of household durables like tapestries, new furniture and utensils is very close. By the end of our period, England not only possessed a transformed stock of houses, but the interior fittings of even poor men's houses had become more ample and more comfortable than at the beginning. The great discrepancies of wealth meant that the life of different social groups remained distinct, but it may not be unreasonable to divide England into two nations, of those already infected by the desire for consumption goods at least partly gratified, and of those—still the majority in 1688— not yet touched by the great changes going on above them. One consequence of long-run price trends after 1662, and especially in the golden mid-century, 1730–55, was to bring more of the population into the market for consumption goods.

Windfall improvements in purchasing power, especially among social groups with little margin to spare, must have provided some incentive for greater and more varied consumption. Equally important, however, in teasing out spending were increases in the range of suitable goods offered at prices which made them attractive to middle- or lower-rank pockets. Any amount of envy would not serve to stimulate imitation unless the price mechanism were flexible enough to comprehend newly created appetites. It was precisely because luxury goods became cheaper and more plentiful that a large-scale trade in them developed after the fifteenth century. But neither price nor emulation can fully explain changes in the structure of demand up to the Industrial Revolution. Another ingredient in the mixture is the fact that so many of the products on the consumer market were new or were improvements upon medieval commodities. Beer, most of the fruit and vegetables with which we are now familiar, rice, sugar, tea, coffee, cocoa, revolutionized dietary habits among the well-to-do before 1680, and were spreading down the social scale well before 1750. Tobacco had become the consolation of poor as well as rich by 1700, and spirits, even though gin had a brief but disreputable heyday as a popular narcotic, had more permanently formed a distinct feature of domestic consumption from the mid-seventeenth century. Although important changes in wine consumption occurred during the period, the wine trade in 1700 probably had no more and no less impact upon English taste than in 1300.

Apart from food, 'new' products included glass, pewterware, Delft pottery, cutlery, worsteds, stuffs, soap, The inventories suggest that such products were widely in use in farmers' and similar town households by the mid-eighteenth century, and they were readily purchasable in local shops by 1670–1720 if not before. But the expanding market is most clearly displayed in the history of tobacco, sugar and tea consumption. Consumption of sugar, for example, had already reached an annual per capita level of 4 lb. by 1740, and tea, which in the eighteenth century was fast becoming a staple of British diet, showed an even more spectacular rise, from about 20,000 lb. in the 1690s to at least 5,000,000 lb. in 1760. That these products had reached the poor was noted by critics like Arthur Young who believed them expensive fads which undermined health and strength. In the century after 1680, moreover, a running battle between domestic textile manufacturers and importers of Indian calicoes indicates how deep the demand for lightweight textiles had become. About 1700 perhaps three-quarters of the output of Norwich stuffs was already consumed at home. Imported calicoes were valued at about £400,000 p.a. in the first half of the eighteenth century.

For the million or so families at the foot of King's social ladder and their kind in earlier generations, the business of spending was still simple. The problem was to find enough to acquire necessary food and shelter. The inelasticity of wage-rates and the marginal surpluses enjoyed by subsistence food producers meant that the poor as a body were especially sensitive to the effects of inflation, because so much of their income was devoted to essential consumption. Per capita expenditure on food and drink in 1688 equalled 45 per cent of total personal expenditure, but the poor consumed at least 70 per cent of what they received in foodstuffs and probably had done for centuries. The impression of constancy, however, is deceptive. Thorold Rogers discerned a 'golden age' for the labourer in England between 1380 and 1510.[1] Thereafter it was not an unrelieved downward slope, for there were several plateaux of stable prices. The depths were plumbed

[1] J. Thorold Rogers, *Six Centuries of Work and Wages* (1887, rep. by Allen & Unwin, 1949), pp. 326 ff.

between 1590 and 1630 and after 1660 the trace of real wages turned upward again for about a century. Rogers calculated the purchasing power of wages, expressed in terms of three qtrs. of wheat, three of malt and two of oatmeal, to illustrate the downhill run. In 1495 a skilled man could earn them in 10 weeks, in 1533 in 15 weeks, in 1562 in 32 weeks, in 1593 in 40 weeks, in 1610 in 43 weeks and the same in 1651. An unskilled labourer could obtain the same food in 1495 in 15 weeks, but a whole year's work was insufficient in 1651. Conditions improved in the next century, but even in the mid-1740s it took several weeks longer for both skilled and unskilled to earn the same quantity of grains than in 1495.

But this long view is hardly relevant to ordinary life, for men seldom make comparisons longer than a decade, a lifetime or at most two generations. They adjust to inflation. How else could they have survived such a deterioration in living standards? Harvest fluctuations were more portentous than 'secular trends' in everyday life. A really critical collapse of living standards occurred precisely when the food supply is known to have been in acute shortage, in the early 1550s, in the 1590s and 1650s for instance. Then, even the small farmers and petty tradesmen were reduced to hardship, to famine stuffs like pease-meal, brank (buckwheat), acorns, beechmast and even sawdust.

Between the extremes of hunger and plenty there was at least a little room for changes in the pattern of consumption among the poor. We should expect a low income elasticity for staple foods, but an unforetold improvement in the disposable income of a family often resulted, for a time, in a substantial increase in the consumption of all foods. Even the backward-sloping demand curve for bread—as incomes rise so more expensive foodstuffs are substituted for bread—needs adjustment, because bread was not a homogeneous commodity at the time. Thus bread was a good indicator of social class and regional prosperity in the sixteenth century. The poor had to make do with what the local soil provided, except in the larger towns, and rye, barley, oatmeal, maslin (rye and wheat mixed), and peasemeal were used as well as wheat for local bread-making until the nineteenth century. But the trend already begun by 1570 was for standardization, based on maslin or wheat alone. Gregory King computed that wheat accounted for 38 per cent, rye for 27 per cent, barley for 19 per cent and oats for 16 per cent of English bread grain. Seventy years later (1764) the number of people fed by wheat was 63 per cent of the population, rye 15 per cent, barley

12 per cent and oats 10 per cent, and in the south and south-east wheat had almost completely triumphed over the rest. The change can hardly have been a matter of cost, for wheat prices moved in sympathy with those of other grains before 1750. In addition to rising expectations after the hardships of 1647–62, the increased cost of fuel, which had already resulted in a decline in home baking away from the coal fields before 1700, encouraged the expansion of retail bakers in rural England. At the same time the palatability of coarse bread was reduced as the preparation of stews and pottages declined in seventeenth- and eighteenth-century England, since rye or barley bread was much improved by soaking. By the 1650s bread and cheese had become the mainstay of many poor households as the consumption of meat declined. When conditions improved, the habit of eating white bread was too ingrained to be reversed.

Although the diet of the poor had declined in both variety and energy value by 1650 to the lowest point since the Black Death, recovery was fairly rapid. By 1700 opinion was unanimous that the English labourer was better fed, better clothed and more self-confident than any of his contemporaries on the Continent. Again this was a respite before another deluge of hardship and high prices at the end of the eighteenth century, but as an interval it was of sufficient moment to affect the whole pattern of domestic demand in Britain. The deceleration of inflation growth was significant for the downward extension of the consumer market in England, although the especially favourable conjunction of 1730–50 perhaps opened a new dimension to the patterns of large-scale consumption in precipitating the Industrial Revolution in Britain.

On the other hand, additional consumer spending was not necessarily the way in which the labouring poor would elect to lay out the margin which accrued to them from a rise in real wages. A potent alternative was leisure, especially when the range of choice among consumables was limited. The obsession with workmen's laziness around 1700 suggests that the educated population at least knew how the choice then was being made. The efforts of Protestant reformers to reduce the number, and increase religious observance, of holy days after 1550 at least halved the days on which men rested from toil, but did not necessarily result in any greater application to work. Time-keeping and organized work discipline were creations of a later age, for when so much was done as outwork or by the piece, erratic behaviour was commonplace. The tempo of work was interrupted by many incidents, by bouts of excessively hard labour, followed by exhaustion, by idleness, bad weather and heavy drinking. 'The most lazy, diligent people in the world' observed such unofficial holidays as Saint Monday, following the excesses of the weekend. Working families were imbued with the habits of taking leisure whenever they could afford to do so. Hence the mer-cantilist belief in 'bread-line' wages was justified as the only effective means of work discipline. It was but slowly modified by awareness of the need to encourage consumer spending among labourers, by paying higher wages in order to improve productivity.

If the poor opted for increased leisure, the well-to-do felt similar constraints upon consumption and saving by the need to give. Private philanthropy in all its forms was one of the most important elements in the distribution of incomes or accumulated wealth. Whether it was more important than public transfers through local rates is difficult to say, but, as Professor W. K. Jordan has demonstrated, the volume of charitable donation from 1480 to 1660 was enormous.[1] Such philan-thropy varied from mere alms-giving, through the provision of pensions, loan funds and preacherships, to the endowment of chapels, bede-houses, hospitals, schools, colleges, etc. In London, Bristol and eight other counties no less than £3,000,000 was donated between 1480 and 1660, four-fifths in the form of capital endowments. Over one-third was for poor relief and over one-quarter for educational purposes. The peak was reached in the years 1610–40, and the greatest philanthropists as a group were the merchants who contributed about half of the total sum in Jordan's sample. At the same time much was given out of income for pensions or poor relief, or in support of a socially useful enterprise like a preachership, a school or an almshouse. Many great landed estates set aside up to 10 per cent of gross income for philanthropic purposes, and on many great Church estates the obligation to fund pensions, donations or benefactions was often much greater. Private giving was as much enjoined upon Protestants who rejected the doctrine of salvation by good works as upon Catholics, but the emphasis shifted from alms-giving and religious offerings to the encouragement of self-betterment by the pro-vision of educational or rehabilitative endowments. Even so, mere relief continued to play a significant part in the impulse for giving after 1560.

Thus there were obvious limits to what a man could or would spend upon direct consumption for himself, even if he had the money available

[1] W. K. Jordan, *Philanthropy in England*, 1480–1660 (Allen & Unwin, 1959), chap. VII.

for his own gratification. We have so far discussed both income and consumption in terms of money. It is clear, however, that almost every household received a good deal in kind, either as production for direct consumption or by barter or payment in goods. Even wage labourers might expect part of their earnings in food or accommodation, while the nobility and gentry fed their households at least in part from their own estates. The use of money, as the dominant medium of exchange, had been spreading down the social scale slowly since the high Middle Ages, and in the two centuries between 1550 and 1750 the 'cash nexus' had obtruded itself more and more into daily life even in the countryside. While the two segments of society most obviously dependent upon the market before 1750 were the rich, who had a considerable cash surplus on top of all their commitments, and the urban poor, we have to assume that several nations of Englishmen co-existed between the top and bottom layers of the pyramid. Geographical differences in aggregate wealth, population and consumption persisted, with little fundamental change, from the fourteenth to the eighteenth centuries. Moreover it is not certain that the gap between the luxurious and the frugal effectively narrowed between 1500 and 1750, but in so mobile a society the barriers established by economic isolation, by traditional attitudes to the maintenance of social apartness through outward display, by the use of money, were rapidly breaking down. The social diffusion of ideas about desired living standards was well in train between 1450 and 1750, even though the will so often outran the deed.

SAVING

The capacity to save is essential for any society preparing for industrialization. But the need to save is axiomatic in any society. Violent fluctuations of output and employment in the pre-industrial world compelled prudent men to lay by some part of their receipts in good years to support them in bad. In an agrarian community, moreover, the importance of the seedcorn or the breeding stock was obvious to everyone. But for development, the stock of capital must by definition be increased, and one of the chief problems was how to tease out savings beyond mere replacement capital into further investment. The temptation to hoard was strong in peasant societies, for gold and silver were palpable symbols of wealth and security, and without strong counter-attractions, the stocking in the mattress continued to serve European peasants as savings banks. The bullionist confusion of specie

213

with wealth remained deep-seated even in the merchant community until after 1750, so that the *embourgeoisement* of society did not necessarily result in any significant dishoarding into investment. Saving indeed may reflect productive capital formation only to a very limited extent, for even Gregory King included, in his category of 'actual stock', items like plate, coin, jewellery and furniture which modern economists reject as reproducible capital. But these items were roughly equivalent to live-stock in King's estimates of national capital.

According to King net savings over consumption in 1688 averaged 4·2 per cent of income. By 1695, with depression, war and taxes, the English were 'dissaving' to the tune of 11s. 0d. per head. If King was right, the English were saving less per head in 1688 than either the Dutch (11·4 per cent) or the French (5·6 per cent). Yet savings for in-vestment were much more widely available in England than in France by 1700–50, which implies not higher incomes in the upper reaches of society but different preferences in the deployment of savings. A good deal of investment in England was productively 'dead' before 1750; in France the percentage must have been notably greater. The English at least employed the mechanism of credit as an outlet for their savings, even in peasant communities, and perhaps had done so for centuries. Money-lending was a relatively simple, and at the village level, safe and reliable way of employing cash surpluses. It has been suggested that by 1650 rural credit was widely diffused through the community. From the evidence of probate inventories, many if not all villagers and townsmen apparently lent their surpluses out to their neighbours, relatives and fellow-workmen. Widows and single folk, who frequently used legacies or the proceeds of dispersal sales as loans, were especially important as sources of local credit. Between 10 and 20 per cent of the aggregate valuations of a sample of inventories, 1660–1720, was in the form of loan capital or sales credit. It is probable that the existence of local 'money markets' of this kind was significant for the development of a specific capital market, not least because a good deal of the money had always been lent on mortgage or bond of debt, which rather resembled a debenture. At any rate, the quantity of cash in hand when the inven-tories were drawn was usually quite small, so that preference for liquidity was not strongly marked even in English peasant communities.

Money-lending was perhaps the main channel through which savings were dishoarded outside the great towns before 1700. The influence of changes in the rate of interest upon investment remains complicated. A major problem is the relationship between rates of interest and the articulation of local money markets, not least because many loans were apparently not charged with interest at all. For commercial or other large-scale transactions the rate of interest was important, since quite early in the eighteenth century some men were already comparing the returns to be expected from land and from secure, interest-bearing investments such as Bank or East India stock. John Locke opposed the proposals of merchants like Sir Josiah Child for a reduction of the official maximum rate of interest because lower interest rates could well have increased hoarding and destroyed the long term purpose of the merchants themselves. 'I averr', said Sir Dudley North, 'that high Interest will bring money out from Hoards . . . into Trade, when low Interest will keep it back'. Yet the secular fall of interest rates, from 10 per cent before 1650 to 4–5 per cent in 1750, belied Locke and North. It was of course realized that fixed interest rates were often evaded because risks varied widely. But the downward trend of prevailing rates reflected, first, the increasing number of 'low-risk' investments available to lenders, and secondly, the growing volume of savings which were attracted into the money market.

CAPITAL FORMATION

Since one man's savings were often transferred to another merely to maintain his consumption or liquidity, the specific problem of reproducible capital formation requires separate treatment. An analysis of King's data suggests that about 3–4 per cent of national income was devoted to domestic investment in 1688. The rate of total capital accumulation was about 5–6 per cent, although the effects of war in 1689–97 were apparently so severe that the national capital had fallen by 10 per cent by 1698. About half the stock of capital was in buildings and about one-third in goods and inventories employed in trade and industry. King guessed, but not wildly, that investment had been increasing at 1 to 1·5 per cent a year since 1600, and that the annual increase of 'stocks' had risen from £1,300,000 in 1670 to its peak of £2,400,000 in 1688. It is possible to conjecture that 'reproducible' capital grew at about 3 per cent per annum during the seventeenth century. Now since no development economist will accept that a rate of annual investment below 5–6 per cent will promote industrialization, the centuries before 1700 hardly seem a fertile ground for development. As a rule, industrialization is said to sustain itself when the rate of investment rises from 5 per cent or less to 10 per cent or more, but this is probably based too much upon extravagant expectations of capital needs before the age of the railway and the large-scale factory. More modest increments of capital could produce quite adequate results before 1830.

The importance of new housing before 1700 has already been mentioned. The Great Rebuilding depended for its vitality upon both social diffusion and geographical extension through time, but for southern and midland England the main 'vernacular' phase was concentrated in the period 1570–1640, which was followed by a later period of expansion after 1740. A modest farmhouse cost £5–20 before 1530; by 1640 the cost had risen to £40–50; and mid-eighteenth century farmhouses cost between £50 and £250 depending upon specification and materials. Great houses often cost fantastic sums—Redgrave £8,000, Audley End £90,000, Hatfield £40,000, Eastbury £140,000—but a respectable gentleman's seat in the later seventeenth century could be built for about £2,000. It is possible to discern a rhythm of activity even in conspicuous investment, with peaks in about 1510–40, 1570–1630 and 1690–1730. Town building was equally active before 1700, partly because urbanization, especially of London, was so important, and partly because fire damage caused so much urban destruction. King suggested that one-quarter of the English population in 1688 lived in 'towns'. If so, the *proportion* had probably almost doubled since the 1520s. The social overheads of town growth, sewers, paving, water supply, were obviously less burdensome than in the nineteenth century, although conduits, schools, churches, chapels, even town halls were constructed in considerable numbers, by private benefaction, public subscription or at corporate expense. For the infrastructure of urban life there was clearly no shortage of capital by the seventeenth century. Rebuilding after fire was accomplished quickly and competently. The Great Fire of London reputedly cost at least £8,000,000, yet by 1670 most private building had been effectively restored.

If we leave aside residential and cultural construction, social capital formation before 1750 was strictly limited. The new transport network of turnpikes and waterways was in the making before Metcalfe and Brindley, but the capital costs are difficult to estimate. Expenditure upon roads may have amounted to £50,000 a year around 1700, much of it raised by the rates and laid out in inefficient public labour, and the cost of waterway improvement between 1600 and 1750 probably did not exceed £500,000 all told. Inclosure and reclamation fit into the same category. Only guesswork could establish the cost of reclaiming or converting perhaps 3,000,000 acres before 1750. The important point, however, is that piecemeal inclosure, but not the larger fenland undertakings, was encompassed by landowners or farmers, in the same way as their rural house-building, without a long-run strain upon their resources. Public ventures in the Fens may have required as large an investment as the rest of pre-parliamentary inclosure put together.

As for agriculture in general, fixed capital, other than the cost of the land itself and of inclosure, was less important than working capital, upon which the farmer's annual profits and the landlord's rent depended. Landlords' responsibility for maintaining their plant was a duty lightly borne before 1750. New farm building on some estates probably dated far back into the seventeenth century, though it is surprising how often farmers continued to take the initiative in promoting new work. The greatest impulse came after the Restoration, in periods of low producers' prices (1665–90 and 1730–50) when owners desiring to keep their tenants offered inducements of new buildings. In the long run, however, the landlord's gross income devoted to investment and maintenance in agriculture seldom exceeded 5 per cent a year—almost the same as the landlord's capital formation in the Middle Ages. The planned farmstead, the estate cottage and the network of drains and fences belong essentially to the era after 1750, despite the precocity of certain estates in different parts of the country. But this overlooks the contribution of tenants in financing as well as initiating capital installations and of the still numerous class of owner-occupiers, whose farmyards, to judge from their inventories, were at least serviceable by the seventeenth century. As for the volume of working capital, little can be said beyond referring to the discussion of agricultural change in Chapter Three. New equipment like waggons or rollers increased the arable farmer's need for capital, but technology changed slowly before the nineteenth century, and the bulk of the farmer's capital was taken up in livestock and seedcorn.

It was the accumulation of such working capital, by inheritance, reinvestment or borrowing, which drove the wheels of agricultural progress. Falling profit margins after 1660 perhaps induced a greater investment in better livestock, more fertilizers, new crops, etc., in order to increase output or to spread risks, although the process of development had begun earlier. Dual occupations, so widespread in rural areas, also affected capital accumulation, particularly by allowing transfers into, or out of, agriculture. The most persistent flow was out of farming, and many small-to-medium commercial or industrial undertakings owed their success to capital derived from the land. Thereby a classic test of economic development was passed—the creation and investment of surpluses generated in agriculture transferred into different and generally more productive economic activities. An immeasurable but certainly modest increase of investment in agriculture transformed the food supply of England by 1750, created additional surpluses to encourage expansion in linked sectors, and finally laid the foundations upon which industrialization as a whole was constructed.

Circulating capital was no less dominant in industrial and commercial investment. The average businessman could expect to hold stock-in-trade three or four times greater than the value of his fixed capital. Ironworks, collieries, watermills, alumhouses, glassworks, required heavier investment in plant, but even the great Ambrose Crowley in 1728 possessed fixed capital of £12,000 beside stocks worth £93,000. A large furnace or colliery perhaps cost £200–£500 to install before 1560, £1,000–£2,000 in the early seventeenth century and over £5,000 by 1750. 'Investment in machinery and millwork in quantities to show up effectively in national statistics did not occur until well into the nineteenth century' (Pollard). In the iron industry, for instance, only 43 blast furnaces, 29 forges and about 20 slitting mills were installed from 1660 to 1760. On the other hand, the adoption of the stocking-frame, the Saxony spinning wheel, iron or copper vats and pans, pumps or presses of many kinds, imposed new capital demands upon industrial entrepreneurs during the period from 1550 to 1750. Many businesses, however, were still conducted from a room in the entrepreneur's dwelling house; and not a few self-employed masters possessed only the tools of their trade when they died, having neither stocks nor plant. It was the merchants or manufacturers who drove a substantial wholesale business, who were the real capitalists of European industry before 1750. Stock-in-trade was so important because, with output slow or irregular, the distribution network imposed demands upon merchants' capital which only accumulated inventories of raw or finished produce could satisfy.

'Market financing' in a modern sense played little part in the provision of this productive capital. Joint-stock companies were not unimportant, at least in overseas trade, and from the second half of the seventeenth century blind investment in East India or Bank stock laid

the foundations of the later capital market. But the long train of investment disasters from the 1560s to 1720 was a serious drawback to the
development of company financing. In 1688, joint-stock capital was
valued at only £630,000, of which 80 per cent was in three overseas
trading companies. The close connection between company finance
and government finance—the need to service the national debt—and
with it the growth of safety-seeking investment was significant more for
social and political development than for industrialization, since the
London capital market and its institutions did not evolve to underpin
industrial or commercial enterprise. Earlier joint-stock undertakings
were, for the most part, associations of gentry or businessmen who knew
the implications of the enterprise even if they were not fully active in it.
Except for the East India Company in 1600, the capital upon which
they floated was small. The Mineral and Battery Company for instance
was set up in 1566 with only £1,752 of share capital.

The circle of 'high risk' investors, small and close-knit before 1600,
widened somewhat in the seventeenth century, but was never very
extensive. Most of the capital not ploughed back from profits was raised
upon credit, but by borrowing of a personal and direct kind. Ambrose
Crowley typically obtained a good deal of his capital for specific
industrial projects in the north-east from a variety of local lenders, and
usually in small sums. Since credit was personal, diverse measures had
often to be taken to secure sufficient investment by entrepreneurs.
Formal partnerships set up to provide share capital, which were not
protected by joint stocks or limited liability, were supplemented as
required by borrowing upon mortgage, bond or promissory note and
even by the manipulation of sales credit in order to maintain the
entrepreneur's liquidity. The history of the period is strewn with
projects which failed for want of capital, but creditworthy merchants or
entrepreneurs sedom found it difficult for long to obtain private loan
capital by the seventeenth century. The deep-seated habit of lending
cash surpluses in English society doubtless helped to transfer funds into
productive enterprises, but certain changes in the legal status of
mortgage or other loans were required before a clearly distinguishable
'capital' market (except in land) could develop. This was achieved by
the later seventeenth century, and in the hands of local attorneys or
money-scriveners, a provincial 'capital market' serving the needs of
particular regions was fashioned, independent of London or the growth
of country banking. It may be too much to say that the Industrial

Revolution was founded upon credit, but without the English willingness to lend, without the appropriate mechanism of credit and without its local or group-centred orientation, many an active entrepreneur would have been hard pressed to stay in business in the seventeenth or eighteenth centuries.

FURTHER READING

J. C. Burnett   *The History of the Cost of Living* (Penguin, 1969).

M. Campbell   *The English Yeoman, 1600–40* (Yale University Press, New Haven, 1940).

J. Drummond and A. Wilbraham   *The Englishman's Food* (2nd ed. Cape 1957).

G. E. Mingay   *English Landed Society in the Eighteenth Century* (Routledge, 1963).

S. Pollard and D. Crossley   *The Wealth of Britain* (Batsford, 1968).

L. Stone   *The Crisis of the Aristocracy* (O.U.P., 1967, abridged edn).

B. Anderson   'Money and the Structure of Credit in the Eighteenth Century', *Business History*, XII, 1970.

B. Anderson   'Provincial Aspects of the Financial Revolution in England', *Business History*, XI, 1969.

P. Deane   'Capital Formation in Britain before the Railway Age', and

S. Pollard   'Fixed Capital in the Industrial Revolution in Britain', both in F. Crouzet, ed. *Capital Formation in the Industrial Revolution* (Methuen, 1972).

R. B. Grassby   'Personal Wealth of Business Community in Seventeenth-Century England', *Economic History Review*, XXIII, 1970.

R. B. Grassby   'The Rate of Profit in Seventeenth-Century England', *English Historical Review*, 84, 1969.

B. A. Holderness   'The Structure of Rural Credit in Europe before the Nineteenth Century', *Agricultural History Review* (1976) (forthcoming).

W. G. Hoskins   'The Great Rebuilding of Rural England, 1540–1640', *Past and Present*, 4, 1953.

A. H. John   'The Course of Agricultural Change 1660–1760', L. S. Pressnell, ed. *Studies in the Industrial Revolution* (Athlone Press, 1960).

E. H. Phelps Brown and S. V. Hopkins   'Six Centuries of the Price of Consumables', *Economica*, XXIII, 1956.

9

Conclusion

In this book I have attempted to describe the extent and direction of social and economic change in England between the fifteenth and eighteenth centuries. 'Change', in this context, is rather an old-fashioned term, for which most modern economists and economic historians would now substitute 'development' or 'growth'. The process of development has indeed become so much a major preoccupation of Western economics and politics that the European past is repeatedly studied for lessons apt for policy-making or for prophecy. Development studies, therefore, have not only become a distinctive branch of economics and sociology in this century, but the dialogue between historians and social scientists, seeking evidence for their hypotheses, has also proved both instructive and, in prospect, quite fruitful. What is meant by industrialization: why Britain should have experienced an Industrial Revolution before its potential rivals: and, even more importantly, how industrial growth was achieved between 1750 and 1870, are questions that are still unresolved, however many attempts have been made since Arnold Toynbee's series of seminal lectures at Oxford in the 1880s first opened the case for studying *recent* economic history.

The answers, if they are ever to be found, will doubtless provide the insights necessary for us to discern an outstanding, if not overriding, line in the process of human development—the logic of economic growth. In the last few years, distinguished economists and economic historians, whose research interests have chiefly centred upon recent times, have fixed their eyes on the long view of Western economic development,[1] and this trend toward generalization may well continue,

[1] See, for example, J. R. Hicks, *A Theory of Economic History* (O.U.P. 1969); D. C. North and R. B. Thomas, *The Rise of the Western World* (C.U.P. 1973); W. W. Rostow,

partly no doubt as a counter-offensive against the Marxian dialectic of history. But, as Arthur Lewis has written, 'Every economist goes through a phase where he is dissatisfied with the deductive basis of economic theory, and feels sure that a much better insight into economic processes could be obtained by studying the facts of history. The instinct is sound yet the enthusiasms of the phase seldom survive any serious attempt to get to grips with the facts of history.' [1] Nevertheless, standard textbooks of development economics, like those of Bernard Higgins or R. T. Gill, contain chapters of 'history' in which the authors deal particularly with the breakthrough from the traditional semi-stagnant world of priests and peasants, craftsmen and bureaucrats, which so resembles a large part of the contemporary underdeveloped world, to one in which economic growth and the fertilizing effects of change have become normal. For example, Professor Higgins observes that, 'The acceleration of economic development in Europe after 1500 ... culminated in the industrial revolution ... [and] has been labeled "the rise of capitalism".' [2] But most of these expositions of the universal framework of economic development do not, and probably cannot, integrate their sketches of history with the hard cases of poverty, backwardness and social rigidity upon which the fieldwork or planning skills of the authors have been deployed in practice.

The lessons of history still remain confused and confusing. We shall mislead ourselves if, in distilling from the medley of natural scents the essence of distinctive social epochs in past time, we fail to recognize that pre-industrial Europe, and to an even greater extent pre-industrial England, were *sui generis*. England's uniqueness, in particular, is confirmed, both by comparison with rival European states, and from the analysis of the precise means by which each industrialized state in turn achieved its own industrial revolution in the nineteenth and twentieth centuries. A mixture of influences, some imported from outside, others the product of internal forces, is in each case peculiar and distinctive, and it should cause no surprise that economists have largely been disappointed in history. Professor Lewis has even gone so far as to doubt

---

How it All Began (McGraw-Hill, New York, 1975); R. M. Hartwell, *The Industrial Revolution and Economic Growth* (Methuen, 1971), ch. 2.

[1] W. A. Lewis, *The Theory of Economic Growth* (Allen and Unwin, 1955), p. 15.

[2] B. Higgins, *Economic Development: Principles, Problems and Politics* (Constable, 1958), p. 161.

the relevance of history for economic theory: '. . . the "facts" which would interest the theorist are not what happened but why it happened; and while history may record what happened, it is seldom able to record why it happened.'[1] Such a cold douche is no doubt salutary, but it is unnecessarily defeatist. We now know far more about the sources of industrialization after a hundred years of historical research into the 'facts' which have been turned up by assiduous digging, than we should have obtained from purely theoretical projections of development. This, however, never sanctions any attempt to produce general laws of economic growth, for history is not, and never has been, a predictive social science. The uneasy alliance between analysis and prophecy is well illustrated in the various sociological explanations of entrepreneurial psychology which are rooted in and have ramified out of Max Weber's identification of the spirit of capitalism with the acceptance of new ethical values in the sixteenth century. But why should the balance between social forces, religious and political morality and economic motives achieved during certain centuries of tension in Western Europe be appropriate as a principle of economic development in totally different conditions? The search for a common denominator in conducting dynamic social change has produced an immense literature, but except for emphasizing the contrast between developed and undeveloped economies in their social organization, the results have not been very convincing.[2] The problem, which itself is a comment upon historical studies in early modern European history, is to distinguish the economic motive, which may well be inherent in all societies in which exchange is commonplace, from the dynamic influence of successful innovation in economic life. Many historians and social scientists, in a very apt cliché, have missed the wood for the trees.

The history of the period from 1500 to 1750 may therefore throw comparatively little light on the intractable problems of modern 'underdevelopment', but its power to attract historians and social theorists remains undimmed. Themes such as the 'rise of capitalism', the 'expansion of Europe', the 'growth of the nation state', the 'era of social revolutions' etc., recur so much in the explanation of economic develop-

[1] W. A. Lewis, *op. cit.*, p. 15.
[2] See especially the collaborative works edited by B. F. Hoselitz and W. E. Moore, *Industrialization and Society* (Mouton, 1960), and P. Kilby, *Entrepreneurship and Economic Development* (Free Press, New York, 1971) for the best attempts at both interpretation and comparison in a difficult subject.

ment that the coincidence of a 'new' polity in early modern England—
the conventional association of Tudors and Stuarts in a unitary period
of study—with a cluster of significant economic changes, nowadays often
described as 'pre-industrial', is readily intelligible. But most modern
historians are inclined to doubt the importance of dates such as 1485 or
1529 in marking a significant turning-point in social, economic or
political history. The pre-industrial economy certainly originated well
before the Battle of Bosworth or Henry VIII's breach with Rome, just
as the accession of George III or Hargreaves' invention of the spinning
jenny in 1768, at the other end of the period, were not in themselves
important events in the transition of the economy from pre-industrial
to industrial 'maturity'. The years from 1500 to 1750 are justified
almost solely as an historian's convenience. But, as F. J. Fisher has
noted, the strongly marked character of medieval historiography, with
its special techniques of research and interpretation, and the increased
statistical bias of recent economic historians who enjoy a much greater
stock of useful economic data in the eighteenth and nineteenth centuries,
create essentially artificial barriers.[1] As a result, early modern economic
history in England has often suffered from the lack of rapport between
specialists whose particular interests at different times would reveal
many parallels and common elements in the structure of the economy
across the centuries. On the other hand, there is much to be said for
describing the whole period from about the time of the Black Death to
the Industrial Revolution as a distinct phase of development which it
may be justified to name as 'pre-industrial', thus ignoring the claims of
Columbus, Alberti, Machiavelli, or Luther as the founding father of a
new epoch of economic and social history.

In fact, the word 'pre-industrial' has so far been used without
analysis and without due acknowledgment of its relatively recent
coinage. As such the word is ambiguous, in spite of its currency among
social scientists, since it may even now refer *either* to the whole expanse
of history before mankind was transformed by the effects of industrialization (in reality, before the nineteenth century), *or* merely to a segment
of that time preceding the Industrial Revolution, in which some of the
necessary *preconditions* of industrialization were already active in
working changes in the structure of the economy. The former inflection
of meaning is much too sweeping to be useful, for the western European

[1] F. J. Fisher, 'The Sixteenth and Seventeenth Centuries. The Dark Ages in English
Economic History', *Economica*, XXIV, 1957, pp. 1–18.

economy (of which the English was a part) underwent so many structural modifications—often described as the 'stages of development'—between the ninth and the nineteenth centuries that no single concept or term will suffice for the passage of time before 1750–1850. It is probably best to consider 'pre-industrial' as a transcription of the German '*vorindustriell*', which has generally been employed to describe that stage in European history between the decay of the manorial system of agricultural production and indirect consumption or the decline of household manufacturing as a system of self-sufficiency and the adoption of power-driven machinery and factory organization. The pre-industrial economy was organized around a mode of production and distribution, with a complicated division of labour that was centred upon the great merchant and the rentier landlord, the commercial farmer and the dependent craftsman, which in effect bridged the gorge between the Fall of Feudalism and the Industrial Revolution. Its convenience in describing what is ostensibly an Age of Transition must not blind us to its artificial character. When all is duly said, the adjective 'pre-industrial' relates essentially to an economic epoch, which resembles the pupal stage in the life of an insect awaiting its metamorphosis into an adult. It is moreover a word coloured by hindsight. Without experience of an industrial revolution no historian could formulate the concept of a 'pre-industrial' economy, and almost all historians and economists therefore look for the potentialities or pitfalls, drawbacks or precipitants of industrialization in their interpretation of that part of the past which contained the foothills leading up to their chosen historical watershed. This is a necessary preoccupation and one which is generally fruitful, but it may nevertheless distort the evidence of economic and social changes in an attempt to fit them into the image of linear growth.

Defining words in abstract is a distinctly arid exercise, and the character of a 'pre-industrial economy' will only emerge if it is fleshed out by the details of what we understand by the term. If 'pre-industrial' is to have a positive significance for historical scholarship in England, the leading elements in each man's interpretation will have to be spelled out. For my part the principal features of the pre-industrial economy in England can be summarized as follows:

(i) The economy possessed a dynamic which absorbed and transmuted the variety of fluctuations and changes which repeatedly perturbed the surface of economic life before 1750;

(ii) it also contained a high degree of specialization in the production of goods and services, from which occurred a corresponding elaboration of the system of distribution;

(iii) as a result, the fraction of the population primarily dependent upon agriculture, already small in 1600 by comparison with many third-world countries today, continued to decline in the next 150 years;

(iv) agriculture, moreover, existed in a state of symbiosis with industry in the countryside, an especially significant feature of industrial organization all over western Europe in the period;

(v) government interference in economic affairs, whether for purposes of promotion or exaction, was never so rigid or pervasive as to inhibit growth, and was, as a rule, responsive to the needs and ambitions of those elements in the social order which bore the charge of economic diversification;

(vi) despite a substantial and important increase in the size of the tertiary (or service) sector of the English economy before 1750, the population contained comparatively few genuinely idle or 'useless' individuals like drones in the beehive;

(vii) by good fortune, the allocation of utilizable resources, of land, minerals and other raw materials, water and wind-power, easy communications, as well as of labour, was particularly favourable for development.

The dynamism of the pre-industrial economy is still disputed, chiefly because of the controversies which have embraced the 'discovery' of industrial revolutions with suspicious frequency in the European past. On the face of it, indeed, J. U. Nef's celebrated Industrial Revolution of the sixteenth century diminished the importance of events in the eighteenth, or, at the very least, supplied valuable ammunition for those historians who have chosen to emphasize the evolutionary nature of industrialization. The arguments stressing the lack of novelty in the technical or managerial developments of late eighteenth-century industrial expansion have foundered, as a rule, upon the sandbanks of subsequent detailed research, and few authorities would at present deny that many of the children of sixteenth- or seventeenth-century ingenuity were misbegotten or intractable creations. But refusing to join Nef on his exposed ledge is not tantamount to a rejection of a dynamic of economic growth before, say, 1650.

The essential question, however, concerns not the timing of the Industrial Revolution, which, by any reasonable definition, must be deferred until 1700, but the quality and the direction of precisely those dynamic elements which are patently obvious in English economic history before the eighteenth century. A pre-industrial economy is not static because it preceded the perceived acceleration of growth associated with the concept of the Industrial Revolution. Change at all events was ever present in the structure of society and its economic organization. The general use of money and the movements of population, for instance, involved a whole gamut of social and economic changes of exactly this kind; and, from the web of recurrent and extraordinary fluctuations which beset economic life before 1750, several strands necessarily led in beneficial directions (i.e. towards growth). The great swings of population between the twelfth and the eighteenth centuries brought about important and far-reaching modifications in the economic structure, which contained within them a process of development, not least because people—in times of plenty or in adversity—are the *raison d'être* of both production and consumption. The current of economic specialization in pre-industrial England depended to a large extent upon changes wrought by the sequence of demographic expansion, decline and recrudescence in the course of history from the high Middle Ages onwards. The tensions between change and continuity in the economic order are immanent at all times and the sequence of adjustment or modification is continuous, though, as French historians are well aware, the result may be circular rather than progressive, when viewed in the longest perspectives of history. Whatever its technical or commercial failures, however rigidly tradition or vested interest confined its enterprise, the English economy before 1700 possessed a dynamic, an ability to absorb and utilize even self-acting changes, which overrode the resistance of traditional immobilities. Change, in other words, began, however slowly, to acquire the momentum of growth.

This is particularly evident in the way in which manufacturing industry expanded and developed after the exclusiveness of corporate gild power had been sapped. The rise of industry as a leading sector in the economy, whether viewed in the social context of capitalist organization, or in economic terms, as a principal component in raising national income or in bringing about the diversification in modes of production necessary to take pressure off the land as the fundamental source of human livelihood, obviously did not begin with the development of modern industry round about 1750–1800. What F. F. Mendels has called proto-industrialization',[1] the elaboration of the development of rural manufacturing and mining, based largely upon merchant capitalism—the putting-out system—with its complex patterns of specialization and employment, was not only appropriate to supply the notably varied markets of Europe and the Atlantic world before the eighteenth century, but could develop in directions where 'heavy technology' (except perhaps in the harnessing of water power) was essentially unnecessary. In modern jargon, the logic of industrial development before 1700–50 lay in the application of an 'intermediate' technology (small-scale, hand-operated mechanisms which reduced laboriousness and speeded up production but, in general, did not cause 'technological unemployment'). The growth of this kind of manufacturing in effect relieved population pressure upon inadequate resources in agriculture, and by encouraging the spread of 'dual occupations' and the seasonal differentiation of work patterns went part of the way to reduce the endemic problem of underemployment. In this sense, the scattered evidence of precocious factories or large integrated plants in European industry before 1750 is less significant as an indication of early industrialization than the number of *households* which had passed beyond primary dependence upon food production in rural society. The former obsession of historians with capital accumulation as a measure of social and economic change is similarly less important than those organizational changes in the economic structure of western Europe. The great economic historian Cunningham could once write that 'capital has been the main instrument in material progress', and he clearly thought of the Oceanic voyages of the fifteenth century as opening up a new era.[2] But the date when this great change reputedly occurred no longer coincides, in modern historiography, with the Renaissance or the Age of Discovery. 'Proto-industrialization' was a progressive phenomenon, but was certainly well in train in some parts of Europe by the fourteenth and fifteenth centuries. The 'symbiosis' of agriculture and industry may have originated far back in time, but it still represented a major change of direction from the early medieval separation of manufacturing and food production within the feudal economy of manors and corporate towns. Legal dispensations in economic life often continued to reflect these ancient vested interests,

---

[1] F. F. Mendels, 'Proto-industrialization. The First Phase of the Industrial Process', *Journal of Economic History*, 32, 1972.

[2] W. Cunningham, *The Progress of Capitalism in England* (C.U.P., 1916), p. 21.

often for good social or political reasons, but the restraints upon freedom of action in mining or manufacturing were often employed to
temper or manipulate such enterprise. Even in regions still dominated
by corporate gild power or by an autocratic central authority in the
seventeenth century, the advantages, indeed the necessity, of industrial
diversity were seldom completely ignored. When the medieval inheritance weighed too heavily on economic life at various times after 1400, it
could certainly reduce once flourishing industrial regions to impotence.
As a rule, however, this pressure forced the pace of change in less
inhibited parts of the country (or of the Continent), and rural manufacturing therefore often coincided with urban decline.

Industrial growth in England between 1500 and 1750 was certainly
uneven, but in several trades, in mining and metallurgy, textiles and in
most of the 'new industries' discussed in Chapter 4, the increased
rate of output was not unimpressive. This development, however, often
occurred along lines of expansion which differed in several respects
from the pattern of industrialization in the late eighteenth and nineteenth centuries. Proto-industrialization was certainly the first phase in
the industrial diversification of the European economy, but it was not
necessarily a preliminary or precipitant stage in the development of
modern industry. The pre-industrial achievement, indeed, often
suffered eclipse in the next stage of development. One consequence of
eighteenth- and nineteenth-century industrialization was a repetition
of the history of decay or decline in less favoured regions of industrial
production.

On the commercial development of the economy, the essential point
is to emphasize the role played by the elaboration of the network of
communications and the greater specialization which progressively
occurred in European mercantile organization from the thirteenth
century onwards. Trade, both internal and external, not only responded
to needs already apparent in the development of the economy, by
forging links between producers and consumers, whether 20 or 2,000
miles apart, or by filling vacant spaces in extant systems of commercial
exchange through the deprivation of incumbent merchant communities
through war or aggressive competition; it also acted as a creative force.
The share contributed by trade, especially by overseas trade, in raising
average per capita income in western European societies before 1700 is
particularly important in attempting comparisons of growth and stagnation in the literate civilizations of the whole Eurasian land mass in

which money and commercial exchanges were well developed. It is also taken by economists as a measure of European superiority in relation to other underdeveloped economies since that time.

But the influence of commercial expansion, of what has justifiably been called the Commercial Revolution, was very much more diffuse. The new commodities, which were introduced into the structure of European demand with the extension of long-range trade into tropical and sub-tropical regions of the world—a process which had begun before the Oceanic trade-routes were opened up—were in themselves innovating influences of profound significance. In the same way the growth of internal trade, especially the new combinations of activity which resulted from the expansion of wholesale and new retail outlets in town and country, both varied and enlarged the schedules of popular demand in early modern England. For development it is scarcely possible to exaggerate the part played by changing patterns of demand, and by the purchasing power which supported these changes, especially during the crucially important century after 1650. The wider social diffusion of the commodity trades is one of the most important features distinguishing the commerce of the seventeenth century from that of the high Middle Ages in Europe. Business organization, new methods of credit dealing, improved techniques of book-keeping, insurance or brokerage, and, at the apex, the involved web of debts and taxes, investment and stock-jobbing, known as the Financial Revolution of 1690–1750—in short, the financial and managerial aspects of commercial expansion—may in fact have been less important for the development of pre-industrial England than the changes and the elaboration which occurred in the pattern of the commodity trades. The distinctive role of commerce was to distribute the agricultural surpluses generated in the mother country or in its dependencies, which were essential to support both industrial diversity and urbanization, as well as the volume of manufactured products which resulted from increasing industrial employment. Its achievement, in tying together diverse elements of pre-industrial production and consumption, essentially justified the contemporary opinion that trade was the Great Wheel of economic change between the fourteenth and the eighteenth centuries.

The part played by governments in planning and controlling developments relevant to the cluster of innovations around which the pre-industrial economy formed was ambiguous. The ideal of state-building by enlightened Mercantilist governments is deep-seated in the consciousness of many historians, and, since Keynes's work in the 1930s, has also become a matter of convention in development economics. But the connection established between growth and nationalist policy-making is unnecessary, at least in the case of England. The rationale of proto-industrialization, agricultural progress and commercial specialization owed little or nothing to far-sighted or resolute policies of Mercantilist governments, except in the comparatively small number of instances when strategic considerations overrode private interests. Early medieval economic expansion, for instance, had taken place in an atmosphere generally free of administrative or bureaucratic restraints, and even at times against the grain of communal interests. The control over 'economic' affairs exercised by late medieval governments marked not so much the advent of rudimentary concepts of planning or social welfare as the growing self-confidence of secular authority, and its need to manage fiscal resources, from the thirteenth century onwards. The rise of the nation state in western Europe was essentially an independent variable in the process of economic development.

On the other hand, the secularization of society had the effect of reducing the fraction of the adult population whose preference for priesthood, petty bureaucracy or mere idleness placed significant burdens upon the producers of goods or economic services. The peasant groaning under the weight of the fat priest or the arrogant nobleman is a recurrent image in the literature of medieval Europe and of the *ancien régime* on the Continent. Moreover in many contemporary under-developed societies, from East Asia to South America, increase of the tertiary sector, swollen by great numbers of 'drones' and their importunate families, has preceded the expansion of the industrial and commercial populations in precisely the same way. Medieval English peasants, as Professor Hallam has shown us, preferred to educate their sons up to the Church whenever the opportunity presented itself rather than leave them in the position of peasant cultivators; the consequence was both a flourishing monastic life before 1350 and an over-large body of clergy engaged in pastoral care, many with no hope of a benefice and few material resources upon which they could live.[1] By 1600, Protestant Europe, and to some extent the more adventurous or secularized Catholic countries as well, winnowed out the superfluous ecclesiastical establishment, but except in Britain and the Netherlands, a privileged

[1] H. E. Hallam, 'Some Thirteenth Century Censuses', *Economic History Review*, x, 1958, p. 356.

nobility and a proliferation of office-holders by inheritance remained to swamp the faltering efforts of an enterprising *bourgeoisie*. The low propensity for idleness in English society, even among the aristocracy and professional classes (including the clergy), the variety and social diffusion of enterprise and the common acceptance of Professor C. B. MacPherson's concept of 'possessive individualism' and 'a possessive market society' [1] were more important as elements in the character of pre-industrial society than the evidence of entrepreneurial weakness and technological shortcomings, however resounding and unsettling particular instances of failure may have been. The acceptance of the market as arbiter of economic change, and of a commercial career as a respectable means of obtaining a living, was more notable in the growth of the 'capitalist spirit' than the more obviously celebrated examples of a few great merchant-financiers, company promoters or industrial magnates whose efforts appear to prefigure the achievements of the eighteenth century.

The final element in the profile of the pre-industrial economy of England, the favourable allocation of utilizable resources, is obviously not specific to any particular phase of development, for in the later period of rapid industrialization the stocks of easily worked coal and mineral ores, agricultural commodities fit for industrial use—e.g., wool, hemp, hides, malt, imported cotton and dyestuffs, brick-earth, water, and so forth—are similarly brought into the explanation of Britain's early start in the Industrial Revolution. Moreover, resources locked up by human indifference or technical backwardness may appear more of a reproach than an advantage in the process of economic diversification. Between 1350 and 1750 the English did not exploit the resources with which their country or their dependencies were endowed as fully as they did in the nineteenth century, but what they did achieve, in mining, manufacturing or the improvement of communications, was at least appropriate to the needs and the demands of the time. Industrial and commercial diversification, and not least agricultural expansion, were not inhibited by insurmountable blockages or setbacks such as those which afflicted France between the Hundred Years War and the 'ups and downs' of the eighteenth century.[2] At the simplest, most funda-

---

[1] C. B. MacPherson, *The Theory of Possessive Individualism* (O.U.P., 1962).

[2] See, e.g., D. Richet, 'Economic Growth and its Setbacks in France from the 15th to the 18th Century', in M. Ferro (ed.), *Social Historians in Contemporary France* (Harper, New York, 1972), pp. 180–211.

mental and most poignant level, the infrequency and comparative mildness of hunger crises in England after 1350 form not only the most obvious contrast between the two chief Atlantic regions of Western Europe, but go far to explain the secure basis upon which English 'proto-industrialization' was established, because economic diversification depended to a large extent—but not completely—upon the ability of the agricultural economy as a whole to produce food and raw-material surpluses. Southern England and northern France formed perhaps the most productive, and naturally most fertile, cereal-growing region in agrarian Europe, and the different experience of the two countries is therefore doubly significant.

Medieval England, indeed, despite its technical backwardness in commercial and some aspects of industrial production, was still one of the best favoured and least precarious economies in Europe. That it held on to this initial advantage in subsequent centuries, building upon and extending the foundations, was in part a matter of chance, the absence of destructive war at home and the ready endowment of natural resources, but the different tenor of historical studies in Britain and France suggests that the historical experience of the two peoples has at least affected their mentalities. The British and Americans have tended to look for the lineaments of growth, or dynamism; the French have sought evidence of cycles, fluctuations, vicissitudes, the circular flow of economic change, and beneath all, the 'immobile' structure of human history. In his inaugural lecture at the Collège de France recently, Emmanuel de Leroy-Ladurie has explained the French view, and revealed the contrast brilliantly. For him, the essential *trait* of economic history before the nineteenth century was the tendency for population repeatedly to outrun resources.[1] Thus the long cycles of European, especially French, history are characteristically Malthusian, and in such long swings of expansion and contraction before 1800 linear growth, leading to a significant change of direction in the economic life of Europe—in short to an industrialized society—was hardly possible. '*L'histoire immobile*', as he has called it, is still barely conceivable in English terms. The contrast between the two societies, not only from 1750 to 1830, but also during the long period from 1350 to 1750, when both, on the face of it, experienced the same long-term trends of population change, has perhaps been overstated, but it is still sufficiently marked in the degree to which each obtained benefits from

[1] E. Leroy-Ladurie, 'L'histoire immobile', *Annales*, vol. 29, 1974, pp. 673–92.

essentially similar opportunities of diversification and entrepreneurial innovation, to contain more than a grain of truth. The English economy before 1750 certainly suffered from setbacks, not at all unlike those which afflicted the French economy, but the consequences were perhaps less serious and the recovery afterwards was apparently more complete or more readily susceptible to the influence of progressive changes. In this respect, the availability of alternative resources, the mobility of capital and even of labour, and the opportunity which a large and flexible market offered, not only distinguished pre-industrial England from France, but, in the end, also gave the country an invaluable advantage over most other rivals even before the eighteenth century. By 1750, Britain was already some way ahead of the field in economic development—the result of a long period of hard training in the exercise yard of the past three or four centuries.

Index